Quit Like a
MILLIONAIRE

No Gimmicks, Luck, or Trust Fund Required

KRISTY SHEN AND BRYCE LEUNG

A TarcherPerigee Book

tarcherperigee

An imprint of Penguin Random House LLC
penguinrandomhouse.com

TarcherPerigee with tp colophon is a registered trademark of Penguin Random House LLC.

Most TarcherPerigee books are available at special quantity discounts for bulk purchase for sales promotions, premiums, fund-raising, and educational needs. Special books or book excerpts also can be created to fit specific needs. For details, write: SpecialMarkets@penguinrandomhouse.com.

Library of Congress Cataloging-in-Publication Data

Names: Shen, Kristy, 1982– author. | Leung, Bryce, 1982– author.
Title: Quit like a millionaire—no gimmicks, luck, or trust fund required / Kristy Shen and Bryce Leung.
Description: New York: TarcherPerigee, 2019. | Includes bibliographical references and index.
Identifiers: LCCN 2019008139| ISBN 9780525538691 (trade pbk.) | ISBN 9780525538707 (ebook)
Subjects: LCSH: Shen, Kristy, 1982– | Finance, Personal. | Thriftiness. | Wealth. | Success.
Classification: LCC HG179 .S46146 2019 | DDC 332.024/014—dc23
LC record available at https://lccn.loc.gov/2019008139

Printed in the United States of America
10 9 8 7 6 5 4 3 2 1

Book design by Tiffany Estreicher

To Kristy's dad, who taught her the meaning of *chi ku*. And to all the readers of Millennial-Revolution.com, who inspired us to write this book.

CONTENTS

PART 3
BECOMING WEALTHY

FOREWORD

Some of you are going to hate this book.

At least you will if you are a proud member of the coalition of nay-sayers, the ones who say that reaching for Financial Independence (FI) is only for the privileged, and that their personal hard-luck situation makes it impossible.

Before you go there, run your story through this filter:

- Did you grow up under a totalitarian regime?
- Did your family ever live on forty-four cents a day?
- Was your first Coca-Cola the most incredible experience of your life up to that point?
- Did the empty can then serve as your most precious possession?

Here's my hard-luck story growing up:

When I was five, I collected dirty pop bottles from the roadside for the two-cent deposit and sold flyswatters door-to-door for a nickel.

Here's Kristy's growing up in rural China:

When she was five, she sorted through a medical waste dump looking for treasures she could make into toys. Wonder if she ever found one worth a full nickel?

My family worried about my father's failing health and business.

Her family worried about Chinese communists bursting through the door and hauling her father off to a labor camp.

As tough starts go, my story doesn't hold a candle to hers, and I'd bet yours doesn't either.

Here's the key: Her beginnings didn't hold her back. Her hardships didn't hold her back. The obstacles thrust in her path didn't hold her back.

They became her tools. Her motivation. Her guides.

This little girl who made toys of medical waste and treasured an empty Coke can now travels the world, eats in fine restaurants, writes books, and created an acclaimed blog.

She takes us on her journey from poverty in China, to being a teased outsider in school in Canada, to university student, to engineer, to investor, to millionaire. To freedom.

This book is going to make some minds explode.

Kristy is going to tell you things like:

Money is the most important thing in the world.

Money is worth sacrificing for.

Money is even worth bleeding for.

Wait! What heresy is this? Isn't money the root of all evil?

Not in this modern world, it's not. It is the single most powerful tool we have. Used well, it makes everything better. Easier. More interesting. It creates wonderful options right out of thin air. It is a magic wand.

What about love? What about family? What about education? What about culture? What about . . .? Aren't these the most important things in the world?

What about them?

You want to take care of your family and those you love? You better have money.

You want to spend more time with them? You better have money.

You want the time and leisure for education? For reading? For culture? You better have money.

You want the best of all those things and the time to fully enjoy them? You not only better have money, you better have money that works for you.

If your mind doesn't explode, Kristy can show you how.

This book is going to make some of you millionaires.

But just some.

You have to be ready to drop your excuses and put in the work. Most aren't.

You have to be ready to take your financial life, and the rest of your life along with it, into your own hands. Most aren't.

If you are that rare person who is, in Kristy you have found your guide.

Along with her story, which reads like a good novel, she'll walk you through the process of building your wealth, protecting it from the tax man and market plunges, and nurturing it into a powerful machine that provides for your needs while replenishing itself.

You'll learn about practical things like the insidious nature of investment fees and how to minimize them.

She details where she has invested and why, and walks you through how to do the same.

She presents cool techniques on managing, moving, and withdrawing your money once it is invested.

You may not agree with it all, but one of my great pet peeves is people who criticize a book because it doesn't conform to their own ideas.

A great book should expand your horizons, not just confirm your biases. The ideas in it should be evaluated not against your own but based on the soundness of the logic behind them and the clarity of the way they are presented.

This book is the soul of logic and clarity.

This book knows the journey can be scary.

Kristy gets that. She shares her own objections, fears, doubts, and stumbles on the path. Then, one by one, she provides tangible ideas and strategies to circumvent them.

She takes us by the hand and explains:

> . . . *money is not this big complicated thing that requires a genius-level IQ to understand. Instead, it's a series of simple lessons that, individually, are not difficult to grasp, but when you put them together they become a superpower.*

She'll introduce you to powerful concepts that help make achieving financial freedom easier and less risky. Things like geographic arbitrage, SideFIRE, and Partial FI.

She examines and explodes the myths that you need a six-figure income to do this, that it can't be done with kids, or that it is not necessary or worth doing if you enjoy your job. Trust me. Everything is better with money backing you up. Especially your job.

For those still skeptical, in appendix B she even details the exact dollar figures, year by year, in her climb to millionaire status.

This book wants you to be rich: in money, in time, and in life.

Of course, you are probably not a whiny, complaining naysayer. You picked up this book. You haven't the time to waste building a case about why you can't do this. You want to get started. You want to know how it is done.

With this book, you have come to the right place. She'll take you through the process step by step. Actionable things that you can do no matter what your age, location, background, or education.

Finally, let me leave you with my favorite line in the book:

> *If you understand money, life is incredibly easy. If you don't understand money, life is incredibly hard.*

Choose easy, I say.

—JL Collins

INTRODUCTION

Growing up, I was told that because I was born poor, didn't speak English, and had the wrong skin color, the opportunities open to other kids weren't open to me. I wanted to get rich, travel the world, and write books for a living. Those dreams simply would never come true, the haters said.

The haters were wrong.

At the age of thirty-one, I became a millionaire and quit my job, and now I travel the world and write professionally.

But before I get into my journey, you should know that this is *not* a happy-go-lucky self-help book. The key isn't to "think yourself rich," or "think positively," or "be in tune with the energy of the cosmos." I've read those books, tried their advice, and none of them worked.

I'm not going to tell you what you want to hear. I am, however, going to tell you the truth.

Getting rich isn't fast or easy. Anyone who tells you otherwise had advantages or is trying to trick you into giving them money. I'm not here to trick you. I don't need your money. I'm already a millionaire, remember?

In fact, this book almost didn't exist at all. Since I didn't buy Apple stock at $10, invent the next Snapchat, or do anything all that exceptional by the time I was thirty, I thought my story wasn't that interesting. If I showed you my university transcript, you'd see I'm not even that smart. Why would anyone care? It took an editor from Penguin Random House, Nina Shield, to convince me that my story is worth telling. She told me that it is valuable *because* I didn't get rich with advantages or luck. This means my journey is accessible to anyone.

My journey also spans the entire socioeconomic spectrum. I was born into abject poverty; at one point my whole family lived on forty-four cents a day. So my hope is that no matter where you are, you'll recognize your experience in mine. Whether you're trying to break out of poverty, or middle-class and wondering how a 401(k) works, or a one-percenter who wants to learn how to tax-optimize an investment portfolio, part of my story runs parallel to yours. You may find these lessons new to you or skim a section because it doesn't apply. Both are fine. Figure out where your path matches up with mine, then copy what I did. We should end up at the same finish line.

Getting rich isn't fast or easy. It is, however, simple and reproducible. I now understand that reproducibility is what makes my story valuable. After I discovered FIRE (short for Financial Independence Retire Early) and created my blog, Millennial Revolution, to teach people how to do it, too, the site quickly became a resource within the early retirement community. Readers implemented my advice—and it worked. The answers to questions such as "Should I buy a house?" or "Should I go into debt to change careers?" became clear once they converted the costs into time spent working for someone else.

At the end of the day, it isn't about money, it's about *time*—and how to use it wisely to live the best life possible.

This book exists because these lessons I learned clawing my way from the bottom 1 percent to the top 1 percent are available to everyone, regardless of race, the amount of money in your checking account, and the privilege you may or may not have inherited.

No matter who you are, everyone should know how to quit like a millionaire.

Let's get started.

—Kristy Shen

PART 1

POVERTY

— 1 —

BLOOD MONEY

One of my fondest childhood memories is digging with my friends in a medical waste heap in rural China. As we sorted through the piles of latex gloves, soiled gowns, and used syringes, a tiny voice in the back of my five-year-old head suggested that maybe this wasn't such a great idea. But that was overridden by a much louder, more hopeful voice saying, "What treasures will I find today?"

Now, don't get me wrong. I didn't live *inside* the medical waste heap—I'm not a troll. But I did enjoy it because unlike in a real store, if I saw something I wanted, I could actually get it. Otherwise, a typical experience went like this:

"Mom," I would say, my face pressed up against a glass case, "I know we're poor and we don't have any money. But one day, when I grow up, and I make my own money, then can I have that doll?"

And somehow the answer was *still* no.

So that's why my friends and I were behind the hospital that day. If I couldn't buy a toy, I reasoned, maybe I could make one.

I did find something, believe it or not, in a seemingly infinite supply of discarded rubber bands. We tied the loops together to form a chain and then made the chain into a Chinese jump rope. The best part was that every time our rope broke I could repair it by just swapping out the wonky rubber band.

These days, this would be considered grounds for child services to get involved, but back then, this was just what life was like. We were dirt-poor. And when you're dirt-poor, your choice isn't between Barbie and My Little Pony. Your choice is between food, heat, and medicine, in that order. Toys never even entered the picture.

According to the US Census Bureau, in 1987, the national average wage in the United States was $18,426.51 per year per person.[1] In China, it was 1,459 CNY, or $327, per year per person.[2] To put that in perspective, earning enough to buy a Nintendo Entertainment System (Deluxe Set) at its then–retail price of $179 would have taken the average American worker less than a week. But for the average Chinese worker? The better part of a year.

Also, $327 per year was the earnings of the *average* individual, which included everyone in major urban centers. We lived in Taiping, a rural village with a population of just three thousand, so salaries were even lower—around two-thirds less.[3] My entire family income, at one point, was 600 CNY, or $161, per year, or 44 American cents per day. My dad, my mom, and I had to live on less than 1 percent of an average American's daily salary.

I'm not telling you all this to crap on my childhood or make you feel bad for me. In fact, I'm pretty grateful that I grew up in this way, because I ended up developing something called the Scarcity Mind-set, which played a big part in making me who I am today.

WHAT IS THE SCARCITY MIND-SET?

To understand the Scarcity Mind-set, let's go back in time.

The year was 1945. On January 27, the Soviet army entered Auschwitz and liberated seven thousand men, women, and children from the largest death camp the Nazis had built. Naturally, the soldiers' first instinct was to open up their army rations and say, "Take it! Take it all!"

Turns out that was the wrong thing to do. The prisoners gorged on the food and ended up becoming horrendously sick, some even dying. They didn't realize it at the time, but giving a starving person too much food causes their blood sugar to spike, which leads to a dangerous drop in electrolyte levels, a medical condition that would later be known as refeeding syndrome.

Near the end of the war, scientists at the University of Minnesota ran a study to figure out the safest way to treat starving people.[4] Thirty-six men agreed to be put into a dorm, starved (sufficiently starved but not dying-starved), and monitored.

Sitting became excruciating. Pillows had to be placed between their bottoms and the chairs because they had lost so much fat it hurt. They swelled up like blowfish. Extra fluid started collecting under their skin—a condition called edema—and caused a semipermanent dimple whenever anything pressed into their bodies. They were so weak they couldn't even take a shower; they just didn't have the energy.

But the most shocking change was to their brains. Constantly being deprived of food does strange things to your psyche. Food became their only preoccupation. Hated Brussels sprouts? Didn't matter. Any food placed in front of these subjects was devoured, the plate licked clean. Some subjects brought cookbooks and menus from local restaurants and read them over and over again. They pored over newspapers, memorizing and comparing prices for tomatoes and eggs. Even watching a movie became a peculiar experience. The volunteers wouldn't remember the plot or the characters but recalled in vivid detail any time the characters ate something.

In a recent study that took place in a lab, subjects were separated into those who had eaten lunch and those who hadn't. When seated in front of a screen flashing words like "TAKE," "RAKE," and "CAKE" for one-thirtieth of a second, those who hadn't eaten correctly identified the food words far more often than the control group did.[5]

When you don't have enough of something, it becomes the most important thing in your life. Everything else is secondary. The experiment changed the subjects not only physically, but mentally as well.

This is the Scarcity Mind-set.

When someone's starving, their brain ignores almost everything—except that one thing it doesn't have.

MY SCARCITY MIND-SET

In 1958, Communist Party leader Chairman Mao began a campaign known as the Great Leap Forward. It was an attempt to rapidly modernize China's economy from agrarian to industrialized in order to compete with the West. Only, it was crafted by someone with the economics knowledge of a toddler. Farming villages were given a quota of steel to produce, despite the fact that the average villager had zero knowledge of how to, you know, produce steel. Villagers abandoned their farming efforts and built backyard furnaces. They melted their pots and pans to meet the quotas.

This quickly caused what became known as the Great Chinese Famine, which ravaged the countryside for three years. Meanwhile, the government exported grain to the West, Cuba, and Africa, despite severe domestic food shortages, to advertise how well Mao's plan was working. People were dropping like flies, while foreign aid was refused. Private ownership of land was forbidden, and growing your own crops was labeled "counterrevolutionary" and punishable by death—assuming, of course, you weren't already dead from starvation.

After every blade of grass, every leaf, and even insects had been picked clean, people started eating clay. The clay was called "Guan Yin" after the goddess of mercy—a fairylike goddess in white robes worshipped for her compassion and kindness. Since this type of clay was white, people thought the goddess of mercy had blessed it to save them. The clay of course had the opposite effect and many people died painfully from bowel blockage. Even so, people still ate it, just to have some relief from their hunger pains.

On his walk to school, my dad would regularly hear a thud and look over to see a schoolmate slumped into a heap. He summarizes this time by saying, "My only wish was to be full."

During the worst month of the famine, my dad's best friend, Wenxiang, saved his life by giving him a bite of a half-rotten sweet potato he found in a farmer's field. It had been missed when the government confiscated the harvest, and if he'd been caught, he would've been executed. To this day, sweet potato is one of my father's favorite foods.

Wenxiang died, like so many of my dad's friends, of starvation, just a few months before the famine finally ended in 1962.

Since then, my dad has gotten his wish of knowing what it's like to be full. But food is still his obsession. I wasn't ever allowed to waste it. Every piece of an animal had to be eaten, from head to tail, the marrow sucked clean from the bones. That's why he found it so strange that chickens in Western supermarkets were packaged as "thigh," "breast," or "wings." Didn't these chickens have heads? Necks? Feet? Thinking of those unwanted parts tossed away made his heart ache.

My dad's story taught me how scarcity takes over your mind. I didn't live through a famine, so my life was already a major step up from his. Even though I didn't own a pair of underwear or socks that wasn't patched and repatched by my mom until there were more patches than sock, even though I got bullied for my thrift-store clothes and DIY haircuts, and even though I became exceptionally good at pretending to be sick to avoid field trips that my parents couldn't afford, I never forgot how lucky I was.

But growing up in poverty created a Scarcity Mind-set in me, too; I was obsessive about money.

In 1988, my dad got a chance to immigrate to Canada for his PhD, leaving me and my mom back in China. On my seventh birthday, he sent me a musical birthday card. Dad told me he had bought it in a dollar store. I did the calculation quickly. One Canadian dollar was around three CNY at the time, which meant that this one card could have fed my family for almost two days![6] It was by far the most precious thing I had ever owned. So of course, I went around the neighborhood, playing it over and over and smacking whoever's dirty hands dared to get near it. I wrapped it in a cloth and kept it under my shirt as if it were a baby bird that needed constant tending.

Several months later, its tiny battery ran out and it died a glorified death. But I'll never forget the time I was the proud owner of the most expensive and special card in the whole world. Two years later, after Mom and I had immigrated to join my dad in Canada, he decided to take me to the toy store for the first time in my life. He picked up a stuffed bear from the shelf. I looked at the price tag and gasped. Five dollars was enough to feed our cousins back in China for more than a week! I returned that overpriced bear to its shelf and pulled him over to the bin with the giant orange sign that said "SALE: $0.50." Afterward, I made him send the remaining $4.50 to our cousins, and I felt amazing every time I thought about how they would be fed for a week because of my sacrifice.

The Scarcity Mind-set does have its downsides, though. When I was nine, we lived in a tiny one-bedroom apartment near Dad's university. The entire place was furnished with mismatched, half-broken furniture my parents salvaged from the curb or picked out from the dumpster. But compared to the concrete box where we had lived in China, with no heating, damp floors, and a bathroom that was just a hole in the ground, it was a palace.

One day I came home from school to find that I had lost my key. After turning my schoolbag upside down and digging through all my books, gym clothes, and pencil case, I still couldn't find it. A cold feeling of dread filled my chest. I delayed the inevitable as long as possible, but after dinner I had to fess up.

For the $30 that was required to replace the lock, I had to pay the price. And by that, I mean my mother beat me. Not only did I gain a crazy-high pain threshold that day (I'm basically Wolverine), I also confirmed my suspicion that when you're poor, money is the most important thing in the world, because money is survival. You don't make careless mistakes because if you do, people go hungry, or even die.

Look: I'm not telling you these stories because I want you to weep over my messed-up childhood or applaud how far I've come. I want to show that you don't need to grow up privileged to become a millionaire. As a child, I couldn't even fathom what a millionaire was. Was the cupboard full or was it empty? That's as much as I knew about money.

My family started off in the bottom 1 percent, which rewired my brain to make it hyper-focused on what we lacked. That Scarcity Mind-set made me prioritize financial security above everything else—and it is precisely that Scarcity Mind-set that got me to where I am today, in the top 1 percent. These days, instead of digging through trash, I travel the world as a thirty-five-year-old retiree. Rather than handicapping me, the Scarcity Mind-set taught me the three lessons that would eventually turn me into a millionaire:

Money is the most important thing in the world.

Money is worth sacrificing for.

Money is even worth bleeding for.

— 2 —

PEACH SYRUP, CARDBOARD BOXES, AND A CAN OF COKE

The first time I felt rich was when my dad gave me a can of Coke. In China, Coca-Cola is called "Kekou Kele," which means "Tasty Fun." Back then I was lucky if my drinking water wasn't contaminated with parasites, so the idea of something being both tasty *and* fun blew my seven-year-old mind. Everywhere I went I saw ads showing rich (I assumed) kids in the West drinking Coca-Cola, and they made me want to be a rich kid so badly.

So, on my first day in Canada, when Dad handed me a can of this "Tasty Fun," my hands were shaking so much I could barely hold it upright. When I took my first sip, my head nearly exploded. (Or so I thought. It was actually my capillaries. The excitement and sugar rush gave me a massive nosebleed.) I was just about to turn eight, and I finally knew what a rich person's drink tasted like.

Most people will tell you that Coke is cheap sugar water that rots your teeth and gives you diabetes. Not only that, pretty much anyone can afford it. But I knew none of that. I nursed mine for a week, savoring every drop. When I was done, Dad tried to throw it out, but that empty can was far too precious to just toss away. It became my cup, toothbrush holder, and hair roller. I named it CanCan and slept with it every night. CanCan was my constant companion until my father bought me that bargain-bin teddy bear.

That Coke was the most luxurious treat I'd ever had, so I protected it, maximized every ounce of enjoyment from it, and didn't let a drop go to waste. I didn't know it at the time, but that was the first lesson of the Scarcity Mind-set.

Business books love to dump on the Scarcity Mind-set, saying that it "holds you back." The idea is that if you focus on what you *don't* have rather than what you *could* have, you tend not to recognize the opportunities right in front of you.

That's fine. In the context of being an entrepreneur, it's probably decent advice. But what those business authors don't understand is that nobody is operating under a Scarcity Mind-set because they *want* to. They are *forced* to, because at some point, they didn't have enough resources, and the Scarcity Mind-set helped them survive. Scarcity isn't always a bad thing. It can even be constructive.

Think back to school. You have a big paper due in a month. You put off writing that paper by chatting up friends on social media, obsessing over the news, and watching reality TV. You procrastinate, because your resources (in this case, time) are plentiful. It's okay to dawdle because there's so much of them.

But if the deadline were in a matter of hours or days, you'd use your time more wisely. You'd ignore that gossipy call from your bestie and that kangaroo video your cousin sent you, even though you know it'll be awesome. Those distractions can go to hell because you are now a tornado of productivity. With the deadline looming, you become laser focused and use every brain cell you have to finish the paper.

This is the Scarcity Mind-set at work. When time is scarce, you push yourself to get as much done as possible, because time is precious.

The same goes for money. When you're flush with cash, you don't appreciate its value since you think there will always be more. But when you're poor, every penny is treasured. I learned to appreciate every dollar my parents earned, every cent I ever made from my newspaper route, and developed a near-photographic memory for prices. Money was the single most important thing in our lives. Scarcity was the constraint that shaped my childhood creativity.

And that was shitty in oh so many ways. But I consider it a net positive, because in order to be truly creative, constraints are necessary. If you've ever tried to write a novel, you know what I mean. Staring at a blank computer screen feels debilitating. With infinite directions to pursue, you end up paralyzed. But by imposing some constraints—like learning how to structure your paragraphs, build a story arc, and write a scene, or doing a writing exercise—you start to see a path forward.

Ernest Hemingway supposedly bet his friends he could write a story in just six words. They laughed at him: how could a handful of words possibly convey the depth of a full narrative? You wouldn't even have space to describe a single eyelash, never mind an entire character. But Hemingway did just that. Not only did he write that story, he even gave it emotional impact. Don't believe me?

"For sale: baby shoes. Never worn."[1]

See how much oomph you can pack into a tiny space? That's what constraints do.

SCARCITY MADE ME STRONGER

I'm no Hemingway, but just as that micro story revealed his ingenuity, growing up poor unleashed mine. Poverty taught me four vital skills that I still use today—skills that I like to call CRAP: creativity, resilience, adaptability, and perseverance (the acronym being a fitting metaphor because of all the crap I had to wade through to get them).

Creativity

When I was ten years old, I dreamed of owning a Barbie Dream House. I had seen the commercial repeatedly because we had only four channels. Even now, more than twenty-five years later, I can remember it vividly: the camera zooming in on the two happy girls putting Barbie on her pink satin bedspread, then pulling back as they flicked on the streetlamp outside her window, giggling. As badly as I wanted it, though, I didn't bother asking for such an extravagant gift for my birthday or Christmas; I knew my parents couldn't afford it. The stupid thing cost so much money, I didn't even think *Santa* could afford it.

But the pull of the dollhouse was strong. So, one day, when I noticed some perfectly good cardboard boxes just sitting in the dumpster outside our apartment, I grabbed them.

Back in my room (which also doubled as my parents' bedroom, a workspace, and storage space), I dug around a desk drawer until I found a pencil and a pair of scissors. I drew squares for the windows, marked the front and back doors, and, with surgical precision, started cutting. By tenting together two pieces of cardboard, I made a roof. Then, by gluing together the cutouts from the doors, I built a mattress. I added the finishing touch by transforming the scraps from my mom's sewing pouch into a floral bedspread.

I stepped back to admire my masterpiece. My scrappy little dollhouse looked nothing like the one in the commercial, but I didn't care. Making it had been so much fun; who cared if it didn't have a parking space for Barbie's car (sold separately) or working light fixtures?

Whenever I got bored of watching infomercials and MacGyver-ing my toys, I went to the library, where I found an entire building full of books, and I could take up to fifteen at a time without anyone's calling the cops! I couldn't believe it.

At first, I could only read in Chinese, so I stuck to the foreign languages section. One day I was walking down the aisle, letting my fingers wander over the spines, when one book caught my eye. It was *A Little Princess*, translated into Chinese. When I got to the checkout, the librarian had to gently coax me into letting go of it, just for a second, so she could scan it for me.

I devoured the book in three days. The story was about a girl named Sara, who's so rich she has her own maid, carriage, and pony. But she's also kind and generous. Her father sends her to a fancy boarding school, so he can go off to war, but not before investing his entire fortune in a diamond mine. Then he dies on the battlefield, and not only that, all the money vanishes. The headmistress steals Sara's belongings to pay for her school fees, and she is forced to work as a servant at the school.

This riches-to-rags story was the exact opposite of my life, which made it intriguing as hell.

I kept reading. I started to read English books, too: the Baby-Sitters Club series, R. L. Stine's Goosebumps, and Christopher Pike's Spooksville. Eventually, I had enough of a grasp of English to write my own stories.

That launched my childhood love of writing, which later morphed into my dream of becoming an author. Twenty-five years later, the culmination of that dream is sitting in your hands.

All because my family couldn't afford cable.

Resilience

When I was thirteen, my right eye swelled shut from a wasp sting. This had the effect of making me look like Cyclops, which wasn't exactly helpful in improving my social status as a self-conscious teenager. But we didn't have the money to buy the $15 anti-inflammatory medication, so I simply put on a pair of thrift-store shades and went to school pretending to be a rapper. Weirdly, this didn't endear me to my peers, who were already bullying me on the regular. But hey, when your parents can't afford to throw money at a problem, you learn to tough it out.

"Nice pants," a schoolmate would say behind my back, voice dripping with sarcasm.

"I know. I have good taste," I would retort, smiling and pretending to brush crumbs off my faded overalls.

"Your parents are poor."

"No. They're billionaires who are just really into hobo chic."

I think this is why years later, when I finally moved from poverty into the middle class on a computer engineer's salary, I never fell into the trap of fear of missing out (FOMO), also known as keeping up with the Joneses. I'd developed Teflon skin early on, so while my coworkers were blowing their incomes on cars, clothes, and houses, and working unhealthily long hours to keep it all together, I didn't give a rat's ass about what anyone thought.

Adaptability

As a kid, we moved around a lot, chasing cheap rent so my parents could send the savings back to our family in China. Every time, I'd end up in a new school district, lose the friends I had been able to make, and have to start all over again.

The first time we had to move, I broke down into sobs. My dad pulled me aside, held my chin between his hands, and looked me directly in the eyes. "I know you're sad you're leaving your friends. But I found a cheaper place that will save us money. Your cousins are counting on this money to go to school, and they have so much less than you. You don't want to let them down, do you?" That shut me up.

This is why discomfort and setbacks never faze me. In university, I figured out how to stretch the money I made from my internships until it covered tuition, rent, food, and everything else. I lived in a $300-a-month basement room, but it was no big deal. Sure, it had its fair share of dust and blackflies, and was scorching hot in the summer without air-conditioning, but that just meant I spent more time at the library, reading. (And, hey, at least I had a bulletproof security system: a branch I used to wedge the window closed!) It wasn't glamorous, but the adaptability I'd honed in my childhood allowed me to cover all my expenses, and I graduated with zero debt.

Perseverance

Getting my degree is one of the most difficult things I've ever done. I was enrolled in one of the toughest undergrad programs in the country, computer engineering at the University of Waterloo (the MIT of Canada, as it's known).

I realized what I was in for the very first week of freshman year. While students in other tracks were making friends, getting drunk, and partying, we were getting our asses kicked by two intense exams; those who didn't pass had to take remedial courses on top of a full course load. (I swear, if you were ever drowning in the ocean, Waterloo would find some way to tie rocks to your feet because life is just too damn easy.) Luckily, I had heard about the exams ahead of time, so I flanked those bastards by giving up my summer to study.

But it all paid off. As soon as I graduated, not only was I able to cover my costs, I had two years of internship experience and a killer résumé. And guess what? I had mediocre grades *at best*. My lab partners always got straight A's, while it would take me ten hours to understand a simple concept, only to end up with a C.

That didn't stop me, though. I knew I didn't have to be the best. If I could just pass and get my degree, this grueling program would pay for itself. If I had to work psychotically hard to force my slow-learning brain to understand impossibly difficult subjects, so be it. If I had to drag my sleep-deprived body through the trenches, so be it. Hell, one time I even went as far as chugging an entire bottle of Buckley's cough syrup (their motto is "It tastes awful. And it works") to stay awake during an exam because I was sick as a dog and hadn't slept for two weeks. (Somehow, I passed, even though I barely remember any of it.)

INVISIBLE WASTE

You'd think reliving these stories would make me sad, but in fact, I look back on my childhood and young adult years with fondness. Not only did I survive, I have some pretty happy memories! Also, my experience gave me an outsider-looking-in perspective on Western culture that has served me well.

People write to me all the time asking if I can help analyze their financial situation, and they send balance sheets showing spending multiple times higher than what I spend each year *now*—as a millionaire. When I politely (or not so politely) point this out, their reaction is, "I can't think of a single thing I can cut back on!"

We'll discuss more about the biochemical reason why this happens in chapter 8, but one of the most valuable lessons I got from growing up poor was the ability to identify invisible waste.

Let me give you an example. When I was a kid, I desperately wanted to get diabetes.

Weird, right? Let me explain.

Diabetes, to me, was the most prestigious disease in the world. Only rich people, or at least people who had enough money to buy piles and piles of candy, could afford to get it. So, once I immigrated, I spent a good part of my childhood eating and drinking a ton of sugar. I especially loved canned peaches. But I never got to eat the peaches themselves, just the syrup. My mom worked at a Chinese buffet washing dishes, and every time the waitresses filled up a container of peach halves for the dessert bar, they'd throw away the syrup. And Mom would be waiting, ready to snatch it before it got dumped down the drain. I got addicted to the stuff, drinking it at all hours of the day. It made me happy, not just because of all that free sugar but because we no longer had to throw away money buying milk or juice. I could subsist on peach syrup, water, and whatever else the restaurant tossed at the end of the day. It was heaven.

I told that story to a friend of mine recently and she was absolutely horrified. But that was my world. I didn't know food groups or recommended daily servings. My food was basically the packaging your food came in. You ate the fruit, I drank the syrup.

If you haven't gotten the theme yet, here it is: other people's garbage was my treasure. And as I assimilated, I realized how much waste is completely invisible. The *Guardian* estimates that as much as sixty million tons of food are wasted every year in the United States alone, just because it's misshapen or discolored.[2] This is a *third* of all the food being produced!

That's just the tip of the iceberg. Americans throw away eleven million tons of clothing a year.[3] Eleven. Million. Tons. That's even worse than the food because it can take hundreds of years to biodegrade, so it just sits in our landfills with all the plastic bags and last year's cell phones, slowly destroying the environment.

Western society always strives for more. But is "more" the key to our happiness? Studies show that any bump in happiness related to financial security maxes out with a $75,000 salary.[4] After that, "more" doesn't actually seem to help when it comes to well-being. Statistics also show that a salary of just $34,000 a year makes you part of the top 1 percent in the world.[5]

If a container of peach syrup can thrill a kid who doesn't know otherwise, then maybe we don't need much either. Some, or even most, of what you're buying isn't making you happy. Some of your spending is waste, plain and simple.

MAKING INVISIBLE WASTE VISIBLE

Let's do an exercise to find out just how much invisible waste exists in your life.

EXERCISE: ELIMINATING INVISIBLE WASTE

MATERIALS: A CLOSET, SOME MASKING TAPE

Open your closet. Push everything to the left.

Take an empty hanger and wrap a piece of masking tape around it, as shown here, and hang it at the far right.

For the next month, every time you wear an item of clothing, after you wash it, hang it to the right of the marked hanger.

Over time, this will reveal how often you wear certain items. The stuff all the way at the right is what you wear most frequently. Toward the center, but still to the right of the marked hanger, are pieces you wear, but not recently. To the left of the marked hanger are clothes you never take out at all. The longer you do this, the more accurate your closet map will become, and you'll be able to get a sense of how much is "active," meaning what is in regular rotation. Similarly, you'll learn the percentage of your closet that's "dormant" and never sees the light of day.

Don't worry; you don't have to toss out the clothes you don't wear. But hopefully you'll start thinking about invisible waste and how easily it can sneak into your life. We'll be using the information gleaned here when we examine in chapter 8 *why* we all buy more than we need.

In our culture, the Scarcity Mind-set is portrayed as pure deprivation, a hindrance to a child's development. But growing up with that perspective helped me in ways I could never have predicted when I was that kid in China pining over a can of Coke. Scarcity is a powerful constraint. It taught me to wade through the CRAP to become more creative, resilient, and adaptable, and to persevere to build the life I have today.

Scarcity also allowed me to quickly identify invisible waste. It's time to start pinpointing it in your life, too.

— 3 —

BE EDUCATED OR DIE

The classroom door flew open. Ten men in bulletproof vests stormed in, assault rifles pointed at us.

"Police! Hands on your heads!"

I did as I was told, but my first instinct was to dive under my desk. Judging by their wide-eyed terror, my classmates felt the same way. The final exam, which had seemed so pivotal just minutes before, was forgotten. Pencils rolled onto the floor and exam papers fluttered in the air.

You know how when there's bad turbulence, everyone turns to look at the flight attendant? Well, our teacher looked even paler than the walls of the classroom. That's how I knew this wasn't a drill. A kid at my high school had been spotted with a gun. It was June 2000, just one year after the Columbine shootings, so the police—understandably—took it seriously. It took thirty minutes, which felt like forever, to search everyone, classroom by classroom, until our principal announced over the intercom that the SWAT team had cleared the building. With shaky legs, we filed out and assembled at a designated area on the football field.

I called my dad to tell him what had happened and ask for a ride home. He said: "If the exam is still on, don't leave."

Even though neither the suspect nor the gun had been located yet.

At the time, I was just a teeny tiny bit peeved about being abandoned in an active-shooter scenario. As I walked home after the test was canceled, I wracked my brain trying to remember the number for child services. It wasn't until many years later, when I asked Dad about how he came to this country, that I began to understand where he was coming from. To me, it seemed as if school were more important to him than my life. To him, school *was* more important than his life.

When my dad was seventeen, he was forcibly removed from high school and sent to the countryside as part of his "reeducation." This happened during the Cultural Revolution, a decade-long period of class warfare exploited by Chairman Mao to take back control over the Communist Party. After his Great Leap Forward—which aimed to convert China from an agrarian society to an industrial one—face-planted, causing three years of famine and killing millions, he realized he had to do something drastic to consolidate power and prevent a coup.

Anyone who was considered "bourgeois" (teachers, doctors, landowners, people who worked for the opposition party) was branded an "anti-revolutionary." My grandfather, having worked as a medic for the Kuomintang, the Nationalist Party, which opposed the Communists during the civil war, fell into that category, along with my grandmother, my dad, and his four siblings. They were all guilty by association.

My dad spent the better part of his youth—*ten years*—doing back-breaking labor in the countryside. Using primitive tools, his job was to haul massive boulders to and from a quarry, under a blazing-hot sun, surviving on meager rations. Once, while hauling a two-hundred-pound rock with a friend, he slipped in the wet mud, rolled down a hill, and almost got crushed to death. He lost hope of having a future or any chance of improving his situation. Every day was as grueling and hopeless as the last.

In 1977, after Chairman Mao died, the new leader, Deng Xiaoping, decided to overhaul the system and reopen the schools. The National College Entrance Exam (NCEE), or Gaokao, which dates back to 1952 and can be taken by anyone, regardless of political or socioeconomic status, was reinstated. It dawned on my dad—a factory worker at this point—that this was his shot.

The three-day exam tested comprehension in every high school subject, despite the fact that during the Cultural Revolution most students had been kicked out of school and never graduated. Dad describes December 10, 1977, as the most unforgettable day in his life. His father woke him up at four thirty a.m. to cook him breakfast, and his parents watched him eat in silent devotion. As he boarded the bus, he looked back at my frail and coughing grandfather, who had been ill for years following the denouncements and hard labor of the Cultural Revolution. Not only did his future rest on the results of this exam, but his entire family's future, including his four siblings', did as well.

So, you can imagine the pressure he was under. *Millions* of people were competing for a coveted university spot; the NCEE was referred to as "a thousand soldiers and their horses trying to cross a log."

The odds were not in my dad's favor. But as you may suspect by now, he got in. In fact, he got 60 points more than the required score and was admitted to a top university. (He found out later that 5.7 million people had taken the exam that year—and only 4.8 percent passed.[1]) The news quickly spread in his small town. Even the people who had previously ostracized my grandparents started treating them with respect.

Education was how my dad got out from under the thumb of a totalitarian government. So, he wasn't overly sympathetic whenever I complained that a subject was too hard or I was too tired to go to school—or the school was closed because a gunman was on the loose. You tough it out. Because your entire family is depending on you. (I still think he should have come and picked me up, though.)

The Gaokao is still the most important exam in a Chinese student's life. I've heard similar stories from Vietnamese friends; for their parents, getting an education was also a matter of life and death. During the Vietnam War, students with the highest marks were kept behind to fill political roles, while their peers were conscripted into the army, which meant that the kids with better grades were the ones who survived. We've all heard of amazing kids like Malala Yousafzai, who faced death threats for going to school, and Ugandan immigrant Twesigye Jackson Kaguri, whose family scrimped and saved to get him a no. 2 pencil, the price of admission to his local school.[2] These are extreme cases, I know, but around the world, education often remains the only way out of poverty. Even in the United States, getting an undergraduate degree increases your average salary by 70 percent. No matter where you are, education has the power to change your life by improving your earning power.

Not only that, one longitudinal study demonstrated that a lack of education can be as harmful to your health as smoking. Education improves your ability to process and understand information. Education also helps you become more curious and self-sufficient and teaches you how to trade short-term pain for long-term gain. People who drop out of high school die, on average, a decade earlier than their peers who have a bachelor's degree. But more than 10 percent of Americans ages twenty-four to thirty-five (over eight million people) don't have a high school degree.

Maybe you're with me. Or maybe you're rolling your eyes, wanting to throw names like Richard Branson and Katy Perry in my face, to prove that it's possible to drop out and still make it big. But (as I'm sure you secretly know) these lucky people are the exception, not the rule. If you want to extend your salary and your life, education is pretty much the best bet.

After all, if it weren't for that exam, I wouldn't be here. Even though I grew up in poverty, too, my father laid the groundwork for my success, and he never let me forget it. It wasn't until he got his PhD after years in Canada that he finally found a job as a research scientist for the government, and that's when things started to turn around. Dad has always played the long game.

And he was right; all the blood, sweat, and tears to get my degree were worth it in the end. But as you'll see in the next chapter, not all college degrees are created equal.

DON'T FOLLOW YOUR PASSION (YET)

While I was growing up, my mom got laid off a lot.

She went from job to job—dishwasher, seamstress, maid—getting the pink slip every couple of months. She blamed racism and her inability to speak fluent English. When I was in high school, she went to community college and got a certification for electronics assembly, which helped her get higher-paying work. She even stayed on somewhere longer than a few months. But then the tech bubble burst, and she was once again let go.

All this instability caused her a ton of anxiety, and she became paranoid and depressed. She rarely slept, and she constantly accused unseen enemies of plotting to kill her. She called the police on our neighbors so many times that 911 blacklisted our phone number. This just fueled her downward-spiraling mental state, which she took out on me and my dad.

When it was time to pick a field in university, I knew I had to be careful. By this time, our family finances had stabilized somewhat, but we were still sending money back to China, and, like my dad forty years earlier, I knew I had exactly one shot. I couldn't risk graduating without being able to find a job. My degree had to help me become independent as quickly as possible. I didn't want to end up like my mom.

WHY I DIDN'T FOLLOW MY PASSION

The year was 2000. The Backstreet Boys were on top of the charts, the world hadn't blown up from Y2K, and for most people, a degree was just a means to an end—getting a job. In fact, even though it seems like it's been around forever, the phrase "follow your passion" is relatively new. According to Benjamin Todd, CEO and founder of 80000Hours .org, the phrase spiked around 2005, when Steve Jobs gave a commencement speech at Stanford, in which he said, "There's no reason not to follow your heart."[1] Nowadays, we hear that advice over and over again, drawing young graduates like moths to a flame. It's sexy and empowering. It's also dangerous.

When it came time to pick a college, I evaluated my options mathematically. I pored over every university's website to figure out how much each degree would cost and weighed that against income statistics. I was most interested in:

1. Writing

2. Accounting

3. Computer engineering

Writing was my number one choice. But was a creative writing degree a good investment? A four-year program in Canada would have cost me about $40,000 (and *way* more if I went with a US school). I learned that writers can make anywhere from $500 to $50,000 to millions per year—if you're Stephen King—with the average income at $17,000.[2] Next, I looked at the hourly minimum wage, which I reasoned was how much I could earn right out of high school. At the then-minimum wage of $6.85 an hour, I'd be looking at $14,248 a year. I subtracted that from my expected salary. This degree was worth . . . drumroll . . . $2,752 a year.

Next, I did the same calculation (using the in-province tuition cost at the time) for accounting and computer engineering. Here's how they lined up:

Degree	Total Cost	Median Salary Above Minimum Wage
Creative Writing	$3,380[3] x 4 = $13,520	$17,000 - $14,428 = $2,752
Accounting	$3,264[3] x 4 = $13,056	$38,200[4] - $14,248 = $23,952
Computer Engineering	$3,622[3] x 4 = $14,488	$55,000[4] - $14,248 = $40,752

I stared at my notepad, the wheels inside my head turning. Grabbing my trusty calculator, I divided the rightmost column by the middle one. This gave me a single number I could use to rank my options—a "Pay-over-Tuition," or POT, score (tee-hee).

Degree	Total Cost	Median Salary Above Minimum Wage	POT Score
Creative Writing	$13,520	$2,752	0.20
Accounting	$13,056	$23,952	1.83
Computer Engineering	$14,488	$40,752	2.81

For every dollar you spend on a degree, multiply that by the POT score; that's how much money you can make above minimum wage after graduation. Every dollar I spent on an accounting degree meant I would earn 1.83 times more than my tuition. Computer engineering was even better, giving me a 2.81 multiplier on my tuition. Unfortunately, creative writing, my childhood dream, came in dead last.

Computer engineering was the clear winner. I chose Waterloo because it had an internship program that allowed me to work while getting my degree, which meant I could pay off my tuition during undergrad. Not only would I end up with zero debt, I'd have two years of experience on my résumé.

I have to admit, the idea of going to university for computer engineering didn't exactly make my heart skip a beat. I grew up wanting to write stories, not code. But I didn't have a trust fund, and my parents needed me to stop adding to their financial burden. I had to make the hard choice, but the one the math told me was right.

But you might say, "What about doing something you love and being fulfilled and all that jazz? Don't you want me to be *happy*?" Of course I want you to be happy. But one of the biggest lies we've been sold is that following our passion is the key. Statistically, following your passion will lead to unemployment or underemployment. Those of us who grew up poor know that we're unlikely to wake up excited each day when we're worried about where the next meal is going to come from or whether we'll have to choose between electricity and hot water this month.

Not only that . . .

Passions Change

People change. What lights you up could be very different a few years from now than it is today. One psychology study at Harvard and UVA found that nearly all nineteen thousand participants reported that their passions had changed significantly over the previous ten years.[5]

Encouraging people to base their career on what they love when they're eighteen is like encouraging them to exclusively dress like their favorite band from high school. In which case I'd be writing this book while dressed like Scary Spice, and nobody wants that.

Passions Don't Necessarily Make Good Jobs

I'm passionate about cat videos, travel, and stuffing my face with pad thai, but that doesn't mean I can turn those interests into a career. And even if I could, it doesn't mean I should. Even now, when I'm doing something I love—writing—there are still days when I want to tear my hair out. There are parts of every passion that, when turned into a full-time job, suck. I love writing, but that doesn't mean I love rewriting chapters over and over again, or getting rejection letters from agents, or poring over the dense legalese of a publishing contract until my eyes bleed.

The only reason I'm able to pursue writing now is because I'm not dependent on it to pay the bills. Work is rarely fun when you have to worry about your next paycheck. Work is even less fun when you're forced to be creative on a schedule because you have no other choice. And this is all assuming you are lucky enough to be working in a field you love!

Passions Don't Equal Happiness

Happiness (which we'll talk about more in chapter 8) has to do with the intersection of expectations and reality. Culturally, we expect our work to be engaging, give us autonomy, pay us fairly, let us collaborate with people we like—and be fulfilling. But the idea that each of these conditions can be met, forever and ever, is false. You can't control how much you get paid, how many jobs exist in a certain field, how great your coworkers are, or whether the job will still exist a year from now.

Follow the Math Instead

I had completely forgotten about that little Pay-over-Tuition exercise until I sat down to write this book. When readers write in for help with their finances, I often say, "Time to math shit up!" before I break down the numbers. As it turns out, I was mathing shit up all the way back in high school! Rediscovering those POT scores inspired me to test them out on all sorts of careers I didn't consider back then. Let's see what this tells us about many of our "dream" jobs using updated numbers from the US in 2018.

Degree	Total Cost	Median Salary Above Minimum Wage	POT Score
Fine Arts	$10,230 × 4 = $40,920	$48,780[6] – $15,000 = $33,780	0.83
Dancer	$10,230 × 4 = $40,920	$35,672[7] – $15,000 = $20,672	0.51
Actor	$10,230 × 4 = $40,920	$36,380[8] – $15,000 = $21,380	0.52

Pretty rough. When readers write in from one of these fields, it's not a surprise if their finances aren't in the best shape. But what does surprise me is when readers from stereotypically lucrative careers like doctors or lawyers write in. How in the world can a doctor be in financial trouble? Well, take a look:

Degree	Total Cost	Median Salary Above Minimum Wage	POT Score
Doctor	Undergrad: $10,230 × 4 = $40,920 Med School: $207,866[9] Total: $248,786	$208,000[10] – $15,000 = $193,000	0.78
Lawyer	Undergrad: $10,230 × 4 = $40,920 Law School: $18,175 × 3 = $54,525[11] Total: $95,445	$119,250[12] – $15,000 = $104,250	1.09

These high-paying careers aren't much better than a career in the arts! Sure, you can expect to make a six-figure salary, but the combination of the length of time to become qualified and the expensive tuition can be lethal. These tuition numbers are for *in-state public schools*, by the way. Go to a private college and the math gets even worse. Plus, we're not even taking into account the loss in earning power from the extended time in school.

It was a lightbulb moment for me: it explains all those doctors who are still struggling with their finances a decade after graduating.

The POT system also reveals that you don't need a degree at all to have a fruitful career. Here's what happens when I run the math for a plumber.

Degree	Total Cost	Median Salary Above Minimum Wage	POT Score
Plumber	$3,660[13] × 2 = $7,320	$52,590[14] – $15,000 = $37,590	5.14

Since being a plumber only requires a two-year associate's degree from a community college, the tuition costs are low, and the median salary is so relatively high that plumbers get an amazing bang for their buck! Not only that, plumbers have a huge built-in customer base (all buildings have pipes, duh), they're impossible to outsource, and in big cities like Chicago and New York, where supply is low and demand is high, they can make as much as $70,000 a year![15]

Who knew?

And by the way, this is a good exercise not just for a high school senior—most of us are long past that point—but for anyone thinking about switching careers.

Now, I realize this chapter might be depressing to some of you. I'm not here to tell you things you want to hear; I'm here to tell you the truth. But remember that the rule is "Don't follow your passion (yet)." I'm not saying you can't ever make money doing what you love. After all, you're only reading this because I eventually *was* able to become an author. But you have to follow the rest of my advice first. Doing what you love and hoping for money to follow is risky. Follow the money first, and you can do what you love later.

Not all degrees are created equal. Don't follow your passion (yet). Follow the POT.

And, yes, I wrote this entire chapter just to be able to close with that line.

I regret nothing.

CHAPTER 4 SUMMARY

- ▸ Following your passion is a bad way to pick a career.

- ▸ Instead, you should pick a career based on its Pay-over-Tuition (POT) score.

  - • POT score = Median Salary Above Minimum Wage / Total Cost of Degree.

  - • A high number means money spent on tuition will have a greater effect on your income.

— 5 —

IOU = I OWN YOU

As I mentioned, growing up the way I did taught me a lot. There was one part of my cultural background that came in especially handy: statistically, Chinese citizens have an average savings rate of 38 percent.[1] That is *massive* compared to the American rate of 3.9 percent and the Japanese rate of just 2.8 percent. What's going on here? Is Chinese culture just naturally more frugal than others?

I went to my best source: my dad. He said that even before the Communists came to power, government corruption was so common it was just a way of life. Whenever someone did you a favor or lent you something, you were expected to repay them, either through political favors or with money. Over time, it became ingrained in the national psyche that being in debt to someone gives them power over you. (During Chinese New Year, you have to settle any debts and start with a blank slate—or be cursed with bad luck all year.)

Admittedly, this is the definition of anecdotal evidence, but there are other explanations. First of all, debt was not available to the Chinese for most of our country's history; the first credit card wasn't even introduced there until 1985.[2] Compare this with the Western world, where credit cards came to the market in 1950.[3] When I was growing up, the concept of credit was completely foreign to me. I didn't know what a credit card was, had never heard of a bank loan, and had no clue how a mortgage worked. If my parents wanted a big-ticket item, like a bicycle or a watch, they saved up. Buying on credit and paying it back later wasn't an option. You simply had the money to buy it or you went without.

Second, due to the lack of a social safety net in China, we have always had to fend for ourselves. Education, health care, retirement? It was all up to us.

Finally, the expectation of catastrophe was drilled into my parents' generation, and that mind-set—that shit can hit the fan at any moment—defined how they saw the world. The idea of relying on the government was laughable. The government's job isn't to help you! Their job is to find new and creative ways of making your life immeasurably worse.

This all taught me that debt had to be avoided at all costs, and that if I wanted something I'd have to earn it. I didn't get a credit card until after I graduated from college. At work, I would sit back and watch as my friends and coworkers went nuts with debt, spending money they hadn't earned, while patting themselves on the back for being fiscally responsible by buying the basic Tesla model instead of the one with all the fancy features.

I've since realized why debt is so destructive. Debt removes the link between time and money. And when that happens, people start making bad decisions that blow up their finances.

HOW DEBT WORKS AGAINST YOU

Einstein is supposed to have said, "Compound interest is the eighth wonder of the world." As you earn and save, your money makes more money, and that money makes even more money. Literally every finance book available talks about this, and all agree that it's a Very Good Thing.

But what's if it's not a Very Good Thing? What if it's a Very Very Bad Thing?

I'm sure everyone's heard that $E = MC^2$. Allow me to introduce you to Luca Pacioli's Rule of 72.

Here's how it works. If you know the return you're earning on an investment (say, 6 percent per year), divide 72 by that number (72 / 6 = 12). This gives you the number of years it'll take for your money to double. If I invest $1,000 with a return of 6 percent a year, it'll compound into $2,000 in 12 years without my investing another cent. That balance goes up over time, because the money I make makes more money, which in turn makes even more money.

When you're an investor, the Rule of 72 is your friend. It helps your money grow. But if you have debt, the Rule of 72 is your enemy. It works against you to take what little money you have. Credit cards typically have interest rates around 20 percent, so if I borrow $1,000 to buy a flat-screen TV, it would take only 72 / 20 = 3.6 years for my debt to *double*. Another 3.6 years and the debt quadruples.

This is why debt is so scary. If you don't kill it, the debt monster gets bigger and bigger until it's consuming everything in its path.

Don't let the monster get that big. We have to slay it now.

FUTURE YOU VERSUS CURRENT YOU

Another reason debt is so dangerous is because debt distorts the value of money.

Back in China, when my parents didn't have money, they couldn't buy anything. There were no credit cards, no lines of credit, nothing. If they couldn't afford something, they simply didn't get it. And you know what? Thinking back, it's a decent system. Nowadays, every idiot and their cat can get a credit card. And when they do, it's so easy to forget how precious money is.

Because money is a stand-in for time.

In order to buy a $100 watch, my parents would have had to earn each dollar through manual labor. At the rate of 44 cents a day, the amount they got paid, it would have taken them 228 days—and that doesn't consider funds set aside for food, clothing, and basic living expenses. One TV would have required at least a *year* of work.

Debt changes all that. Debt allows someone to get that TV right *now*, using money that seemingly appeared out of nowhere. Down the road, that TV will cost double or more, but that's a problem for Future You. Present You is busy enjoying their brand-new TV!

By disconnecting money and time, debt screws over your future self.

These days, Americans owe $13 trillion[4] and Canadians $1.8 trillion,[5] and it's no wonder. When the value of things we purchase is no longer tied to the number of hours we had to work for them, it's easy to take this "funny money" and blow it. The problem is, eventually Present You will become Future You. And then what are you going to do?

First, do whatever you can to avoid going into massive debt. It's the worst financial mistake you can make. That being said, a lot of us are already far down that road and trying to make our way back to financial freedom. What are we supposed to do then?

Glad you asked.

CONSUMER DEBT

When it comes to types of debt, consumer debt is by far the worst. It's a blood-sucking vampire. Not only does it bleed you dry, it makes you terrified of the sun by trapping you indoors, shopping for crap you don't need, and/or shackled to your desk for years.

Since consumer debt has the highest interest rate, you want to slay this bad boy first. Consumer debt should be treated as what it is: a financial emergency that you have to take care of *now*. Here are a few things you can do to sharpen your stake.

1. **Cut expenses to the bone, even if it hurts.** Consumer debt has the highest interest rate of all and, as per the Rule of 72, doubles faster than any other type of debt. You need to treat this as a crisis. There is absolutely no point in investing or even saving much cash if you're carrying debt with a 10–20 percent interest rate. Paying it off should be your number one financial priority. If you need to get a side gig or a roommate, or learn to say no to dinners out, do it.

2. **Order your loans based on interest rate, highest to lowest.** If you have several vampires at your neck, kill the one with the highest interest rate first. That one sucks the most blood *and* grows the fastest, making it doubly dangerous.

First, pay the minimum monthly payment on all of your cards to make sure you don't go into default (which would make things even harder to deal with). Next, make the biggest stake ever (all the cash you can scrape together) and stab the nastiest bloodsucker (the one with highest interest rate) straight in heart. Paying off the smallest loan might make you feel better, but you're trying to kill a monster here, not boost your self-esteem. Remember, your goal is to let the credit card companies take as little of your hard-earned money as possible—so you can invest it (which we'll talk about in chapter 10) and taste that sweet, sweet freedom sooner.

3. **Refinance your loan**. Many credit card companies run promotions allowing you to transfer balances between cards and pay 0 percent interest for a set period of time, usually a year. These help you along by reducing your debt's interest rate. Don't simply transfer your debt around; do this only if you're sure you can pay it off within that grace

period. These companies are hoping you *can't*, because then the interest rate skyrockets and you get screwed again. Be careful!

When readers ask me how to invest while they're carrying consumer debt, I tell them they're trying to run a marathon with a parasite on their back. There's no point. You'll run out of energy in the first mile. No matter how good the returns, the interest rates on your debt will immediately devour them. Slash your expenses and destroy that vampire first.

STUDENT DEBT

In terms of interest rates, student debt is the second scariest. Even though it typically carries a lower interest rate than consumer debt (4–8 percent instead of 10–20 percent), it's the only debt you can't discharge in bankruptcy—you can run and hide, but it's always following, like that red ghost from Pac-Man. However, this is only true for Americans (there are complex rules for Canadians, but you can do it).

This is why it's critical to figure out your POT score from chapter 4 before choosing a field, if possible. If not—if you're reading this knee-deep in debt without a job that pays enough to help you out of it—you still have options.

Payment Reduction

Most student debt is held by the federal government, which has some advantages. Namely, it provides ways to reduce how much you owe each month if you don't make enough money or unexpectedly lose your job. This doesn't reduce the total balance, but it prevents you from defaulting, which would make the situation way, way worse. Using a payment reduction plan is like eating one of those white pills in Pac-Man: it doesn't make the ghosts go away, but at least they stop chasing you for a little while.

There are four types of income-driven repayment plans.

REPAYE—Revised Pay as You Earn

REPAYE has the lowest barrier to entry and is the most forgiving income-driven repayment plan. It's open to all graduates with federal direct loans, regardless of when you took out the loan. You are even eligible for loan forgiveness in twenty years for undergraduate degrees and twenty-five years for graduate degrees.

On this plan, the maximum you will ever pay is 10 percent of your discretionary income, which is defined as after-tax income minus 150 percent of the federal poverty level.[6] At the time of this writing, if you're single, the US poverty level is $12,140, so 150 percent of the poverty level is $18,210 ($12,140 × 1.5). If your after-tax income is $30,000, your discretionary income would be $30,000 − $18,210 = $11,790 per year, or $982.50 per month. Under REPAYE, your monthly payment would be limited to 10 percent of $982.50, or $98.25.

PAYE—Pay as You Earn

PAYE is an older version of REPAYE with more red tape. Generally, you are only eligible if you graduated college in 2012 or later. (This is because you can't be a new borrower as of October 1, 2007, and have received part of the loan on or after October 1, 2011.) Like REPAYE, your monthly payment is limited to 10 percent of your discretionary income, and your loan is forgiven after twenty years.

IBR—Income-Based Repayment

IBR limits your payment to between 10 and 15 percent of your discretionary income depending on whether you're a new borrower after July 1, 2014. Outstanding loans are forgiven after twenty-five years if they were taken out before July 1, 2014, and twenty years for loans taken out after that date.

ICR—Income-Contingent Repayment

ICR limits your payment to 20 percent of your discretionary income but calculates discretionary income slightly differently, as: After-Tax Income − 100% Federal Poverty Level. Outstanding loans are forgiven after twenty-five years.

Summary

Plan	Payment Amount	Forgiveness Period
REPAYE	10% of discretionary income	20 years (undergrad), 25 years (graduate)
PAYE	10% of discretionary income	20 years
IBR	10–15% of discretionary income	20–25 years
ICR	20% of discretionary income	25 years

Remember, these plans don't magically make the loan go away; they only keep you from defaulting if you aren't able to pay them back at the moment. They do, however, make you eligible for loan forgiveness twenty to twenty-five years down the road, but we'll discuss why this isn't a silver bullet either. Each program has eligibility requirements depending on what type of loan you have, so contact your loan provider or go to StudentAid.ed.gov to see your options.

Loan Forgiveness

Let's talk loan forgiveness. It sounds like signing up for a repayment plan is a no-brainer given that they have loan forgiveness options, right? Well, not exactly. In the United States, student loans that are forgiven are added to your taxable income, so while your loan may go away, a portion becomes an IRS debt. If you don't have the cash to pay off that tax bill, you then have to negotiate with the IRS to see if you can get on one of *their* repayment plans or try to discharge the tax debt through bankruptcy—which could take years. You could easily be in your fifties by the time you get rid of that damned debt. See what I meant when I said that student debt is like the red ghost that just follows you around forever?

The big exception is the Public Service Loan Forgiveness program. If you work for a nonprofit or the government, the PSLF forgives all your debt after ten years of income-based payments, and that amount actually does go away. No surprise tax bill, just bye-bye, debt.

The strangest thing about this program may be how little people seem to know about it. Most folks think it only applies to charity workers, but many jobs qualify. Teachers are generally eligible since they tend to work for the state. Health care workers, too, if they work for a nonprofit hospital; ditto for academics at universities run by the state. If your employer has any connection to the government whatsoever, check with your HR department to see if you qualify. You can have any of these loans:

- ▶ Federal Subsidized/Unsubsidized Stafford/Direct Loan

- ▶ Federal Direct PLUS Loan

- ▶ Federal Direct Consolidation Loan

Look closely. Even if you have the wrong type of loan, you might be able to consolidate it into a Federal Direct Consolidation Loan, and then all of a sudden, it's eligible!

The really tragic thing about the PSLF is that in order to qualify, you have to make ten years of payments toward the *right* loan type. If you've been making payments on an ineligible loan, they don't count toward the ten-year time frame. But if you work for a qualified employer, have a qualified loan (or consolidated it), sign up for one of the repayment plans above, and make your payments on time for ten years, it's possible to get rid of your student loan once and for all.

If you're Canadian, I'm happy to report that navigating your student loans is far simpler. The Canadian government has something called the Repayment Assistance Plan, which, depending on family income, will reduce the monthly amount you pay toward the loan. For Americans, if their reduced payment is less than the interest they owe, their loan gets bigger, but for Canadians, the government will pay any interest, preventing the loan from increasing. Additionally, your loan will be forgiven after fifteen years, with none of that taxable-income crap that the Americans have to put up with. It's a federal program, so it's available to everyone (cue "O Canada").

There are also more-specialized programs, depending on your field and province. If you're a nurse or family doctor, there are separate assistance programs for you. If you live in British Columbia, there's one for you, too. And if you live in Newfoundland, you don't have to pay it back ever, since they converted all their student loan programs into a grant-based system back in 2015! So, check with your province, and see what you qualify for. You may be pleasantly surprised.

Refinancing

Refinancing is your final tool. Refinancing transfers your loan from a public to a private lender, which can reduce your interest rate. Be *super* careful here, because once you do this, you lose the safety net of a federal loan, like the ability to lower your payments using income-based repayment programs, and your loan is still nondischargeable in bankruptcy! You also can't have your loan forgiven through the PSLF. For this reason, I generally advise people *not* to refinance their student loans unless their job is super stable and, even then, to only refinance the portion that they can repay within a year. For example, if you're a highly paid doctor with a whopping balance, and you can put $50,000 toward your loan this year, then go ahead: refinancing can help you save interest for the year while not sacrificing PSLF eligibility for your entire loan.

MORTGAGE

Last, but definitely not least, is mortgage debt. Mortgages are generally the heftiest and most common debt people carry in their lives, and while housing is way too big a topic to discuss here (we'll deal with it in chapter 9), here are a few quick notes.

Because mortgages are secured against your home, the interest rates tend to be low. While consumer debt typically has rates of 10–20 percent, and student debt 4–8 percent, mortgages are as low as 3 percent. For that reason, it can make sense to not pay off a mortgage and invest instead, since even a conservative investment portfolio can make around 6–7 percent annualized.

We'll cover both investing and housing later on, but for now, a rule of thumb is:

If a mortgage has an interest rate of . . .	Then . . .
< 4%	Pay the minimum, invest the rest.
> 4%	Pay off the mortgage first, or refinance to below 4%.

Getting into debt is one of the things that prevent us from living the life we want, because it can quickly snowball. While the best strategy is to avoid it in the first place, if you're already in debt, these tools will help you get out of it before it destroys your finances. Sharpen that stake, and good luck.

CHAPTER 5 SUMMARY

- ▸ Debt uses the power of compound interest against you rather than for you.

- ▸ Credit card debt is the most dangerous category and should be paid off ASAP.

  - Cut expenses to the bone.

  - Pay off credit cards with the highest interest rate first.

  - Consider taking advantage of cards that allow you to transfer balances for a temporary 0 percent interest rate to give you some breathing room.

- ▸ Student debt is the next most dangerous category because of how difficult it is to forgive.

  - Depending on the type of loan, you may be eligible for a payment reduction program such as REPAYE or IBR.

  - If you work for a nonprofit or a government agency, you may be eligible for the Public Service Loan Forgiveness program (PSLF), which will annul your loan after you make ten years of qualified payments.

- ▸ Mortgages are the third type of debt most people encounter.

  - If your mortgage rate is less than 4 percent, pay the minimum and invest the rest.

  - If your mortgage rate is higher than 4 percent, pay down the mortgage before investing.

NO ONE'S COMING
TO SAVE YOU

You know how in North American preschools there's a slot reserved for snack time? In China, we had smack time. And smack time was *all the time*. Napping too long? Smacks. Playing incorrectly? Smacks. Smacking each other? Oh God, so many smacks.

"NO! VIOLENCE!" my teacher would scream at my classmates while raining down blows upon our three-year-old heads.

Now, before you dismiss my culture as barbaric, try to understand that growing up in China isn't like growing up in the West. Because of the sheer size of the population, school is a highly competitive system in which you are expected to do what you're told or face swift consequences.

It was in this environment that my father first introduced me to the concept of "*chi ku*," which translates to "eat bitterness." Eating bitterness is seen as strength in our culture. Accepting and pushing through pain without complaint or anger is how you build character. During the Great Famine, my dad's generation ate bitter melon, an almost inedible vegetable, because it was one of the only foods available. Dad still eats bitter melon from time to time, to remind himself what suffering tastes like.

The Chinese can be a tad melodramatic.

When my teacher slapped me for fidgeting in my seat, I *chi ku*'d. When she kicked me for being unable to nap (for some reason I was nervous around her and couldn't sleep), I *chi ku*'d. And while I never really told my dad what was happening, he had an inkling when I clung to his leg every morning, refusing to let go. Thirty years later, he admitted he considered taking me out of that school. But for him reality always overrides empathy. Sometimes your entire life turns upside down through no fault of your own, and you have to learn how to tough it out and survive. No one is coming to save you. He thought about helping me out. But he wanted me to learn how to *chi ku*. He wanted me to learn how to save myself.

The problem was that despite the stereotypes associated with Asian mental prowess, the fact of the matter is that I'm not particularly smart and I wasn't that good at math. It can take me days to understand a basic concept that others breeze through. In junior high, I failed a reading test that 70 percent of the class passed, despite spending all my free time in libraries. In high school, physics and computers were my worst subjects. The first exams I ever took in those subjects I scored a shameful 60 percent. Luckily, my dad, being a mechanical engineer, was able to tutor me in those courses. But in English and reading, my parents couldn't help at all. I stayed up late every night to painstakingly make my way through Shakespeare and guides on essay writing.

I knew I needed to work ten times as hard as my peers. I gave up my summers to take extra courses. That way my workload was reduced each fall and I had more time to digest everything. I used that extra time to get a leg up on the textbooks and the practice questions. By the time I graduated high school, those 60s had turned into 90s, and I got into the computer engineering track at the notoriously brutal University of Waterloo. Which, of course, just made my workload problem even worse. I was a regular fixture in the labs, study rooms, and libraries, studying for twelve hours at a stretch and occasionally all night.

It was all worth it.

Even in high school, I knew that getting the right degree was my ticket. And even though I graduated near the bottom of my engineering class, because I worked my ass off with lots of unpaid overtime during my internship, I quickly landed a full-time job. My boss didn't care about my mediocre grades; he hired me because of my insane work ethic. Whenever he had extra work for me, I always said, "Bring it on!"

Don't get me wrong, I'm not just bragging about how I became successful because I worked hard. What I realized much later was that I worked hard because I was afraid. I was afraid that this was my one and only chance at a good life, and I didn't want to blow it. I was afraid of becoming a burden on my dad, who at the time was supporting our extended family back home. I was afraid that if I failed, I'd drag our family back down into poverty, after all the sacrifices he had made to get us out.

To paraphrase the words of Ed Harris's character from *Apollo 13*, failure was not an option.

SCARCITY MIND-SET VERSUS ENTITLEMENT MIND-SET

Many of my peers grew up way differently than I did. They had gone to summer camp and had gotten cars or tickets to Europe as graduation presents, but after graduation they ended up unemployed and living in their parents' basements. This baffled me. I had started off poor and made it to middle-class; they'd started off middle-class, so shouldn't they have been ahead of me?

What I later realized is that for them, that ingrained fear of failure was simply . . . missing. When I asked what they were doing to improve their lot, they would say, "I'm sure things will work out," or "I don't know, work's not my thing."

For them, failure was *totally* an option.

I was born into a situation where scarcity was all I knew. But, as we've discussed, that mind-set ended up being a blessing in disguise. Since I knew that things could *always* get worse, the Scarcity Mind-set taught me that money was precious and if I wanted security and autonomy in life, I'd have to earn it.

Look, I'm not trying to shit-talk my fellow millennials. We've been maligned as the "Me Me Me Generation" for long enough, told we have an Entitlement Mind-set that mistakes privileges for rights. This is an insanely broad generalization that doesn't consider the economic collapse that happened right around the time we were making our way into the workforce. But sometimes I did feel like I was on another planet from my peers. When you're poor in the developing world, there is no safety net. But here, there are systems in place to help you get on your feet. That's a great thing—but when it runs up against that Entitlement Mind-set, people can become *dependent* on that assistance, which often comes in the form of Mom and Dad.

According to business and economics professor Paul Harvey, "a great source of frustration for people with a strong sense of entitlement is unmet expectations."[1] If you believe that you're special, and all you have to do is find your singular passion and turn it into a perfect job, that's a recipe for disaster. The reality is that the world owes you nothing. You only become "special" by developing skills that are in demand, which takes focus, grit, and long-term work. Other people can help along the way, but in the end, we have to save ourselves.

WHY YOU NEED TO SAVE YOURSELF

I didn't learn to swim until I was twenty-four years old. That surprises my friends, since after retiring at thirty-one, I got my scuba certification and have since gone diving in Thailand, Cambodia, the Caribbean, and the Galápagos. But it wasn't that long ago that I was terrified of water. There weren't any recreational pools in my small village in China. After we emigrated, a few near-drowning incidents made me swear off swimming forever. So, it wasn't until I was a full-grown adult that I decided to conquer my fear. I signed up at the YMCA, embarrassed but also determined. At first, I gripped the flutter board to my chest as if it were the precious birthday card my dad had sent me as a kid. But one day my instructor swam over and smacked it out of my hand. "If you fall off a boat, do you expect a flutter board to just magically appear?" He was right: it was time to give up my crutch. Learning how to swim has been one of the most satisfying things I've done.

When things don't go according to plan, you won't always have a backup. Given our economic reality of declining job stability and disappearing pensions, you can no longer rely on the government or your company to take care of you in retirement. My readers frequently write in with stories about how they were able to escape their bad circumstances. Some had help along the way, others had to struggle alone, but ultimately, they all saved themselves. For example:

Susan grew up in Alberta, Canada, with blue-collar parents. Her father, having gambled away the family savings on a failed business, abused alcohol. They lived in poverty and tiptoed around him. She knew she'd been dealt a difficult hand, but that didn't faze her. Since her parents couldn't afford to put her through university, she opted to go to community college, working part-time to pay her tuition and picking a program that let her complete her degree in two years. After graduation, she got a job working for a shipping company, which paid around $35,000 per year. Over time, she got a programming certification and became a software developer, making $45,000 per year. After seven years there, she got a PMP (Project Management Professional) certification, which, combined with her experience, enabled her to become a consultant earning $100,000 per year. She beat the odds of her background to make six figures after twelve years in the workforce.

Melissa grew up in Chicago in shelters, feeling so hungry at times that she developed an unhealthy relationship with food. She got good grades but hadn't ever considered that college might be within reach. But her teachers didn't give up on her. They even paid for her SAT and

ACT exams and helped her enroll in an early college program. After obtaining *five* degrees and a PhD, she now earns a six-figure salary in the public sector.

Nick grew up in Dallas, Texas, with a successful salesman father. Nick's dad was making a killing—but also got into a killer amount of debt. Nick grew up with the kind of life most kids can't even dream of, but when it was time for him to go to college, his dad lost his job. The tuition money went to pay for the house, the maid, and the BMWs. For the first time in his life, Nick had to fend for himself. He worked his ass off, paying off much of his student loans by working part-time jobs while still in college. He chose a field—petroleum engineering—with robust job prospects and paid off the rest within a year of graduation. Nick tells me his dad's refusing to give him money was the best thing that ever happened to him. While his siblings are still struggling with bad financial habits like their father and racking up mountains of debt, he's built a portfolio big enough to enable him to travel the world and retire overseas.

BUILD YOUR OWN SAFETY NET

The Scarcity Mind-set teaches us that money is precious. The Entitlement Mind-set enables us to kick the can of personal responsibility down the road. But we all need to learn to protect ourselves from those scary inevitabilities like layoffs and outsourcing.

We need to learn how to save ourselves. To do that, we build our own safety net. Your safety net needs to feed you, clothe you, and pay for the occasional kick-ass vacation to Aruba, all without relying on a job or the government—neither of which is as reliable as it used to be. If you become your own safety net, it won't matter whether you started off with a Scarcity Mind-set or an Entitlement Mind-set. You'll win either way.

I spent the nine years after graduating college coming to this realization, and my journey there was twisty and turny, full of mistakes and false starts and things I wish I had done differently. That first day, as I settled into my new job, I thought that I was on easy street. Smooth sailing from here on in. My time to *chi ku* was over.

Turns out, things were about to get so much harder than I ever thought possible.

PART 2

THE MIDDLE CLASS

— 7 —

CONFESSIONS OF A FORMER PURSE JUNKIE

I've been talking about my Scarcity Mind-set and how it impacted me. But the truth is, I haven't always been good with money.

Sometimes immigrants like me who escaped poverty in developing countries experience what I call the "Immigrant Money Rebound Effect." First, the initial shock upon discovering the abundance of the First World: "Holy Christ, it's a can of Coke!" Second, as the family transitions to middle-class, the realization that your hard-earned money isn't going to be confiscated by the government: "I can spend this on *whatever* I want?!" Third, the self-destructive foray into Western-style overconsumption: "I'm going to buy all the things!"

After getting my first full-time job, I realized that, among women, purses are a symbol of wealth. Whenever my colleagues paraded their Louis Vuittons around the office, our female coworkers would treat them like the queen of England, cooing and stroking their monogrammed trophies.

Purses were a sign of *success*. Since I was successful, I reasoned, I wanted—no, *deserved*—one! I decided that Coach was "my" brand and proceeded to become an absolute scholar of their product line. I knew how to spot fakes. I could tell where a purse was made based on its serial code. I could instantly identify the exact make and model hanging off a stranger's arm from twenty feet away.

I was obsessed. Every time I bought one, I would do this definitely-not-crazy thing where I'd stick my entire face inside it and inhale deeply. *Mmmm. New-purse smell.*

One day, my husband, Bryce, came back from work to find me sitting in front of the computer, my eyes glued to the screen. I gestured him over. "This is a genuine Penelope with jacquard fabric and all-brass hardware!"

He stared at me like I had grown a second head. "What the hell are you talking about?"

"Come look!" I insisted. An eighteen-year-old girl was oohing over the Coach Penelope leather satchel while carefully removing it from its box like a newborn baby.

"Is this the entire video?" Bryce asked, incredulous. "She's just . . . unboxing a purse?"

I didn't respond. I was too busy inputting my credit card information.

I know now that I had a full-blown addiction. Shopping is the easiest and fastest way to get a hit of dopamine, the pleasure hormone. Since this is the same chemical that's released when we eat tasty things, have sex, do drugs, or accomplish something we're proud of, I was hooked. Just pull out your wallet; you don't need to push through the boredom and frustration of mastering a skill, face the ups and downs of nurturing a human relationship, or *do* anything. (We'll talk more about the neurological reasons why this happens in chapter 8.) In short, buying Coach had turned me into a lab rat. It was as if an electrode connected my brain to a big red button, and every time I pushed it, my pleasure receptors would light up. It was *so* easy.

I bought five purses in the span of a few weeks. Every time, I'd purr over my new purchase for a couple of days. But those jolts of happiness were short-lived. I'd inevitably get bored and start shopping for a new one. The hunt was intoxicating but the good feels never lasted. Many immigrants I know have experienced something similar. It's like driving a starving man to a Golden Corral; he may just eat himself to death. I almost did.

But one day, as I was fawning over yet another bag, out of the corner of my eye I saw something: a half-finished Coke. I had been drinking it when the doorbell rang, and I had abandoned it as soon as the delivery person arrived, bearing my latest acquisition.

Something inside me broke. When I had arrived in this country, a Coke can had been my most precious possession. And here I was, two decades later, treating it like an afterthought. All because of . . . an empty bag.

I didn't like who I had become. I put down my new bag and canceled my order for the next one. Then I finished that damn Coke.

YOUR PAST DOESN'T DEFINE YOU

One of the best pieces of life advice I have ever gotten was from a man named Mario Haddad. Mario was Bryce's new manager at a computer chip design company and Bryce was heading to San Jose, California, to meet him for the first time. Bryce had heard that Mario was "unusual" and that in Silicon Valley, he was known as "the Fixer," someone they sent in whenever shit hit the fan. Bryce spent his flight wondering, *What's he like? What's his deal? Is he a psychopath?* (Shockingly common in upper management.) There's always dirt somewhere. When you're high up in the chain, you're bound to have pissed someone off. But it seemed like everyone from sales to customer support to corporate to the engineers loved Mario, and those four never agree on anything!

After Bryce met Mario, it all came into focus. A major client had threatened to pull their hundred-million-dollar contract because their servers were down, and the product was to blame. Everyone had been running around, calling senseless meetings and finger-pointing—desperate to save their jobs. With all the commotion, no one was focused on actually fixing the problem. Then Mario arrived.

"Guys! It doesn't matter whose fault it is—I don't care. What do we do now?"

Immediately, everyone shut up. Because Mario didn't care about assigning blame, Bryce's coworkers were stunned into silence as their brains slowly switched from politician mode back to engineering mode. Every time someone started dredging up past mistakes, even if it was the CEO, Mario shut it down and kept everyone moving forward. By the end of the crisis, people who had been at each other's throats were patting each other on the back for pulling together.

When Bryce asked Mario how he learned this mind-set, Mario replied, "I grew up in a war zone."

Mario is Lebanese and from the 1970s to the early 2000s, Lebanon's history can be summarized as a mixture of "horrible civil war" and "horrible regular war." When a bomb obliterates a building or explodes in a crowded marketplace, you don't have the luxury of dwelling on the past. Questions like "Why did we have to come to the market today?" and "Why did we choose to live in this neighborhood?" are pointless. In that moment, you have two choices:

1. Pick up a bucket and help put the fire out.

2. Watch more people die.

Fortunately, Mario's family managed to immigrate to America. Now the only bombs he has to deal with are of the Jäger variety, but those experiences shaped him permanently and gave us a life-changing piece of advice: "The past doesn't matter. What do we do now?"

When readers complain about their finances, their regrets always feature prominently in their excuses: "I'm in too much debt." "I picked the wrong degree." "I'm too old to change." I get it. You've made mistakes. I have, too. We're all human. But the difference between success-ful people and everyone else is that successful people, like Mario, don't spend time on what-ifs. They spend that time finding a solution. Don't worry about how far you've fallen. Keep climbing.

If you're in debt, didn't pick a degree with a good POT score, or just feel stuck, repeat after me:

"The past doesn't matter. What do we do now?"

THE PAST DOESN'T MATTER

My friend Joe's dad was a successful businessman in Thailand and his mother a college professor. When Joe was just twelve years old, his dad's electronics retail business failed and the whole family immi-grated to the United States to start over. They arrived with only three suitcases and hardly any English to work unstable minimum-wage jobs. Joe's dad took midnight shifts at a gas station, delivered pizza, and picked up odd jobs. Their entire family of five slept in one room. Their lowest point came one day when Joe's dad was out on a pizza delivery.

A customer refused to pay and when Joe's dad didn't give him the pizza, the man attacked him with a baseball bat. At first, Joe's dad re-fused to go to the hospital because he had no health insurance, but the pain got so bad he paid out of pocket for surgery on his broken arm. After this, the bottom fell out. Joe's dad couldn't drive with one arm in a cast. Both of Joe's parents were now unemployed.

They almost gave up and moved back to Thailand. But one day, their luck changed. Joe's mom found a Thai restaurant for sale, a forty-five-minute drive away from their home. The seller was going through a divorce and, desperate to cash out, agreed to cut his price down to $9,000 from $16,500. Because Joe's parents had lived so frugally, they were able to come up with the $5,000 down payment.

They had no experience running a restaurant, but Joe's dad was de-termined to make it work. He learned how to cook, and his wife ran the front. The kids helped out in the evenings and on weekends, and that hole-in-the-wall restaurant eventually put them all through college. Joe's dad could have dwelled on the mistakes he had made in Thailand with his business or wondered why he hadn't just given up that stupid pizza. But he didn't. He was too focused on his next move.

Let me also tell you about Bill.

Back in 2002, Bill was a twenty-one-year-old college student who loved to party. Having tried pretty much every drug known to man, he was also the dealer for his friends. One night, he brought some drugs to a party, got high, and then went home to sleep.

The next day, hungover from the night's debauchery, he called his friend to head to class. But it was his buddy's roommate who picked up the phone, and he was yelling, "He's dead! He's dead!" Turns out the drugs he brought to that party had been (unbeknownst to him) laced with fentanyl, which had killed his friend in his sleep. "You have to get out of there now!"

Bill sprinted into the hallway, but he didn't get far. At the end of the corridor was a pair of cops, handcuffs in hand. Bill was convicted of "reckless homicide by delivery of a controlled substance" and sentenced to ten years in jail. On that day, multiple lives were turned upside down and two families destroyed by his recklessness. Bill thought his life was over. By the time he'd be released, he'd be thirty-one, and what kind of a future is there for a thirty-one-year-old ex-con with no college degree?

But Bill didn't give up. After getting out of prison in 2012, Bill started from the bottom. He went back to school, then got a $9-an-hour job stacking boxes. After that, he began selling sporting apparel. A lot of doors were slammed in his face. Eventually he managed to earn $1,000 one month, then $1,500 the next. He's now managed to amass a quarter of a million dollars in net worth and teaches others about finances and how to come back from a massive failure on his blog Wealth Well Done.

Bill's story is proof that you can come back from anything. He could have wasted his time in prison blaming the cops, blaming his luck, blaming society, but he didn't. He made a horrible mistake, got taught a brutal lesson—and came back stronger. He is the epitome of Mario's approach.

If you picked the wrong degree, or didn't get a degree, and are living paycheck to paycheck, it's not the end of the world. It's time to roll up your sleeves. The only thing you can control is what you do now.

There is always a way out. The key is to remember:

The past doesn't matter. What do we do now?

— 8 —

THE DOPE ON DOPAMINE

I refer to my time as a purse junkie as a mistake, but I don't regret it. What I learned completely changed my approach to money—and happiness.

I meticulously researched my first bag, spending hours on You-Tube. When I made my purchase (a lime-green Penelope shopper), my heart was bursting with excitement. This was the first fancy thing I had ever owned, officially marking my entry into the middle class. I stayed up all night smelling the fabric and caressing the leather, whispering, "My precious" . . . You know what? When I write it out, it sounds nuts, so let's move on.

That first purchase made me legitimately happy. But my second bag (a gold Ashley carryall) didn't. I was so confused. I had spent just as much time researching it and spent just as much money, but it wasn't the same. I didn't get that same high. By the time I was on to bag five, it was such a nonevent I don't even remember it. Soon, I got so bored of my purses I sold or gave away all but one.

I had inadvertently gotten on the Hedonic Treadmill.

When we buy something special or get a raise, we're happy because we perceive a positive change in our life. Similarly, when something bad happens, like a blown tire or a health issue, that negative change bums us out. But over time, we get used to the new normal and return to our baseline level of happiness. Psychologists Philip Brickman, Dan Coates, and Ronnie Janoff-Bulman first noticed this phenomenon in a 1978 study in which they tracked the happiness levels of two groups: lottery winners and recently injured paraplegics. As expected, the lottery winners reported a much higher level of happiness than the control group, and the paraplegics a much lower level. But over time, both groups adapted to their circumstances, and after a year their self-reported happiness returned to the levels at which they were before their lives had changed.[1]

Happiness is relative. Understanding that not only explains the diminishing returns of luxury purse buying, it applies in all areas of your life. In the 1970s, Vicki Robin, author of the *New York Times* bestseller *Your Money or Your Life*, began running the finance seminars that made her a household name. She would ask the audience to write down how much they earned and how much they thought they needed to earn to be happy. On average, people thought they needed double what they earned. It didn't matter if they made $30,000 or $100,000; the threshold was relative to their current salary.

So, are we simply incapable of being satisfied with our lot? On the surface, it seems so, but as I dug deeper, I realized that the Hedonic Treadmill—on which no matter how much we run, we always stay in place—is more than a psychological phenomenon. It's biochemical.

BLAME YOUR BRAIN

Your brain is a complex machine and neuroscientists are only beginning to understand it. What neuroscientists do understand pretty well is the mesolimbic pathway, which is part of the reward system in the brain. It contains pathways that trigger feelings like cravings, hunger, desire, and pleasure. The mesolimbic pathway incentivizes us to seek food when we're hungry and water when we're thirsty. It's also responsible for the positive reinforcement we feel when we get them.

Which brings us to dopamine. Dopamine, the "pleasure chemical," is the main neurotransmitter coursing through the mesolimbic pathway. When something good happens, dopamine gets released and we feel pleasure. At least, that's what we've been led to believe. In reality, it's a bit more complicated. The mesolimbic pathway also contains a structure responsible for processing dopamine called the nucleus accumbens, which houses neural pathways sensitive to dopamine. These are the *real* gateways to pleasure and happiness. This distinction is why the narrative of "more dopamine = more happiness" isn't actually true.

In 2006, neurologists in Germany conducted an experiment on the nucleus accumbens. What they found explained the Hedonic Treadmill. Subjects were asked to play a game of identifying simple objects like circles and triangles. If they won, they'd get one euro. If they lost, they got nothing. Before starting they were given a percentage likelihood of winning.

You would think that people would be pumped if they won money no matter what, right? Wrong. Turns out, if people were given a high chance (like 100 percent) of winning, when they did, an fMRI showed no additional activity in the nucleus accumbens's dopaminergic receptors. Conversely, if they had a low chance of winning (like 25 percent) and they did, the fMRI showed a spike of activity in those same dopaminergic receptors. Conversely, if the person was given a high probability of winning (like 75 percent) and they didn't, the fMRI showed a *decrease* in dopamine activity.

The nucleus accumbens reacts to both the presence of a positive stimulus and also the *expectation* of that stimulus. In other words, pleasure isn't based on an absolute level of dopamine in the brain, but rather on the *relative* level versus the *expected* level of dopamine in the nucleus accumbens.

Relative, not absolute.

Yay for Cocaine!

The results were published in an academic paper titled "Prediction Error as a Linear Function of Reward Probability Is Coded in Human Nucleus Accumbens."[2] This title both amuses and nauseates me, as a former engineer and current writer, in its complete inaccessibility. Anyway, as boring as all the scientific terms are, this is one of the few attempts to study the brain's reward system as it relates to finances.

In fact, we only know as much as we do about the human mesolimbic pathway because of research done in the context of addiction studies. Specifically, cocaine studies, funded by the DEA, CDC, and WHO, to understand and treat drug addicts.

So . . . yay for cocaine?

Cocaine, amphetamines, and other drugs operate by disrupting dopamine reuptake and reabsorption, causing the chemical to overwhelm the mesolimbic pathway and overstimulate its pleasure centers to the point of madness. But because the nucleus accumbens is involved, your brain resets to the new normal. That's why the next time a cocaine user takes a hit, the high isn't as strong. Their baseline has recalibrated; they need more cocaine to get the same high. Two things can happen next. Either the user gets bored by the decreasing effectiveness of the drugs and stops using—or they double down. Every addict knows that experience as "chasing their first high."

The Hedonic Treadmill works the same way. Each time you spend money on a big-ticket item, you get a little high, because your nucleus accumbens is detecting a change for the better. But after you buy that purse, or that TV, or that Xbox, it acclimatizes. Your level of pleasure steadily declines with each new purchase of a similar item; while the stimulus remains the same, your brain's expectations have increased.

Not All Spending Is Created Equal

Here's the part where I'm supposed to scold people who spend too much money. Sorry to disappoint. The lesson here isn't exactly what you may think.

Once I figured out what was happening, I realized that this diminishing-happiness effect only applied to possessions—not to experiences. Maybe it's because I spent most of my childhood stuck in small towns, but I've always loved to travel. When we were working, Bryce and I would plan two vacations a year to Europe or the Caribbean, with the bill for each averaging $2,500—not chump change, by any means. And I had a great time, every time. We looked forward to our next vacation, reading travel guides and watching *No Reservations*. And then the day would come and we'd be like, "Wow! We're in Rome!" Afterward, we'd go through our photos over and over and compare notes of our warm, fuzzy memories. The point is, it always felt worth it. That spending didn't have the same drop-off that spending on stuff did, so we kept doing it.

Around that time, I started to notice a strange pattern among my friends and family (which was later reinforced when I started my blog and readers emailed me their financial situation to analyze). The more *stuff* people owned, the unhappier and more stressed they tended to be. Conversely, the less *stuff* people owned and the more they spent on *experiences* like travel or learning new skills, the happier and more content they were. Possessions give you an initial burst of dopamine that fades as your nucleus accumbens acclimatizes, causing you to continuously chase that high. People who spend on experiences get way more bang for their buck.

Stuff tends to snowball, too. I have a friend who collects art, but it's never just about the piece; he also has to pay for it to be framed, reinforce a wall in his condo so it's strong enough to support it, buy special lights to display it the way the artist intended, insure it . . . The list goes on and on. And every time he finds out about a new expense, he flies into a rage about the scuzzy vendors "taking advantage" of him!

Not all spending is created equal. Unless you are in true dire straits, day-to-day expenses like rent, groceries, heating, electricity, etc. don't tend to bring you great happiness or unhappiness. At a certain point, they blend into the background. These are baseline costs.

Spending increases your happiness when it brings something new to your life, whether that's a possession or an experience. These are splurges. However, that happiness is temporary for possessions but not for experiences.

Some spending *decreases* your happiness. These expenses—like insurance and maintenance—are necessary when you own things. Nobody enjoys spending money on a flooded basement or a flat tire. They are unexpected costs.

When I was growing up, I thought the key to happiness was more stuff. If one Coke could make me so happy, then thirty Cokes should make me thirty times as happy! But the truth is, if someone had given me thirty Cokes, I would have panicked and started digging a hole under our chicken coop to hide my fortune from my neighbors. Then I would have sat on my porch, forever on guard for anyone who looked suspicious to keep them from murdering me and my family to steal my reserves.

That's the problem with possessions. You get the initial bump, but then it fades, and if that possession is expensive, you worry about it. If it breaks, you have to spend money to fix it. If, for example, one of the chickens pecked open one of the Coke cans, I would have had to kill that chicken. Then I'd have been down one can of Coke *and* one chicken, which we would have had to pay money to replace. Possessions convert splurges into unexpected costs.

Think of my friend the art collector. His initial purchase gave him a burst of happiness. But over time, that happiness faded because his nucleus accumbens acclimatized.

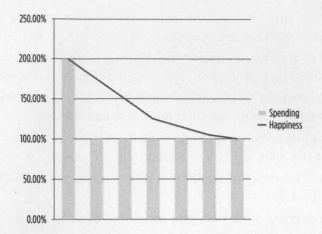

When the expensive purchase caused him to spend money to insure and maintain it, the spending didn't make him happy. It had the exact opposite effect.

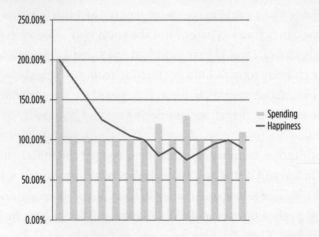

But now let's look at someone who spends money on experiences. Since every experience is different, your happiness spikes each time. Not only that, once the experience is over, you don't own anything, and as a result you don't need to protect it. So, you don't get that conversion of splurge–to–unexpected cost spending. Instead, your spending and happiness look like this:

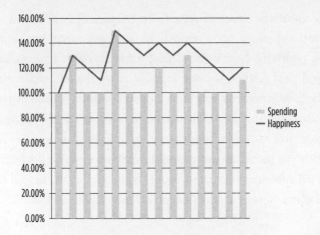

Not All Cuts Hurt

This realization lit up my brain with possibilities. If all spending isn't created equal, does that mean not all cuts in spending will hurt? If certain expenditures don't increase your happiness, doesn't that mean eliminating them won't affect it one way or the other? If certain expenditures *decrease* your happiness, wouldn't eliminating them make you happier?

Everyone thinks budgeting is like being on a diet. If you spend less, you're less happy. But in actuality, *certain* spending doesn't decrease your happiness. In other words, not all cuts hurt.

One summer in Toronto, the Transit Commission, which runs the subways, decided to go on strike. For weeks, the city's subway system ground to a halt and TV stations filled with angry Canadians (it doesn't happen often, but when it does, watch out!). Rather than pay for taxis daily, I decided to jog to work. To my surprise, it didn't take as long, nor was it as difficult, as I'd imagined. I even lost weight and was able to cancel my gym membership. So, when the TTC got back online, I continued jogging to work, saving almost $200 every month that summer. I felt physically amazing and loved seeing those extra dollars in my bank account.

Remember the closet exercise from chapter 2? I asked you to track your clothing usage for a month to sort out what you're actually wearing regularly. Now pretend that a fire started in your closet and destroyed your clothes. If you lost the stuff on the left, well, you barely wore them anyway. You might be bummed, but it wouldn't really affect your day-to-day life. Conversely, if you lost all the clothes to the right, you would *feel* it. They were the pieces you wore every day. Whenever you picked an outfit, you'd miss the ones that got burned up.

Not all spending is created equal. And as a result, not all cuts are created equal. Some cuts hurt deeply. Others don't hurt at all.

This Time It's Personal

I have a confession to make. I find personal finance books annoying. They tend to make you feel bad about spending money, berating you for buying a cup of coffee every morning. If only you'd invest it, that $3.50 would be worth a hundred thousand in thirty years!

Bull. Shit. While I don't doubt the math, universal advice like that is idiotic. Some people don't care about coffee (like me). But other people love it—it truly makes their day better. I'm from Sichuan Province, where all our food is covered in chili oil. If someone told me that not eating spicy foods would extend my life expectancy, I'd respond, "Why would I want to live a longer life without my favorite food?"

The secret to budgeting is not to imitate some template but to find the budget that works for *you*.

Step 1: Eliminate Baseline Costs That Don't Make You Happy

First, find the easy stuff. Pore over your monthly expenses and look for spending that can be easily eliminated without any real hit to your quality of life. Bank fees are a good example. By opening accounts at zero-fee online banks or credit unions, you can eliminate bank fees (which will make you feel awesome):

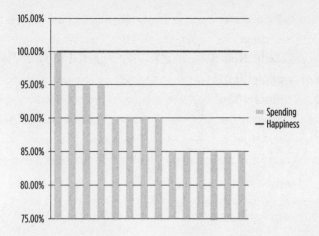

Give it a shot. Sometimes you'll find spending you weren't even aware of. I once had a friend discover she was still paying for hosting for a website she no longer owned!

Here are a few suggestions to get you started.

- Bank fees

- Subscriptions to things you no longer use

- Cable packages for channels you don't watch

- Landline (who uses landlines anymore?)

Step 2: Eliminate Baseline Costs That Hurt but You'll Get Used To

Next find ways to make expense cuts that may cause you some amount of discomfort but you'll get used to. For me, it was jogging to work. For you, it may be cooking at home, biking to work, or buying used things instead of new. There will be an adjustment period, but once your nucleus accumbens kicks in, your happiness level will return to baseline.

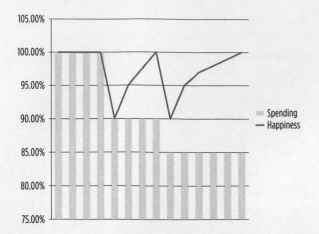

There are some expenses that you'll find simply can't be cut without permanently affecting your general well-being. If for whatever reason I lost access to spicy Sichuan food, my happiness level would look like this:

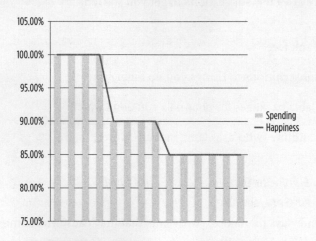

Finding the appropriate expenses to cut for your personal situation is the key to successful budgeting. None of this "just quit buying coffee" crap. Your spending is personal and specific to *you*, and no book can tell you exactly what to do, no matter how hard they try to convince you. The only way to find out is to try it and give it some time. If you find yourself missing that thing too much, undo it!

Here are a few items that may fall under this category.

- ▸ Buying lunch at work

- ▸ Eating out

- ▸ Going out with friends

- ▸ Gym membership

Step 3: Reduce the Expensive Things You Own
That Cost You Money

In this step, we take a hard look at the expensive items you own. Specifically, things that cost you money to maintain, insure, repeatedly fill up with premium gas, etc. The goal is to reduce or eliminate unexpected costs as much as possible.

The two most common items people own that contribute to their unexpected costs are their car and their home.

Let's talk about cars for a minute. Readers often write in to say how they try to save and be responsible, but bad things continue happening to keep them from getting ahead. Digging deeper, often it turns out that their overreliance on their cars is the cause of their bad luck. Not only do cars decrease in value the second you drive them off the lot, they are money sinks. One blown radiator can destroy months of diligent saving.

Sometimes, people misinterpret my advice as meaning they have to get rid of their cars. Not so. Remember, most of a car's unexpected costs are dependent on miles driven rather than ownership of the car itself. Gas and maintenance costs go down the less you drive, and you can reduce your insurance premiums if you don't drive every day. If you can find a way to use your car less by, say, biking to work or taking public transportation, you can keep your car while reducing most of its unexpected costs. Plus, it's good for the environment and your waistline. The goal is to turn this . . .

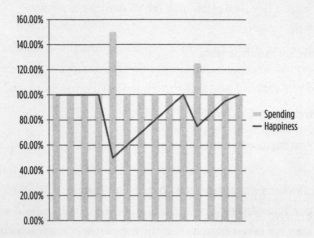

. . . into this:

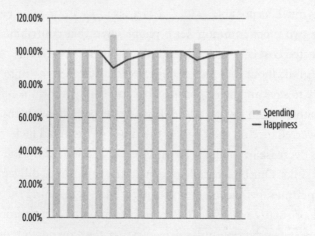

A house is the second major item in this category, but housing is such a big topic that we devoted an entire chapter to it (chapter 9). In short, people justify the unexpected costs of owning a house by pointing out that houses tend to appreciate in value, so the costs are always offset by this investment, while renting is throwing money away. We'll debunk this myth in the next chapter.

Step 4: Add Splurges

By the time you've reached this step, you've gone through your spending and found what you can cut painlessly. You've also realized what you can't live without and added it back. Finally, you've looked at your most expensive items (cars, mainly) and either reduced your reliance on them or eliminated them completely.

Now let's have some fun! Add up all the spending you've cut. Then take a part of that and allocate it toward splurges. You don't have to decide what you're going to spend it on (in fact, it's better if you don't so you can make it spontaneous), but this is "fun money" you can do whatever you want with. For me, this usually means traveling, but it could be anything. Want to go to a concert? Go for it! Go scuba diving? Sure! Go to Vegas for a wild weekend? Well, clear it with your significant other first, but why the hell not? I would encourage you to splurge on experiences over possessions to get lasting happiness, but it's up to you. As long as the amount allocated is less than the amount you saved by cutting, then you have successfully saved money while increasing happiness!

UNDERSTAND YOUR BRAIN, UNDERSTAND YOUR BUDGET

Budgeting does not have to be the soul-sucking chore that everyone thinks it is, because budgeting isn't simply about cutting. You just need to understand two truths about the human brain, namely:

- ▸ How you derive satisfaction from your spending is determined by your brain.
- ▸ Everyone's brain is different.

The process of finding your optimal budget is different for everyone. My budget will not work for you and vice versa. But by understanding the link between dopamine, happiness, and spending, and by following the steps outlined in this chapter, you will hopefully take a budget that looks like this, the budget of a typical consumer who owns too much and is perpetually unhappy because of high baseline costs and unexpected costs . . .

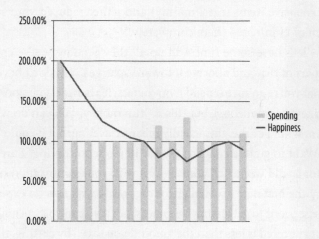

. . . and turn it into this, one with low baseline costs, no unexpected costs, and lots of happiness-producing splurges:

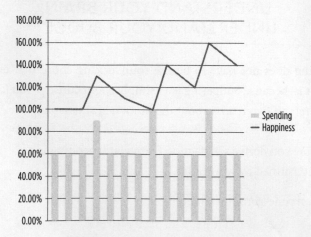

In the process, you will discover the most efficient way of turning dollars into dopamine that works for you and you alone. If you're anything like me, you will find it incredibly liberating, and you'll be happier and healthier, with more money than you ever thought possible.

Now on to something a bit controversial. It's time to talk about why owning a home sucks.

CHAPTER 8 SUMMARY

- ▸ Spending money is addictive because our brains reset our expectations and we no longer get the same amount of dopamine with repeated spending.

- ▸ There are three different types of spending:

  - • Baseline Costs: Day-to-day costs that you get used to, like rent or utilities. These don't increase or decrease your happiness.

  - • Splurges: An occasional purchase that makes you happier.

  - • Unexpected Costs: Unexpected costs to fix something that's gone wrong. These decrease your happiness.

- ▸ How people budget varies per individual. You have to experiment and see for yourself which cuts hurt and which don't.

- ▸ To find a budget that works for you:

  - • Step 1: Eliminate baseline costs that don't make you happy.

  - • Step 2: Eliminate baseline costs that may hurt to get rid of but that you'll get used to living without.

  - • Step 3: Eliminate as many unexpected costs as you can by reducing high-maintenance things you own.

  - • Step 4: Add splurges back into your life.

YOUR HOUSE IS NOT
AN INVESTMENT

I've talked a lot about my upbringing already, and you might be thinking there were a lot of ugly moments. Please understand it's not my intention to depict my culture as being all about physical abuse and abandonment issues; there are downsides as well. Namely, our attitude toward housing. As we discussed, when famine and instability can instantly destroy your sense of peace, your approach to money naturally becomes conservative. We don't waste anything. We hoard our savings. We fear debt. These attitudes have generally served us well in helping us become resilient as we assimilate into new communities and cultures.

But all these lessons fly right out the window when it comes to housing. In Chinese culture, a house is the be-all-end-all status symbol and the only thing we throw our hard-earned money at. It's also the only thing that we are willing to go into debt for. I've seen friends who spend hours clipping coupons to save a dollar off toilet paper overspend by hundreds of thousands of dollars on a condo, caught up in the excitement of a bidding war. This obsession is anything but benign. Our hatred of debt, our ability to live on almost nothing, and our emphasis on education are powerful tools that allow tons of immigrants like my family to escape poverty. But it's still rare for those same immigrant families to become truly rich. The reason for this, as it turns out, is housing. My own parents, who lived through a famine, who survived on $0.44 USD a day for *years*, started asking me a few weeks after I had graduated when I was going to buy a home. (And they've never stopped asking.) At the time, I didn't know better either, so after I settled into my first full-time job, my then-boyfriend, Bryce, and I started to look for a house.

THE TERROR OF THE HOUSING MARKET

I've been through a few legitimately terrifying experiences in my life. Facing my kindergarten teacher was one of them. Being trapped in a high school with a suspected gunman was another. But all of that pales in comparison to shopping for a house.

I grew up counting pennies; now I was being asked to spend hundreds of thousands of dollars, all at once, based on a ten-minute open house. I hadn't been working that long and that amount of money seemed unimaginable. And here's what really irritated me: what I could get didn't even seem that *good*.

"How much would it cost if the roof needed repairs in the next year?" I asked one real estate agent.

"Oh, maybe ten thousand dollars. Maybe more."

"And would this be covered under a warranty of some sort?"

He chuckled. "That's . . . not how things work."

What was most surprising was how accepting everyone was of these asinine conditions. My friends and colleagues who wouldn't have bought a cell phone without a one-year warranty were gladly signing on to thirty years of debt with no guarantee that their house wasn't being held together with duct tape.

As I said, even my parents got in on the act. "You have to stop being so picky," my mom would say, sliding a flyer across the table. "Here's one your dad and I found for you." The same woman who beat me for costing her $30 to replace a house key wanted me to spend $800,000!

My uneasiness came to a head with what I like to call the "Scary House." In my neighborhood, there was a house that looked possessed. Someone had put up signs in front about secret government drones and written "UFO" across the windows in red paint (or at least I *hope* it was red paint). One day, we noticed holes, six feet deep, all around the property. I thought, *Welp, this house is going to be on the news tonight!* as we hurried past.

Then a For Sale sign appeared in the front yard.

"Who the hell is going to buy that thing?" I asked Bryce. "There are probably bodies buried underneath the floorboards!" Not to mention the walls and roof were falling apart from neglect.

A few days later, the sign had a sticker: "Sold." For half a million dollars.

I thought that was the stupidest thing I had ever seen, but it got worse. The buyer turned out to be a property flipper, who moved in with a crew and, over the course of a few weeks, did a half-assed renovation to make the house look superficially presentable and then put it back on the market.

A few days later: "Sold." For $800,000.

Now I was pissed. Not only was real estate expensive, it was a scam.

WHY HOUSES ARE A SHITTY INVESTMENT

Something about housing makes people insane. Even rational people like my parents turn into debt-accumulating monsters. I don't blame them, though. The marketing, after all, is pretty slick.

Renting is throwing your money away.

Owning a home is investing in yourself.

A man's home is his castle.

They're not making any more land.

Housing always goes up!

We've all heard these lines. They sound reasonable, so we assume owning a home is a rite of passage into adulthood. But when I started looking into it after the Scary House incident, what shocked me most was the math. Owning—not just buying—a home is incredibly expensive. (Note that even though my statistics are from the United States, the numbers are pretty much identical north of the border.)

Ready? Here we go.

According to the US Census Bureau, the average American family stays in a home for about nine years. The average American family also keeps the bulk of their net worth in their home, under the assumption that a house is a good investment that always increases in value.

Let's see what happens to this average American family over these nine years.

Historically, housing tends to appreciate at the rate of inflation, but for the purposes of this example let's give housing a big boost and say that it increases at the same rate as the stock market, an average annual rate of 6 percent. If this were to happen, then over nine years a house purchased for $500,000 will increase to a value of $844,739, for a total gain of $344,739. By the time that family sells they expect a nice fat check, and everyone is ecstatic! Awesome, right?

Well, not quite. The problem is that owning a house costs money way beyond the purchase price. It costs money to buy, sell, finance, and appraise it, and to insure and maintain it each year, which we logically know but basically just dismiss when we're digging deep for that down payment. I did too, thinking, *How much could that be?*

Turns out, *a lot*. First, there are fees involved in the purchase. Buyers have to pay for a title search at their land registry office, which costs an average of $100. Then to register their purchase, they have to pay a title recording fee—$150. In some states, they have to pay a lawyer to do this for them, which is about $1,000. So far, we're up to $1,250. Still sounds like small potatoes, doesn't it? Well, in the immortal words of

Samuel L. Jackson in *Jurassic Park*, "Hold on to your butts." You have to insure the house. Rates vary by city and state, but the average national cost is about 0.5 percent of the home value, per year. This gets paid annually, so over nine years that's $500,000 × 0.5% × 9 = $22,500. You have to pay property taxes; the average annual rate in the United States is about 1 percent. $500,000 × 1% × 9 = $45,000.

This stuff is starting to add up, isn't it? And houses cost money to maintain. Roofs collapse, pipes burst, ghosts of Civil War soldiers haunt your cellar. Realtors recommend setting aside between 1 percent and 3 percent of your home value every year for maintenance. So conservatively, this would be $500,000 × 1% × 9 = $45,000.

At the end of those nine years, our average American family wants to sell. Selling costs money, too. First, you have to pay your real estate broker. A typical commission is 6 percent, which gets calculated on the final sale price, not the original purchase price. Six percent of $844,739 is $50,684. Also, don't forget about land transfer taxes, which are paid to the city and can vary from almost nothing (0.01 percent in Colorado) to ridiculously high (4 percent in Pittsburgh). The national average is about 1.2 percent, and 1.2 percent of $844,739 is $10,137.

And that damn lawyer fee of $1,000. You have to pay that *again*.

If all these numbers are making your head spin, you aren't alone. Here's a summary of all these costs we've talked about:

Title Search	$100
Recording Fee	$150
Lawyer Fees	$1,000 × 2 = $2,000
Insurance	$500,000 × 0.5% × 9 = $22,500
Maintenance	$500,000 × 1% × 9 = $45,000
Property Tax	$500,000 × 1% × 9 = $45,000

Broker Commission	$844,739 × 6% = $50,684
Land Transfer Tax	$844,739 × 1.2% = $10,137
Total Cost	$175,571

In total, this family has paid a whopping $175,571 just to own this house. So that $344,739 gain they were anticipating? Fifty-one percent of it got eaten up!

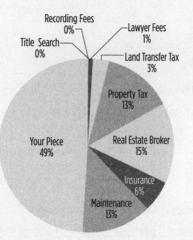

Your piece of the pie is only 49 percent of the total gain of the house.

Maybe you're thinking, *That's not so bad; that's still six figures of gain.* Here's the thing. In this analysis, I've assumed that this family bought the house outright with a suitcase full of cash. As we know, almost no one does that; they borrow the money in the form of a mortgage. So, let's add that in. The typical down payment on a first-time home purchase is 10 percent, and to cover the balance, our family walked into their local bank and got a mortgage. As of 2018, the interest from this mortgage no longer makes sense to deduct, since the standard deduction got raised in the Tax Cuts and Jobs Act, so our family gets no tax break from loans of less than $600,000.

After nine years, our typical American family will have paid $162,033 of interest to their bank! That's money they're never getting back.

So now let's add that onto our costs.

Title Search	$100
Recording Fee	$150
Lawyer Fees	$1,000 × 2 = $2,000
Insurance	$500,000 × 0.5% × 9 = $22,500
Maintenance	$500,000 × 1% × 9 = $45,000
Property Tax	$500,000 × 1% × 9 = $45,000
Broker Commission	$844,739 × 6% = $50,684
Land Transfer Tax	$844,739 × 1.2% = $10,137
Mortgage Interest	$162,033
Total Cost	$337,604

Our typical American family has now paid $337,604 for the pleasure of buying their home! That's *98 percent* of the gain they were supposed to get!

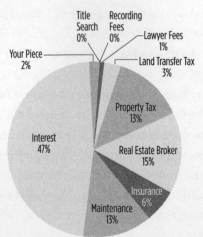

QUIT LIKE A MILLIONAIRE

They're left with that tiny slice at the top: 2 percent.

And remember, this is all based on the wildly optimistic assumption that their house will appreciate at the rate of the stock market (6 percent) year after year. If the house appreciates any slower, then they're actually losing money. This is why the typical family who keeps the majority of their net worth in their property never accumulates much money. They *think* they're getting ahead as they see its value go up, but they don't realize that all the extra costs add up to the point where most of their gain has vanished.

A house can be a *great* investment—for real estate brokers, the government, insurance companies, and banks. Basically, for everyone except the owner.

For the owner, a house is a *terrible* investment.

Now, to be clear, I'm talking about primary residences. In other words, a house you buy, move into, and live in. Housing *can* be a good investment if it's purchased to rent out to a tenant. However, landlording is a whole other topic that's beyond the scope of this book, so I'm not going to talk about it. There are tons of great resources on that topic; go read one of them.

THE RULE OF 150

This all begs the question: does it ever make sense to buy rather than rent?

The math may make it seem like the answer is no, but everyone has to live somewhere. (And obviously, in an extreme case where a mortgage costs $1 a month and rent is $1,000,000, then buying would make sense despite the extra costs.) What is the tipping point where the decision to rent becomes the decision to buy?

A real estate broker would tell you that if the monthly mortgage payment equals the rent of an equivalent place, then it makes sense to buy and pay yourself rather than paying a landlord. However, this conveniently ignores all the ownership costs we discussed. We know now that for the average American family, the cost of buying, owning, insuring, and selling a home equals the interest costs for a typical mortgage over a nine-year period. We also know that in the first nine years of a standard thirty-year mortgage, around 50 percent of your total payment goes toward interest, while the rest goes toward paying down the principal. In order to figure out when it makes sense to buy, we have to take the interest, add the extra costs of owning that home, and compare that to the rent you'd be saving.

This is where the Rule of 150 comes from. Since the extra ownership costs are approximately equal to the interest of a typical mortgage over nine years, and the interest is approximately 50 percent of your mortgage payment during that time, you have to multiply your monthly mortgage payment by 150 percent. This is how much your house will *actually* cost per month, once all expenses are factored in. If that Rule of 150 monthly cost is higher than your rent, then it makes sense to rent. If it's lower, then it makes sense to buy. The moral of the story isn't to never buy a house, it's to "math shit up" before you do.

At the time that we were looking for a home, my Rule of 150 number was way higher than what I was paying in rent ($850 a month for a one-bedroom apartment). So after "mathing shit up," I said no thank you to the housing market and kept my money.

WHAT DO RICH PEOPLE DO WITH THEIR MONEY?

The math made sense, but this opened up an unexpected can of worms. If I wasn't going to blow my savings on a house like everyone else, what was I supposed to do with it? Nothing in my background could provide guidance, so for a brief period, I felt lost. Then I decided to start learning how rich people did things. When it came to managing money beyond paying for food and rent, I was clueless, and my parents were clueless as well. I had to start looking for answers, and who knows better how to grow their money?

To learn what they knew, I read. I spent countless hours in libraries, checking out book after book and reading *Forbes* and the *Wall Street Journal*. This was the start of a nearly decade-long fascination with rich people that eventually culminated in my becoming one of them. What struck me most was how much conflicting information was out there. Some of these authors advocated buying houses; others advised renting instead. Some started companies while others played the stock market. It was a dizzying landscape of information that took me many years to sift through and come up with a pathway to wealth.

But I did discover a path—a mathematically reproducible one. While I've spent the first third of this book talking about the lessons I learned about money from poverty, now it's time to turn to the lessons about money I learned from the rich.

The first lesson came from Robert Kiyosaki, in his bestselling book *Rich Dad Poor Dad*. In it, he claims (and I'm paraphrasing here):

Poor people buy stuff. The middle class buys houses. Rich people buy investments.

Rich people buy investments.

Hmm . . .

Well, I thought, while I was more than happy to be middle-class, it certainly didn't hurt to learn how to invest, right? I called up my bank and made an appointment for the very next day.

CHAPTER 9 SUMMARY

- ▸ Housing is expensive to own.

- ▸ When you factor in the additional costs of buying and owning a house outside of the mortgage, it can eat up the majority of your housing gains.

- To get a more accurate estimate of your housing costs, use the Rule of 150:

  - Take your monthly mortgage payment and multiply it by 150 percent.

  - If that Rule of 150 monthly cost is higher than rent, rent. Otherwise, buy. Always "math shit up" before you buy.

- Poor people buy stuff. The middle class buys houses. Rich people buy investments.

— 10 —

THE REAL BANK ROBBERS

Imagine this. You're sitting at your local bank, chatting with a salesperson about how to invest your retirement money, when a group of armed men burst in. They're wearing trench coats, and one of them is obviously Keanu Reeves, so, you know, your typical Wednesday in LA.

"Whoa, you should, like, totally give me your wallet!" Keanu slurs at you while slow-motion cartwheeling around the lobby. You've seen a movie or two, so you recognize that a heist is under way—but there's a twist. The bank robbers aren't the real villains in this scene. That would be the nice salesperson sitting in front of you. The armed men just want your wallet. That'll cost you $60 and the time and inconvenience of replacing your credit cards and ID. The bank wants your savings—specifically, a percentage of it, every year, forever.

The real bank robbers work for the bank.

THE POWER OF MORE

The main challenge for a young person who has just started full-time work is the art of "adulting." Paying bills, finding a place to live, cooking, that sort of thing. For me, it was adjusting to the shock that the money I earned was mine to keep. That's a whole lot of Cokes. It was mind-blowing.

Right out of college, my money management approach was simple. Income went into my checking account and was then reluctantly spent on necessities like food and rent. After six months, my contract job converted into a full-time position, and I learned about fancy things like employer-based retirement accounts (which we will discuss in chapter 12) that I was now eligible for. When I found out that my work would give me extra money with an employee matching program, I immediately signed up—and quickly realized I had to start making decisions about how to invest that cash. That's how I found myself sitting down with a dude from my bank.

What he told me didn't exactly inspire confidence. He kept recommending me this one mutual fund run by the bank but couldn't answer basic questions about it.

"So, this fund invests in stocks?"

"Yes."

"Which ones?"

"Those are determined by the fund manager."

"How does the fund manager know which stocks to pick?"

"He uses an algorithm to select them."

"Can I see this algorithm?"

"Unfortunately, no. It's proprietary."

"Okay . . ." I sat back in my chair, suspicion blaring like an air-raid siren in my head. "How do you know this manager knows what he's doing?"

"Well, he runs a mutual fund, so he must be pretty smart."

"That's not answering the question."

"What would you like me to do to convince you?"

"I'd like to meet him."

The bank salesperson scoffed. "Yeah, that's not happening."

"So, let me get this straight," I replied, reaching for my jacket. "You want me to trust my money to a person I've never met, can never meet, using a proprietary algorithm to pick stocks that will never be explained to me—"

"Look." The salesperson bolted upright, sensing correctly that he was not making a sale today. "Most people don't have a problem with this kind of setup."

I walked out of his office and never looked back. One perk of being an engineer is that I've developed the habit of checking and double-checking the math before making any financial decisions. So I knew which products had the highest commission rates, incentivizing the banking officer to peddle them to unsuspecting customers. The mutual fund he was trying to sell me that day paid the highest commission of all. Not only that, when I dug in, I found that the fund I was being pushed toward "wrapped" multiple funds—all run by the same bank, each with its own manager—into one superfund! The superfund manager would have gotten a cut as well, and the salesperson would have gotten a commission on top of that!

How many people in this bank would have been leeching off my money if I had listened to him?

When Percentages Beat Dollars

Around that time, I noticed what might be the biggest difference between how lower- and middle-class people think versus how rich people think. The lower and middle classes are obsessed with *adding* to their wealth: getting an education or a higher-paying job, that kind of thing. Rich people are obsessed with *growing* their wealth. They generally don't talk about how much they make as a dollar amount, but rather as a percentage of their net worth.

"I only make six dollars an hour!" a poor person says.

"I only made three percent last year!" a rich person laments.

When you're poor, percentages mean nothing. Ten percent growth is meaningless when you have no money; after all, 10 percent of $0 is $0. The vast majority of investors are people like you and me: working stiffs trying to improve their savings, starting off with a few thousand bucks at most. A percentage point is worthless, because 1 percent of $1,000 is just $10 a year. Who cares? But to the people *running* these mutual funds, 1 percent is a lot of money.

An equity fund I just chose at random has a management fee of 1.7 percent; that is, they charge 1.7 percent of the net value of your investment to select which stocks and bonds to put your money in. To an individual customer, that 1.7 percent seems like no biggie, but here's the thing: that apathy is the exact reaction the bank is hoping for. At the time of this writing, this particular fund had assets under management of $700,000,000. To them, 1.7 percent is worth almost *twelve MILLION* dollars each and every year. And each of those twelve million dollars is handed over by someone saying, "Eh, who cares about one point seven percent?"

Percentage points matter. That was one of the first lessons I learned from rich people that helped me to become one of them.

What Exactly Are You Paying For?

When I started learning about investing, I thought it was about picking individual stocks: grabbing up Apple shares at $10 and later selling them at whatever ridiculously high price they're trading at now. But that felt uncomfortably close to betting on horses at a racetrack, and I do not, nor will I ever, gamble. I've seen firsthand how that particular vice can wreck people's lives, and my dad taught me that it's one of the most expensive addictions you can get; you can drink only so much alcohol before you pass out, but with gambling you can lose your entire life savings. So, stock picking never sat right with me.

That's when I learned about index investing. I first heard about it from bestselling author JL Collins, author of *The Simple Path to Wealth* and founder of JLCollinsNH.com. I've since met Jim and had the opportunity to thank him in person for teaching me about this, because it was the first time investing ever made sense to me.

Every day people like us get up, brush our teeth, and go to work. That labor, whatever it is, makes money for our employers. No one can tell whether the work I do for my company is more valuable than the work someone else does for theirs. All we know is that money is being made. Index investing takes the guesswork out of trying to predict which company will rise or fall, and instead bets on the total growth of the stock market.

That, I could get behind. In any given race, I'd have no idea which horse is going to win or lose, so I'd never bet on any individual horse. But would I bet on the casino? Absolutely. Because no matter which horse wins or loses, the casino makes money.

Index investing allows you to bet on the casino.

Your Investments Can't Go to Zero

What's everyone's biggest investing fear? Having all their money disappear, right? At least, that was my biggest fear—the guy in charge of my stocks picks a bunch that go bankrupt. Index investing doesn't have this problem. Since the index owns all companies, it's impossible for it to crash to zero. Individual companies may go bankrupt, but unless every single company goes bankrupt at the same time, the index never hits zero. (And if it does, the aliens have probably invaded, *Independence Day* style, and who cares about your 401(k) balance then?)

Index investing also has an elegant built-in barometer in that it owns shares weighted by market cap. In other words, if a company is worth more, the index owns more shares of that company, and vice versa. This is the most intuitive way of creating a gauge for the stock market as a whole, which is why most major indexes, like the S & P 500, which tracks the five hundred biggest companies in the stock market, are constructed like this. That means that when a company releases a cool new smartphone and their stock soars, the index will automatically pick up more shares. And when another company steps in it and their stock plummets, the index will dump shares. For the S & P 500, once a company drops in value from number 500 to number 501, it's dropped from the index altogether.

JL Collins brilliantly described this as a "self-cleansing" mechanism, and that's exactly what it is. Owning the index means you only own the biggest, healthiest companies and makes sure you get rid of shares of bad companies before they hit zero.

(Note that the only major American index *not* to use this methodology is the Dow Jones Industrial Average, which is price weighted rather than market-cap weighted.)

Index Investing Lowers Fees

One of the most frustrating things about evaluating actively managed mutual funds is that they don't explain how they pick their stocks. They'll throw around terms like "proprietary algorithm" or "high alpha and low beta," but at the end of the day the fund manager's not going to tell you because if they did they'd be out of a job.

The power of indexing is how simple it is. You could probably run an index fund yourself: just throw all the companies in the stock market into a spreadsheet, sort by market cap, and pick the top five hundred. Done. You've just created an index fund. And because it's so simple, there's no fund manager to pay.

In the United States, actively managed mutual funds charge MERs (Management Expense Ratio fees) north of 1 percent annually. In Canada, it's even worse, with a typical mutual fund charging around 2 percent. But a typical index fund tracking the American stock market

(NYSE: VTI) charges only 0.04 percent! That's twenty-five times lower than the fee for an actively managed one.

The sneaky thing about management fees is that you don't get a bill at the end of the year. If you did, you would say, "Wait, I have to pay a thousand dollars? For what?!" And then you would call up your bank for an angry conversation. Instead, that fee is taken out of your investments silently, every month. You never get a bill and you never see those charges broken out in a statement. That fee is baked in. The intent is to quietly take small amounts out of your pocket each month and hope you won't notice. In fact, you can't even see the fees unless you compare a managed fund to an index fund.

This is five years of the S & P 500's price history, from 2013 to 2018:

S & P 500 Performance 2013–2018

Now let's see what would happen if we added a 1 percent management fee to this fund:

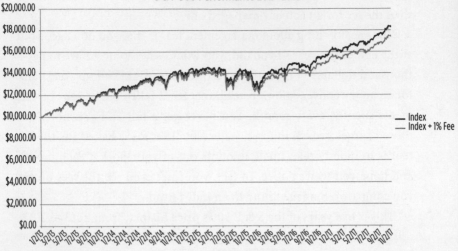

S & P 500 Performance 2013–2018

After five years, that 1 percent really adds up. For a person investing $10,000 at the beginning of 2013, they're giving up $900, or almost 10 percent of their initial investment! Imagine how many cans of Coke you could buy with that! And this effect just gets worse as time goes on. One percent may not seem like much right now, but over a typical retirement time frame of twenty-five years, it snowballs.

S & P 500 Performance 1993–2018

QUIT LIKE A MILLIONAIRE

For that same person investing $10,000 over twenty-five years, this adds up to $13,500! This isn't even Coke money anymore; that's more than their initial investment!

Index Investing Beats Most Actively Managed Funds

And here's the most infuriating part: those actively managed funds charging those high fees aren't even good. If you were paying someone thousands of dollars to paint your house, you'd expect it to be painted. If you were paying someone thousands of dollars to fix your car, you'd expect it to be fixed. But just because you're paying a mutual fund manager doesn't mean they'll make you money. They get paid whether their fund goes up or down.

Think about that for a second. If your job was to manufacture chairs, and on your first day you inadvertently started a fire, destroying some chairs, you'd have managed to manufacture *negative* chairs. Do you deserve to get paid? Probably not. Do you deserve to keep your job? Probably not. But that's the deal many fund managers have. If they do a good job or do a bad job, they still get paid—by you.

And for all these fees, what value do you get? Turns out, not much. If you were to poll all active managers who are trying to outguess the stock market, you might expect about 50 percent to have beaten the index and 50 percent to have underperformed. But that's not the case, and the reason is the management fees. Active managers don't work for free. That means they have to beat the index by 1–2 percent just to make up for their own fees.

Would you like to know how many active managers manage to beat the indexes after fees in any given year?

Fifteen percent.

That's right. Only 15 percent of active managers manage to beat their benchmark indexes after fees. And because there's no reliable way to tell which of the active managers will turn out to be among that 15 percent, there's no reliable way to pick which actively managed mutual funds will outperform—especially if the fund manager won't even meet with you.

That's when I realized it was really very simple. Index investing beats 85 percent of actively managed mutual funds.

How to Steal from Wall Street

If you ever want to see a banker sweat, try this: walk into your bank, ask to see a salesperson, and ask to put your savings into index funds. It's the funniest thing ever.

Armed with the knowledge of why index funds outperform actively managed funds, I did exactly that. I had done my homework. I knew the literature and research cold; I knew the statistics. I had looked up the commission the salesperson would earn on an index fund: precisely $0. So, I was expecting an amusing spectacle.

And boy did I get it. That salesperson spun story after story about why I was making a huge mistake, and I slammed down chart after chart onto his desk proving him wrong. Eventually, he resorted to outright lying. This account, he claimed, couldn't purchase those types of investments. But after I asked to speak to his supervisor, he relented. I got my account set up, and I invested in my index funds.

Here's the deal: Wall Street *hates* index funds. Inside those shiny glass skyscrapers is basically a giant collection of stock traders. They have thousands of analysts working long hours, poring over the press releases and financial statements of every publicly traded company. They then feed this information in the form of tip sheets to traders on the floor of the New York Stock Exchange. Those traders then place orders based on that information. If that info suggests a company's stock is trading below its true value, then the traders place a buy. If that info suggests it's trading above its true value, they place a sell.

This is an oversimplification of a complex system, of course, but at the end of the day Wall Street's job is to price how much a company's shares are worth and to make money if they find a discrepancy. The effect of all this activity is the day-to-day movements of each stock's price, as well as the overall movement of the stock market as a whole. Over time, this will cause a company's share price to reflect what that company is truly worth.

However, someone has to pay all these people to do this work. That's where actively managed mutual funds come in. By setting it up so the fund charges a percentage of all assets under management, and tricking investors into thinking that a percentage point or two isn't a big deal, Wall Street manages to make money whether their traders guess correctly or not. The managers and their staff get paid—with your money—regardless of whether they do a good job.

Index investing is different. When you bet on the entire stock market, you are taking advantage of all the work those traders are doing trying to research and price out each individual stock in that index. And because there's no fund manager, you don't pay them or the legions of staffers who work for them.

When you use index investing, you are getting money *back* from Wall Street.

I left my bank that day with this strange sense of satisfaction. When I sat down in that salesperson's office, he had every intention of screwing me. *He* was the robber.

But when I left, *I* was.

CHAPTER 10 SUMMARY

▸ Index investing allows you to invest in all companies at once rather than trying to pick out the winners.

- Indexes can't crash to zero.

- Index funds have lower fees.

- Index funds beat 85 percent of all actively managed mutual funds after fees.

— 11 —

HOW TO SURVIVE A STOCK MARKET CRASH

I've been talking a lot about my life, and it might seem that I learned everything myself, but the truth is that my husband, Bryce, was with me through it all. We met in university as lab partners (nerd love!) and since then we've been navigating the big scary world of finance and adulting together. I'm mentioning him now because when it came time for me to put everything I'd learned together and figure out what exactly to do with our savings, Bryce saved my butt not once but twice.

I knew that index investing was the way to go, but selecting the right funds and designing a portfolio were different. The first means picking the best bricks in a pile; the second uses those bricks to build a house. Should we throw all our money into one index (S & P 500)? Spread it out among the Toronto Stock Exchange and international indexes such as the MSCI EAFE? What about bonds? Night after night, our account stared at us, all in cash. And I stared right back, paralyzed with indecision.

At the time, Bryce was earning his master of engineering degree at the University of Toronto and taking an economics course. While most of the material was dry and not useful unless you're in supply chain management, one article jumped out at him. It was about the Nobel Prize–winning concept created by economist Harry Markowitz in the 1950s: Modern Portfolio Theory.

WHAT IS MODERN PORTFOLIO THEORY?

Modern Portfolio Theory says that assets boil down to two measurements: expected return and volatility. Expected return, measured as a percentage, is the expected annualized return of an asset. Volatility, measured as a standard deviation, is the day-to-day gyration of said asset. The higher the standard deviation, the more volatile the asset.

Let's take two assets: equities, as represented by the S & P 500, and bonds. If we were to plot the risk/return numbers of these two assets, it would look like this:

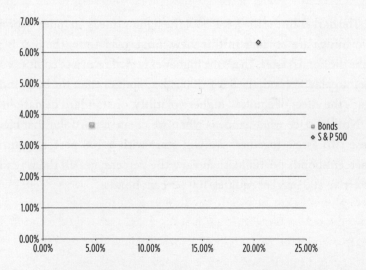

On the vertical axis is expected return, and on the horizontal axis is standard deviation. The S & P 500's position at the top right indicates that it's a high-return, highly volatile asset, while bonds, on the bottom left, are lower return and less volatile.

Let's look at the day-to-day price chart of those two dots:

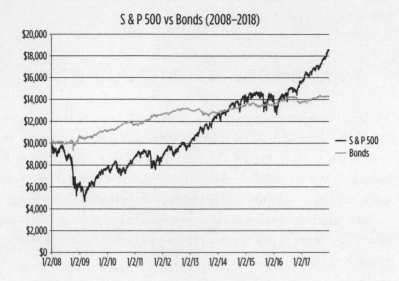

S & P 500 vs Bonds (2008–2018)

The darker line is the S & P 500; the lighter line is an index of bonds. Two things are obvious in this view. First, over time, the S & P 500 kicks the bonds' asses. That's the higher expected return of equities coming into play. Second, the S & P 500 is *way* spikier than the bond index. That's the effect of equities' higher volatility, or standard deviation.

Now let's see what happens when we create a portfolio that blends these two assets together. We will start with a 100 percent equities/ 0 percent bonds portfolio, then vary the percentages all the way until we arrive at 0 percent equities/100 percent bonds:

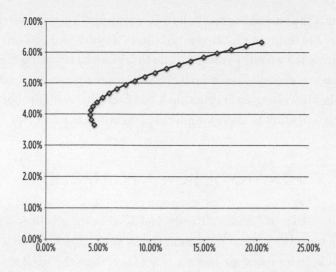

This is what Modern Portfolio Theory calls the efficient frontier, and if we were to look at these portfolios on our price chart, they would look like this:

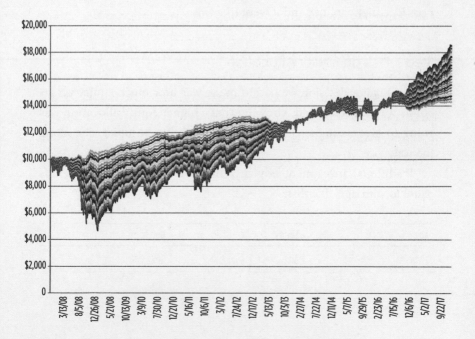

This is the second key to Modern Portfolio Theory: every asset can be scored in terms of expected return and volatility, and you can control how much volatility you're willing to take on by adjusting the percentages you allocate to each asset class. A higher equity allocation will result in higher long-term gains but a bumpier ride. A higher bond allocation will result in lower long-term gains but a smoother ride.

HOW TO DESIGN A PORTFOLIO

Learning Modern Portfolio Theory and combining it with index investing was my big "aha" moment. I finally understood how rich people think. Index investing was my way of accessing the stock markets safely, preventing my portfolio from dropping to zero, and avoiding the nasty management fees that would drag my performance down over the long term. Modern Portfolio Theory allowed Bryce and me to build an investment portfolio that worked for us. I now had a blueprint I could actually follow, and it went like this.

Step 1: Pick an Equity Allocation

The first major decision we had to make was how much equity versus bonds we wanted to hold, knowing that a higher equity allocation was going to give us higher long-term returns but a bumpier ride along the way.

Traditional investment advice is to hold a percentage of bonds equal to your age, like this:

Age	Equity	Bonds
20	80%	20%
30	70%	30%

Age	Equity	Bonds
40	60%	40%
50	50%	50%
60	40%	60%
70	30%	70%
80	20%	80%
90	10%	90%
100	0%	100%

The idea is that when you're younger, you don't care about volatility since you don't need the money right away. The compounding effect of the higher expected return of equities is more important. But as you get into your sixties or seventies, you care more about stability since you need the money to live on. Lowering volatility then becomes more important. Also, when you're younger, your total portfolio is smaller. A 50 percent crash in value doesn't mean as much when your portfolio is worth $50,000, for example, as when it's worth $500,000 when you're older.

Both arguments are solid, and they make sense, in theory. But there's a problem. When you're learning about investing for the first time, you're inexperienced and nervous. The age-in-bonds rule operates under the assumption that people in their twenties will be okay with a 50 percent drop in their portfolio because they have a long investing time horizon.

Here's a short list of people who aren't okay with that:

Me.

So, while Bryce wanted to follow this rule and proposed an 80 percent equity/20 percent bond allocation, I was far more conservative and wanted to go 50/50. We compromised and set our initial target allocation at 60 percent equity/40 percent bonds, with the intention that as my comfort level increased, I would gradually increase it to our age-based target.

Starting at 60/40 turned out to be an unexpectedly good decision, and I'll get to why that is in a bit. But first, on to . . .

Step 2: Choose the Indexes to Track

After you pick your overall equity/bond allocation, the next step is to choose which indexes to track. If you're American, you're probably going, "Well, *duh*, the S & P 500." And in response to that, I'd like to introduce the concept of Home Country Bias.

Home Country Bias is the well-documented tendency of investors to overweight their domestic market. Now, before you accuse me of scolding Americans for thinking they're the center of the universe, we *all* do this. Surveys show that investors all over the world prefer investing in their own countries, holding about 75 percent of their equity allocation at home. This is, understandably, because people tend to invest in markets they're familiar with. In America, you can't turn on the news without hearing about the daily performance of the Dow or the S & P 500, but you've likely never heard of the TSX (Toronto Stock Exchange) or the FTSE 100 (London Stock Exchange).

America is the world's biggest economy, no question about it, so for Americans, the majority of your equity holdings should be American. However, that doesn't mean you should ignore the rest of the world (we'll get to why in a second). Fortunately, there's an index that captures the developed world outside of the United States and Canada called the MSCI EAFE Index. MSCI is the company that maintains it, and EAFE stands for "Europe, Australasia, and the Far East." Like the S & P 500, it works nicely as a market-cap-weighted index of the developed world outside of North America and is the oldest international stock market index out there, having been founded in 1969.

If we were to look at an index of international companies like the

FTSE Global All Cap Index, which sorts companies all around the world by market cap, we'd see that the USA makes up about 50 percent. So, if we want to be globally balanced and reduce risk, we would pick an equity weighting representative of the US economic weighting relative to the rest of the world (50 percent US, 50 percent international).

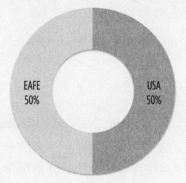

If you live outside of the United States, avoiding Home Country Bias is even more important. America has been the undisputed economic powerhouse since World War II, and if Americans overweight their domestic economy and get it wrong, they won't hurt their portfolio too badly. America is number one. At worst, they'll fall to number two. Big deal. But for countries with smaller economies, the effect of overweighting domestic equities can be devastating, even though the temptation of investing patriotically is strong.

I love my adopted home. Canada has *infinite* Coke cans and *zero* Communists trying to murder my family! It's fricking awesome! But when it comes to my finances, I have to remember that the population of Canada is about thirty-five million. California's population is forty million. Our entire economy is about the size of *one* US state! So, I have to be realistic. Investing completely in Canada would be dumb, because we're tiny compared to the rest of the world. But completely ignoring Canada doesn't make sense either, since there are tax advantages that come with investing in domestic equities (which we will discuss in chapter 13).

Here's the allocation we ultimately chose:

And again, this is a guideline. We went with this because:

▸ We wanted the majority of our holdings to be outside of Canada.

▸ We chose our US weighting based on its economic weighting vs. the rest of the world.

If you think one slice will do better than another, feel free to shift a few percentage points from one and add it elsewhere. If you're right, you win. But if you're wrong, you won't decimate your investments.

Step 3: Pick Your Investment Funds

Once you've decided on which indexes to track and the weighting, it's time to pick your funds. When we started investing, mutual funds were pretty much the only game in town, but nowadays there are much better options available. Specifically, I'm talking about exchange-traded funds, or ETFs.

ETFs are similar to mutual funds in that they invest in a basket of stocks or bonds, but unlike mutual funds they trade on the open stock market. This gives you two advantages:

1. They're cheaper. When someone buys/sells units of a mutual fund, someone working at the mutual fund company has to process those orders and assign you the units. With ETFs, the stock exchange does that, and the process is automated by computers, so their fees (MERs) tend to be much lower.

2. Anyone can buy them. Typically, if you want to buy a bank's mutual fund, you have to invest with that bank. This gives the bank many ways to screw with you, like charging all sorts of fees on your account. With an ETF, any brokerage account that can trade stocks, like Fidelity, Vanguard, or Questrade (for Canadians), can trade ETFs.

That being said, there can be one disadvantage with ETFs. Mutual funds typically don't charge a commission per trade, but ETFs sometimes do, depending on your brokerage. This is because stock brokerages charge $5–$20 to execute a trade, while mutual funds bake that charge into their MERs. Back when we started investing, I was transferring money to our portfolio every paycheck (every two weeks), so my buys were frequent. This would have resulted in a *lot* of fees, so I opted for index mutual funds instead.

But these days, there are lots of brokerage accounts that offer free ETF trading. That means there's little reason to use mutual funds anymore. So, what ETF should you buy? The cheapest one that tracks the index you want. As an index investor like me, you're not shopping around for the fanciest fund manager. You know which indexes you want to track, so find the best index ETF with the lowest fee.

For a reference, here are some popular indexes and the ETFs that track them:

Index	ETF Name	Symbol	MER
S & P 500	Vanguard Total Stock Market	VTI	0.04%
TSX	BMO S & P/TSX Capped Composite Index	ZCN	0.05%
MSCI EAFE	Vanguard FTSE Developed Markets	VEA	0.07%
US Bonds	Vanguard Total Bond Market	BND	0.05%
Canadian Bonds	BMO Aggregate Bond Index	ZAG	0.09%

Note that your employer's 401(k) plan may not offer these specific ETFs. That's okay. Simply pick the lowest-fee index ETF or mutual fund from the list of whatever your 401(k) provider has available. Then later on, when you retire or switch employers, you can transfer everything to a self-directed traditional IRA account and switch them for the ones you really want. We discuss this process in more detail in chapter 13.

MY FIRST PORTFOLIO

So, there we were in our first apartment, two years into our careers, huddled around the computer with printed-out charts and papers scattered throughout our bedroom. The research was done, our portfolio designed, our investment funds picked out, and our combined life savings ($100,000) sitting in our brokerage accounts, waiting for their marching orders. Here's the portfolio Bryce and I decided on:

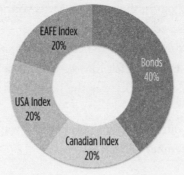

It had a 60 percent equity/40 percent fixed-income asset allocation, with the equity portion split evenly among Canada, the United States, and EAFE.

"Ready?" Bryce asked.

"Yes. I . . . I think . . . ," I stammered.

My heart raced. This was the first truly "rich person" thing I had ever done. I had gone from being relieved to have any money at all to learning how to grow it. The girl who dug for toys in a medical waste heap was about to invest in the stock market. But what if I screwed up? Would I squander every sacrifice my dad had made to escape the Communists for a better life in the West?

I knew I wasn't making this decision lightly. I'd read the papers, I understood the research, and above all I trusted the math. So, with a tentative nod from me, Bryce put in the buy orders and together, we hit the Submit button.

Almost immediately, our portfolio went up.

It was only $10, but it was the first time I really *saw* how money could make money. During my childhood, money had been solely a tool for survival; now I understood how rich people saw it. *This is how the rich get richer.*

The next few weeks were magical. Every time we got paid, we put as much as we could spare into the portfolio and it kept growing. Soon I was up $100, then $500, then $1,000! I couldn't believe it. Specifically, I couldn't believe how easy it was. Why had I been so scared? I felt like an idiot for missing out in the past, but I was young, so I had plenty of time to ride this cash cow.

That night, as Bryce and I lay in bed, he asked me how I was feeling.

"Like a million bucks!" I felt like we had made it. We had learned the secrets of the rich; the sky was the limit. Dad was going to be so proud of me.

Before turning out the light, I checked my watch. It was just past midnight—on September 1, 2008.

THE GREAT FINANCIAL CRISIS

"SHITSHITSHITSHITSHIT!!!!"

"Everything okay?" Bryce called from the front door, having just returned home from work.

"No, everything is not fucking okay! Have you been paying attention to the stock market?!"

The Dow had just plunged over three hundred points, the papers had been screaming about something called the "subprime mortgage crisis" that I didn't understand, and most important, we were losing money—about 20 percent of our portfolio. (See appendix B for details of our exact numbers.)

"So, it's a down day." Bryce shrugged. "It'll be fine."

I grabbed a copy of the paper and shoved it in his face. "This is not just a down day! Everything is *not* fine!"

"Okay, calm down, calm down," he replied while making soothing ocean noises. "Remember, volatility is all part of the process. Sometimes there are up days, and sometimes there are—"

"You don't understand!" I was hyperventilating at this point. "If you screw up, your parents will come save you. If *I* screw up, I'll drag my parents down with me. I can't . . ."

Now, I'm not going to pretend I'm perfect. Far from it. I'm pessimistic, I have crippling self-confidence issues, and I panic easily. All three traits were on display in that moment. And since he's the eternal optimist in our relationship, that was the second time Bryce saved my ass. Because what I didn't mention is that at the moment he arrived home, I had my finger over the Sell All button, and he managed to talk me out of it.

The next few months, unfortunately, didn't help my anxiety at all. Two weeks later, Lehman Brothers filed for bankruptcy and the Great Financial Crisis was in full swing. Both the TSX and the Dow regularly dropped by more than a thousand points. I remember vividly losing $1,000 in a single day. That was more money than my entire neighborhood made back in China!

Bryce would wake up to find all the hair I had stress-shed overnight covering my pillow. He used to try to hide my own hair from me, so it wouldn't stress me out even more, but I always caught him.

"What are we going to do?" I asked in bed after another day of watching our life savings plummet.

"You already know what to do," he replied. "Go back to the research."

Step 4: Rebalance

There's a fourth step to Modern Portfolio Theory. It sounds relatively simple but there's a lot of nuance behind it, and it saved us during the Great Financial Crisis. Here's how.

Modern Portfolio Theory states that after you pick your asset allocations, you need to monitor how your holdings fluctuate over time, and if they start to deviate too much from your allocation targets, you should rebalance. So, for example, if my initial portfolio targets changed like so, then Modern Portfolio Theory would instruct me to do the following:

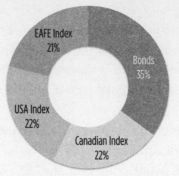

Asset	Action	Amount
Canadian Index	SELL	2%
USA Index	SELL	2%
EAFE Index	SELL	1%
Bonds	BUY	5%

While this simple act of rebalancing may not seem like that big of a deal, it allows the investor to do some pretty clever things. First of all, it prevents you from permanently losing money. Stock markets may go up or down day-to-day, but over time the index always goes up. Since its inception, this is what the S & P 500's performance has looked like:

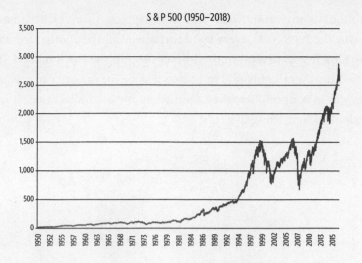

S & P 500 (1950–2018)

This period covers the Cold War, the Cuban Missile Crisis, 9/11, and every disaster that's happened since 1950. The index recovered every single time. If an index investor is caught in a downturn, to get their money back, they just have to wait. I know this may sound counterintuitive—after all, when you see a dip, your natural instinct is to sell—but staying the course is always the smartest approach, which is what Bryce knew that day in 2008. The only way to permanently lose money would be to sell during a dip and miss out on the recovery. Rebalancing prevents you from doing this; you only sell an asset when that asset's allocation is *above* target. In other words, you can only sell things that have gone up. You can't sell things that have gone down.

Secondly, rebalancing enforces good investor behavior. Like I said, you're only allowed to sell assets that have gone up. On the flip side, you're only allowed to buy assets that are sitting below target. In other words, you can only buy assets that have gone down.

Buy low. Sell high. The definition of how to make money in the stock market.

Finally, rebalancing forces you to ignore your two major investing emotions—greed and fear. And if it's not obvious why overriding your emotions is important, let's see what happens in a crash situation. During the 2008 crisis, every few days there would be another stomach-churning five-to-seven-hundred-point drop in the stock market. This caused my overall portfolio to go down since the majority of my holdings was in equities. But when I pulled up my asset allocation, it actually looked something like this:

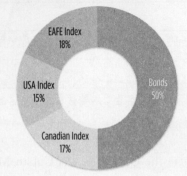

Even though the overall size of my pie was shrinking, my bond holdings were going *up*! This is because in times of financial crisis, money flows from things that are risky (stocks) into things that are safe (bonds). Surrounded by alarming headlines and our dwindling portfolio size, every instinct in my body screamed at me to sell it all, run shrieking into the woods, and never invest again. Modern Portfolio Theory told me to do something different. It said to sell the only asset that wasn't on fire (bonds) and buy more stocks even as the markets continued to plummet.

I didn't know it at the time, but this turned out to be the exact right thing to do.

Limits to Rebalancing

Before I go any further, I have to warn you about a few limitations to this approach.

First, Modern Portfolio Theory only works if a portfolio has some fixed income as well as some equity. This system breaks down if you're too tilted one way or the other. For example, during a stock market crash like the one we had, if I had been holding 100 percent equity, rebalancing wouldn't work. As the stock market plummeted, there would have been no complementary asset that would rise, so my allocations wouldn't have changed and I'd have had nothing to rebalance. That's why I advise not going above 80 percent equity, even if you're an aggressive investor.

Second, Modern Portfolio Theory works best if all your assets are in index funds. If there's even a single individual stock in your portfolio, it could lead to trouble. While it's impossible for an index fund to go to zero, it's entirely possible for an individual stock to go to zero. And if that happened, rebalancing would guide you to sell off every other asset in order to buy more of the failing stock until it was all you owned and the company went bankrupt, swallowing your entire life savings along with it. Don't own individual stocks in a portfolio that you plan on managing with Modern Portfolio Theory!

Surviving the Crash

As I stared at my crumbling portfolio, every instinct told me to cut my losses and run, but the research (and my boyfriend) was telling me to buy more.

Listening to the math and to Bryce had never let me down, so I went with them. Every two weeks, Bryce and I would pool our paychecks, figure out how much money we needed to pay for food and rent, and throw the rest at a stock market that was collapsing. One day, I bought $1,000 worth of index funds, only for my portfolio to immediately plummet by $1,000.

"Where the *fuck* did my money just go?" I yelled at the screen.

Even though it felt like setting money on fire, my ownership of those indexes was going up and up. I just couldn't see it through my fog of panic.

It took until March 2009 for the market to find a bottom and start to rebound. Stock markets had crumbled around 50 percent peak-to-trough, but because our portfolio was only 60 percent invested in the stock market, our portfolio was down about half of that, 20–25 percent.

Here's where things got interesting.

Because we had bought into the market as it fell, I now owned significantly more index fund units than when I had started, and at a significant discount. So I participated in the upside more strongly than the downside.

It took three and a half years for the S & P 500 to return to its pre-crisis levels in April 2012.

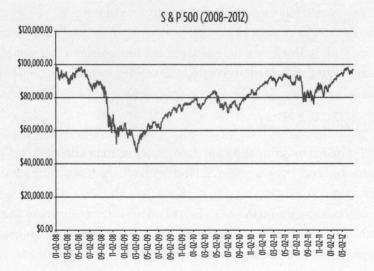

S & P 500 (2008–2012)

Here's how long it took us.

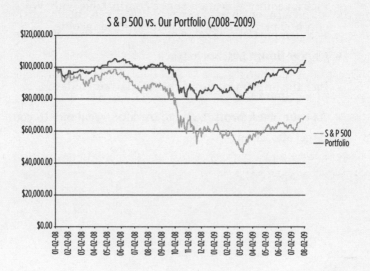

S & P 500 vs. Our Portfolio (2008–2009)

Just two years into the Great Financial Crisis, we had completely recovered our money even though newspapers were still screaming about how screwed the world was. While Wall Street reeled, we emerged without losing a dime. With index investing and Modern Portfolio Theory, we had beaten most of the professional hedge fund managers at their own game.

The day that happened, Bryce greeted me at the door waving a pair of blue-and-silver pompoms.

"What? Why?" I demanded. That's when he showed me our accounts, back at our break-even level.

"Whoa," I exclaimed, dumbfounded. "It worked!"

CHAPTER 11 SUMMARY

▸ Modern Portfolio Theory boils assets down to two metrics: expected return and volatility.

- ▸ To design/maintain a portfolio:

  - Pick an equity allocation you're comfortable with. We chose 60 percent equity, 40 percent fixed income.

  - Choose which indexes to track.

  - Pick the investment funds that track those indexes.

  - As your investments fluctuate in value, rebalance to your target allocation.

— 12 —

TAXES ARE FOR POOR PEOPLE

Most of the time, my dad exists in a state of tranquility, which is how he was able to handle both crippling poverty and murderous Communists with a dignified grace. A grace I don't possess. I fly into a rage *all the time*, as my readers know. And when I started working, a frequent target of my anger was people who were born rich.

Anyone who grew up poor will identify with my love-hate attitude. I loathed rich people yet wanted to be them. I was in awe of their success yet got annoyed when they flaunted it. What annoyed me most is that the rich seem to play by a different set of rules. Where we have to bust our butts to make a living, they can sit there and let the money roll in. Where we have to pay taxes, they, well, don't. As Warren Buffett once remarked, he pays a lower tax rate than his secretary. And the title of this chapter was inspired by Leona Helmsley, an arrogant New York real estate baron (hard to imagine, I know) who famously said, "We don't pay taxes. Only the little people pay taxes."

In a progressive tax system (like in the United States and Canada), you are taxed based on how much you make. Poor people pay little tax because they need every cent of their income to live. Middle-class people pay more because they can afford it. Rich people pay the most because they have money to burn.

Or at least, that's what we've been led to believe. In reality, here's how it works: Poor people pay little. Middle-class people pay more. Rich people use tricks and loopholes (bought with their lobbyist friends) to pay as little tax as possible while the rest of us pick up the slack. This is a major contributing factor to income inequality in the United States. The more money you have, the more loopholes are available to you. And as a result, the less taxes you pay. And as a result, you make more money. It's a vicious cycle. Oh, and by the way, it's all completely legal.

I spent a significant part of my life being angry at these rich bastards exploiting the system. But one day, Bryce, evidently sick of my ranting, threw up his hands and asked, "Instead of bitching about something you can't change, why don't you steal their secrets and use them for yourself?"

That stopped me in my tracks. It's true, complaining about rich people's exploiting loopholes wasn't going to stop them from doing it. And as long as they did, and I didn't, I would fall farther and farther behind while they pulled ahead. But if I stole their secrets and started using them? Maybe I could catch up.

That's exactly what I did. Despite the fact that I've been a millionaire for more than three years, and I've made hundreds of thousands of dollars from my investments since then, so far, I have yet to pay a *single dollar* in taxes. Why? Because investment income is taxed more favorably than earned income. That's why employees get screwed while investors get richer. And let me tell you, it's *way* more fun being on the inside looking out than on the outside looking in.

I want all of you to feel what that's like, too.

THE DIFFERENCE BETWEEN A TAX SHELTER AND TAX DEFERMENT

The first lesson I learned was simple: not every tax break is scuzzy. Leona Helmsley, also known as the "Queen of Mean," may have been sentenced to sixteen years in prison for tax evasion (ah, sweet justice), but there's a big difference between legal and illegal tax avoidance.

When I first started out, I didn't have nearly as many tax-avoidance strategies as the rich did, but there are a few available to anyone, and taking advantage of every opportunity is absolutely critical.

Tax sheltering means putting your money someplace where taxes no longer apply. Think of taxes as gravity in *The Matrix*, or logic in the Transformers movies. Even if it *technically* exists, it doesn't apply to you. For example, if you invest in an index ETF and it goes up, it's not reported on your tax return. If you earn interest on that account, ditto. Once your money is inside a tax shelter, you never get taxed on it again. This is because the money that goes into a tax-sheltering account has already been taxed.

Tax deferment, on the other hand, is the process of taking a chunk of your income and choosing not to pay income taxes on it that year. Here's how it works: You contribute a portion of your income to a tax-deferred account. The amount you contribute reduces your taxable income for that year, and accountants would call this contribution "deductible." So, if you made $50,000 one year, and you chose to defer $10,000, then that year you would only be taxed as if you earned $40,000. That $10,000 you deferred gets put into a special account where it can grow tax-free, but if you withdraw it, it will be added on to your taxable income and you'll pay taxes on it then. This is because money going into tax deferral hasn't been taxed yet.

To recap . . .

	Tax Shelter	Tax Deferral
Contributions are ...	*Not* deductible	Deductible
Growth/interest/dividends are ...	Tax-free	Tax-free
Withdrawals are ...	Tax-free	Taxed as income

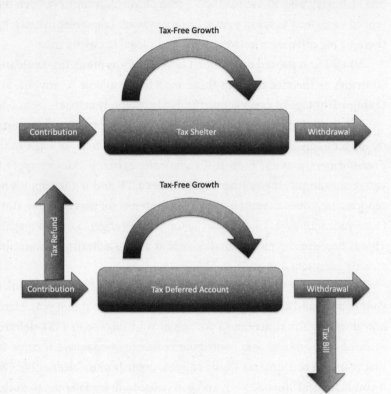

The government allows this because they want you to save for retirement and providing tax breaks incentivizes you to do it. They know Social Security isn't enough to completely provide for you after you stop working, so they want you to save enough to make up the difference. And since they *also* know that retirees are the most active voters, they want to keep them happy.

QUIT LIKE A MILLIONAIRE

SO HOW DO I DO THIS?

The system of opening either a tax-shelter or tax-deferral account is a nonsensical mishmash of numbers and letters. It's not too complicated once you take the time to learn how they work, but it can be intimidating because of the sheer number and types of accounts available. Let's walk through them together.

Retirement accounts in the United States are divided into two major types: employer-sponsored and individual.

Employer-sponsored accounts are the ones that you get through your job. The most common one is the 401(k), but there are others, depending on your employer.

Account Type	Typical Employer Type
401(k)	Private for-profit company (most common)
403(b)	Not-for-profit company or registered charity
457	State employee
TSP	Federal employee/armed forces

These are typically tax-deferral accounts and operate similarly. You put money in, which reduces the amount of tax you pay that year. The money then grows tax-free until you withdraw it many years later, at which point it becomes taxable. As of tax year 2019 you can contribute a total of $19,000 a year for each account type, plus another $6,000 if you're fifty or older.

Employers often match a percentage of employee contributions as part of their salary, but you have to make that contribution to get it. So, if your employer has a 401(k) contribution-matching program, get in on that, because if you don't, you're flushing away part of your paycheck. No rich person ever flushes away part of their paycheck. Ever. If you're not sure whether your employer offers a sponsored retirement plan, find out today! Or, you know, Monday if you're reading this on a weekend.

The other major type of retirement account is the individual retirement account, or IRA. IRAs were designed so that if your employer doesn't offer a retirement plan, you can get similar benefits anyway. An IRA can be opened at any major financial institution and comes in two different flavors: traditional IRA and Roth IRA.

A traditional IRA acts like a tax-deferral account. You put money in, which becomes deductible, which reduces your tax bill, and the money is taxed when you withdraw it.

A Roth IRA acts like a tax shelter. You put money in, and it is *not* deductible, but you can withdraw it without paying taxes on it. That's because your contribution is after-tax money.

Between the two types of accounts, you are limited to a total contribution of $6,000 per year if below the age of fifty, and $7,000 if you're fifty or above (as of tax year 2019) combined. The IRS also imposes limits on how much you can contribute overall. If you have access to an employer-sponsored 401(k) plan and you make more than $74,000 as a single person or $123,000 as a married couple per year, you can't contribute to a traditional IRA and get the tax deduction. Similarly, if you make over $137,000 as a single person or $203,000 as a married couple per year, you aren't allowed to contribute anything to a Roth IRA. Check the IRS website at the beginning of each year before making contributions to see what the limits have been updated to.

The most common US retirement savings accounts in a nutshell:

Account	Shelter/Defer	Contribution Deductible?	Tax-Free Growth?	Withdrawals Taxed?	Annual Contribution Limit
401(k)	Defer	Y	Y	Y	$19,000
403(b)	Defer	Y	Y	Y	$19,000
457	Defer	Y	Y	Y	$19,000

Account	Shelter/Defer	Contribution Deductible?	Tax-Free Growth?	Withdrawals Taxed?	Annual Contribution Limit
TSP	Defer	Y	Y	Y	$19,000
Traditional IRA	Defer	Y	Y	Y	$6,000 (combined with Roth IRA)
Roth IRA	Shelter	N	Y	N	$6,000 (combined with traditional IRA)

For those keeping score, *six* different types of accounts are available, and that's just for regular jobs. The accounts available for self-employed people are a whole other story, so if that's you, check the IRS website or talk to your accountant.

Now, let's go through the (totally legal) loopholes that rich people use to minimize their taxes.

Loophole Alert #1: Double-Contributing to Your Retirement Accounts

Depending on how your company is structured, it may be possible to qualify for two employer-sponsored retirement accounts. For example, if your employer is both a nonprofit *and* is paid by state funds, you could qualify for both a 403(b) and a 457. Hospitals tend to be both; universities, too. Government contractors, including lawyers, architects, and defense workers, can also double-qualify, depending on how their businesses are structured. Amazingly, the contribution limits stack up, meaning you'd be able to tax-defer $19,000 in the 403(b) and $19,000 in the 457, for a total $38,000 deduction! And if you're fifty or above, the extra $6,000 you can contribute also stacks up, for a total of $50,000!

Here's the sneaky part: this is almost never openly advertised to the employees. If you suspect you may be eligible, go to your HR department and ask point-blank whether you qualify to open up another retirement account. Many of our readers have been surprised to find out they could double their contributions!

Loophole Alert #2: Back-Door Roth IRA

Remember when I said if you made too much money you couldn't contribute to a Roth IRA? That's only partly true. If you make too much money to shelter any funds in a Roth IRA, you can still contribute that amount into a nondeductible traditional IRA. A traditional IRA saves you from paying taxes when you contribute but adds them to your taxable income when you withdraw. A nondeductible traditional IRA takes away the first part: the tax savings on contribution.

On the surface, it seems completely batty to do this, since you just eliminated the best part of this account, but it can be a good deal. While the IRS applies income tests to direct Roth IRA contributions, those income limits don't apply when doing a traditional IRA–to–Roth IRA conversion. So, while a high income would prevent you from contributing to a Roth IRA directly, you are legally allowed to do the following:

1. Open up a traditional IRA account.

2. Contribute the maximum ($6,000 in 2019) as a nondeductible contribution.

3. Ask your financial institution to convert the entire account over to your Roth IRA.

Voilà! You have just completed a back-door Roth IRA contribution!

See what I mean when I say rich people don't play by the same rules as everyone else? Even though there's an explicit regulation preventing people who make too much money from avoiding tax, they found a way to do it anyway. The rich always take advantage of a legal gift from the government. And now you can, too! (Note that it gets a little more complicated if you already have a traditional IRA with money in it, or multiple traditional IRA accounts. It's still possible, but there's an additional step of consolidating all your traditional IRA accounts into an employer-sponsored 401(k) plan first in order to get around what's known as the IRA pro-rata aggregation rules. Consult a financial professional for details if you're in this situation.)

"But what about the Canadians?" said no American ever. Well, don't worry, fellow Frozen Northerners, I've got you covered, too. For the people in the Frozen North, the same principles of tax deferral and tax sheltering apply, but fortunately the retirement system is simpler. Instead of six different account types with complicated rules, there are only two.

The Registered Retirement Savings Plan, or RRSP, is the Canadian tax-deferred account. Like the 401(k), you put money in, the contribution becomes deductible and reduces your taxable income, it grows tax-free, and it becomes taxable on withdrawal. RRSP contribution limits are calculated as 18 percent of the previous year's income, subject to a cap of $26,500 in tax year 2019. So, if you made $100,000 last year, you can contribute $18,000 this year. If you made $50,000 last year, you can contribute $9,000 this year.

The other option is the Tax-Free Savings Account, or TFSA. This is the Canadian tax-sheltered account. Like a Roth IRA, you put money into it and the contribution isn't deductible, but it grows tax-free and you can take it out without paying any additional tax. The TFSA annual contribution limit is just a straight $6,000, similar to the Roth IRA.

See, wasn't that much simpler?

Account	Shelter/Defer	Contribution Deductible?	Tax-Free Growth?	Withdrawals Taxed?	Annual Contribution Limit
RRSP	Defer	Y	Y	Y	18% of income
TFSA	Shelter	N	Y	N	$6,000

HOW MUCH SHOULD YOU CONTRIBUTE?

Now that you understand all the ways to shelter or tax-defer your income, how much should you contribute to each account? A rich person would say max them all out. Because rich people don't need to worry about their checking account balance, contributing is just a matter of moving money from one place to another. It's still their money, but now they owe less in taxes, so it makes sense to go all-out. But maxing out the limits would require an American to save $19,000 + $6,000 = $25,000. If you make over $100,000 a year, that may be doable. But if you make $50,000 a year, you have to prioritize. Maybe you can't save $26,000, but what about $6,000? Or $1,000? Which account should you fund first?

First of all, if your employer offers any kind of 401(k) matching program, fund it up to the cap to maximize the matched contribution. Otherwise, you're letting your boss off the hook for not paying part of your salary, and nobody ever got rich by letting people screw them over.

After that, answering this question gets a little tricky. To start off, let's take a look at the US federal tax brackets as of 2019:

Rate	Individuals	Married Filing Jointly
10%	Up to $9,700	Up to $19,400
12%	$9,701 to $39,475	$19,401 to $78,950

Rate	Individuals	Married Filing Jointly
22%	$39,476 to $84,200	$78,951 to $168,400
24%	$84,201 to $160,725	$168,401 to $321,450
32%	$160,726 to $204,100	$321,451 to $408,200
35%	$204,101 to $510,300	$408,201 to $612,350
37%	Over $510,300	Over $612,350

Remember, for tax-deferred accounts you save taxes when you contribute, but you pay taxes when you withdraw. So, you get the most benefit from deferring if you contribute at a high tax bracket and withdraw at a low tax bracket (which we will talk about in chapter 13). If you contribute at the 10 percent bracket and withdraw later at that same bracket, you haven't really done anything useful. But if you contribute at 32 percent and withdraw at 10 percent, you've avoided 22 percent worth of taxes! And again, these tax breaks are completely intentional. Uncle Sam *wants* you to save for your retirement, because a retiree with a lot of money is going to do their own thing and not ask for much.

In short: which account you should fund depends on what tax bracket you're in. At 10 percent or 12 percent, you're not getting much benefit from deferring your taxes, so it makes more sense to fund your Roth IRA first. At higher brackets, like 22 percent or above, it makes more sense to fund your tax-deferred accounts first. Put money into your 401(k) and traditional IRA until you hit the maximum. After that, put money into your Roth IRA using a regular contribution or a back-door contribution.

To recap:

If your employer has a 401(k) matching program . . .	Fund your 401(k) first.	Many employers cap how much they will contribute per year, so fund your savings up to the cap.
If you're in the 10% or 12% tax bracket . . .	Fund your Roth IRA.	

If you're in the 22% or higher tax bracket . . .	Fund your 401(k), then your traditional IRA.	Be careful to pay attention to the contribution caps put in place by the IRS for the traditional IRA. Check the IRS website for the most up-to-date figures.
Once you've maxed out your 401(k)/traditional IRA . . .	Fund your Roth IRA.	Normal or back door, depending on the contribution caps.
Once you've maxed out your Roth IRA . . .	Have a glass of wine.	Congrats! You are now as tax-efficient as you can get.

Here are the Canadian tax brackets, according to the Canada Revenue Agency as of 2019.

Rate	Individuals
15%	Up to $47,630
20.5%	$47,631 to $95,259
26%	$95,260 to $147,667
29%	$147,668 to $210,371
33%	Over $210,371

It's the same decision-making process. If your company offers an RRSP matching program, contribute however much you need to in order to take advantage of it. After that, if you're contributing to your RRSP at a 15 percent tax bracket *and* withdrawing at 15 percent, you're not getting the tax benefits of an RRSP, so it makes more sense to contribute to your TFSA. In fact, unlike the American 401(k), any contribution room you don't use in an RRSP is carried over to the next year, so if you're in a low tax bracket this year it makes more sense to save that RRSP contribution room for later when you might be earning a higher salary. At higher brackets (20.5 percent and above), however, contribute to your RRSP first. Only when your RRSP is maxed out do you then contribute to your TFSA.

If your employer has an RRSP matching program . . .	Fund your RRSP first.	Many employers cap how much they will contribute per year, so fund your savings up to that cap.
If you're in the 15% tax bracket . . .	Fund your TFSA.	
If you're in the 20.5% or higher tax bracket . . .	Fund your RRSP.	Pay attention to the contribution caps put in place by the CRA. Check the CRA website for the most up-to-date figures.
Once you've maxed out your RRSP . . .	Fund your TFSA.	
Once you've maxed out your TFSA . . .	Have a mug of beer.	Congrats! You are now as tax-efficient as you can get.

What About State and Provincial Taxes?

You may have noticed that I've ignored state/provincial taxes in this analysis. This is because for the purpose of deciding which accounts to fund, they don't change much. For example, if you're in a 10 percent federal tax bracket and your state adds another 5 percent, the decision you need to make—whether to fund your 401(k) or your Roth IRA—won't change. Your lowest total tax bracket is now 15 percent, but it's still the lowest tax bracket. Just because the number is higher, it doesn't change the conclusion: it never makes sense to contribute to a tax-deferred account if you will withdraw it at the same tax rate.

The only time state/provincial taxes might change your decision is if they were reverse-progressive, meaning that they charged a higher tax rate at the lower incomes, and a lower tax rate for higher incomes.

But as of this writing, no state or province has done this, because they aren't insane and don't want to be attacked by a pitchfork-wielding mob. So that's why we can rely on federal tax rates for the right answer.

WAIT, HOW DO I GET MY MONEY BACK?

Now you know how middle-class working stiffs can shelter as much of their money as possible. But the question arises, how do I get that money back? Don't I have to pay taxes when I take it out again? For Americans, there's even a 10 percent penalty if I withdraw from my 401(k) before the age of fifty-nine and a half! How does that affect my retirement plan?

Fortunately, there is a way to get all that money out, tax-free, and circumvent any penalties, using—you guessed it—a rich-person loophole (which we'll talk about in the next chapter)!

CHAPTER 12 SUMMARY

▸ Tax-deferred accounts allow you to save taxes now and pay them later, when you withdraw.

▸ Tax-sheltered accounts protect your investments from taxes, but you don't save taxes when you contribute.

▸ The most common American tax-deferred accounts are the 401(k), 403(b), 457, TSP, and traditional IRA.

▸ The most common American tax-sheltered account is the Roth IRA.

▸ You can contribute up to $19,000 per year into your 401(k), 403(b), 457, or TSP, plus an additional $6,000 if you're fifty or older.

- You can contribute up to $6,000 per year into your traditional IRA or Roth IRA, plus an additional $1,000 if you're fifty or older.

- Try to max out contributions to all accounts to save the maximum amount of taxes.

  - If your employer has a 401(k) matching program, max that out first.

  - If your salary is in the first or second tax bracket, prioritize the Roth IRA.

  - If your salary is higher, prioritize the 401(k)/traditional IRA.

- Loopholes exist, such as the double contribution and back-door Roth IRA.

  - Double contribution: Some employees are eligible to contribute to both a 403(b) and 457 if their employer is considered a nonprofit and state employer.

  - Back-door Roth IRA: Can be used for tax sheltering if your salary is above the limit for the Roth IRA.

Note: All advice outlined above was accurate at the time of writing. However, laws can change, which may render this advice suboptimal. Consult a certified public accountant before implementing anything.

— **13** —

NEVER PAY TAXES AGAIN

The tax-reduction strategies you learned in chapter 12 are the bread-and-butter techniques available to middle-class workers. Maxing out every tax-deferral and tax-sheltering account I had was the first step in getting rich, but I wanted the next-level goodies. What do millionaires do when it comes to tax time that allows them to pay so little? I spent months researching that question.

Big mistake.

The sheer volume of techniques and tricks threatened to overwhelm my bookshelf (and my sanity). So many books have been written on the subject, I didn't know where to begin. Was I supposed to set up an off-shore company? An income trust? Buy a plane ticket to Switzerland and open up a bank account there? The more I read, the more confused I got, and quite frankly, the dirtier I felt. Many of these schemes were unabashedly sneaky and borderline illegal, and for every book or article that espoused the values of offshore banking, I saw a headline that read "Person arrested for evading taxes using shell company!" No, thanks.

Whatever I was going to do, I wanted it to be 100 percent above-board. Everything had to be legal, with no sleazy tricks. Every strategy or tax break I employed needed to be an *intentional* one provided by the government. I did not want to escape my cubicle prison only to land in a real one.

This "no sneaky tricks" restriction had the benefit of eliminating 90 percent of my reading material, and once the noise was gone, the answer was simple. I could eliminate my tax burden, using legal tools available to everyone: tax-deferred accounts like 401(k)s, tax-sheltered accounts like Roth IRAs, the standard deduction, and the stock market. Fit these puzzle pieces together in just the right way and you can kiss taxes good-bye—forever.

HOW DIFFERENT TYPES OF INCOME ARE TAXED

The first thing we need to discuss is how different types of income are taxed.

Employment income is income you earn from your job. This is the most common type of income and it is taxed according to your tax bracket, marital status, etc.

Interest from a savings account or a bond is taxed the same way as employment income.

Dividend income is income paid to you by a company whose shares you own. Here's where things start to get interesting. Dividends are taxed at far *lower* rates than employment income. As of 2019, here are the federal tax rates for dividends, assuming no other income:

Single Taxpayers	Married Filing Jointly	Dividend Tax Rate
Up to $39,375	Up to $78,750	0%
$39,376–$434,550	$78,751–$488,850	15%
Over $434,550	Over $488,850	20%

Note that these tax rates apply for qualified dividends, which are defined as being issued by US or foreign-domiciled companies with which the US has a comprehensive tax treaty, and for shares you've owned for more than sixty days.

So right away you can see the tax advantage of dividends over regular income. That first bracket of 0 percent is especially juicy, and in the next section we'll talk about how to fully take advantage of that, but first let's run through the other categories.

Capital gains are income you derive from selling stocks that have gone up in value. If you bought a stock for $10 and sell it for $15, then you have incurred (or "realized") $15 − $10 = $5 in capital gains per share sold. Long-term capital gains, meaning capital gains that were realized for shares you've owned for over 365 days, are taxed at the same rates as qualified dividends. Short-term capital gains, which are capital gains realized for shares that you've owned for under 366 days, are taxed as ordinary income.

Property is taxed each year as a percentage of that property's value. The rate is based on the city you live in, and you can't change this. Property taxes are one of the only ways to effectively tax wealth rather than income. This is because when governments (like France or Cyprus) try to tax bank accounts rather than income, rich people simply transfer their bank accounts out of the country. You can't do that with a house, so homeowners have to suck it up and pay.

There are many other types of income and tax structures, but for a typical worker, those are the most relevant.

TAX OPTIMIZATION AND WHY YOU WANT IT

Based on how different types of income are taxed, you can already see that some are better than others when it comes to hanging on to your cash. Property is the worst, since you're taxed every year whether your house goes up or down in value. Employment income and interest are slightly better, because they're taxed only when you make money. Qualified dividends and capital gains are the best. Theoretically, if you had no other income, you could make $78,750 per married couple in dividends or capital gains and pay $0 in tax.

This is the key insight into tax optimization: certain income is more tax-efficient than other income.

When you're working, your paycheck is employment income, and aside from deferring taxes as I discussed in the last chapter, there's not much you can do to reclassify it. But if you were to stop working, your employment income would drop to $0. And if you were to structure your portfolio such that it earned money as dividends and capital gains, you could end up never paying taxes again.

This is how rich people *legally* avoid taxes. In chapter 9, I explained how houses aren't effective at making you money. Even when the value of your home goes up, those gains end up making the bank, real estate agents, and your local government rich while you're left with a tiny slice of the pie. Rich people understand this, and they also understand that property tax is a wealth tax that they can't get around. That's why rich people tend not to hold a lot of their net worth in their primary residence, whereas middle-class people often do (one reason why it's hard to break out and become rich). Instead, rich people tend to hold the majority of their wealth in investments. Specifically, they hold investments that return money to them as dividends or capital gains.

Let's play a game. You have a million bucks. It's fun to dream, isn't it? You've been working and saving for years, shoving money away into both your tax-deferred and your tax-sheltered accounts. Your accounts look like this:

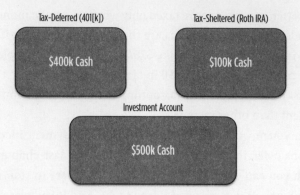

Tax-Deferred (401[k])

$400k Cash

Tax-Sheltered (Roth IRA)

$100k Cash

Investment Account

$500k Cash

Now you want to build an investment portfolio consisting of only two things: a bond ETF and an equity ETF. Let's keep it simple and split that portfolio equally into a 50 percent bond/50 percent equity allocation.

Asset	Amount	Yield	Income Type
Stocks	$500,000	2%	Qualified Dividends
Bonds	$500,000	3%	Interest

Which accounts should you put these ETFs into?

Well, you know that interest is taxed as regular income, so if you put the bond ETF into the investment account, you'll get taxed on that as if it were salary. But if you put it in the 401(k) and the Roth IRA instead, you get that interest tax-free. Meanwhile, you know that you can make up to $78,750 per married couple in qualified dividends without paying taxes. So if you put that in the regular investment account, you'll be able to earn those dividends tax-free. Now your portfolio looks like this:

QUIT LIKE A MILLIONAIRE

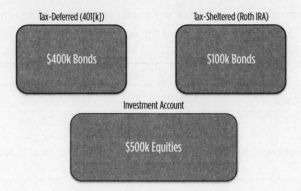

You would report 2 percent of the $500,000 (or $10,000) equity ETF in dividend income on your tax return, and not report anything in interest since those bond ETFs are in tax-sheltered and tax-deferred accounts where investment gains are tax-free. Your total tax bill comes out to $0.

What you've done is tax-optimize a portfolio. Under current rules, this portfolio will never pay a single dollar in tax again, and all you did was move the right ETFs into the right accounts. It's not rocket science, and when you get the hang of it, it's fun!

Let's play again, but with a more complicated scenario. Let's once again pretend you have a million-dollar portfolio, structured like this:

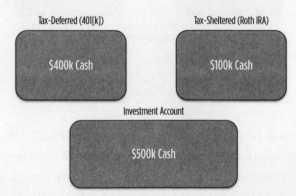

You want to assemble a portfolio that looks like the following table. (There are some asset types here we haven't discussed yet, but all you need to know for now is how much each type of asset yields in income, and how that income is classified for tax purposes.)

Asset	Amount	Yield	Income Type
Stocks (Domestic)	$400,000	2%	Qualified Dividends
Bonds	$200,000	3%	Interest
Real Estate Investment Trusts (REITs)	$200,000	5%	Rent/Non-Qualified Dividends
Preferred Shares	$200,000	5%	Qualified Dividends

Knowing what you know about the different tax-deferred and tax-sheltered accounts, where should these assets go? Well, you know bonds throw off interest, so those should definitely go into the 401(k). We are picking the 401(k) over the Roth IRA, in this case, because we're saving our Roth IRA room for stocks. I'll explain why in a second.

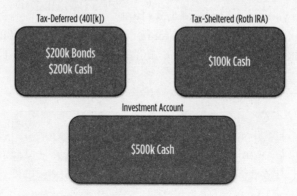

REIT stands for "real estate investment trust," which owns real estate assets like apartment buildings and commercial storefronts. That income is classified as non-qualified dividends, which basically act like regular income. So those go into the 401(k) with your bonds.

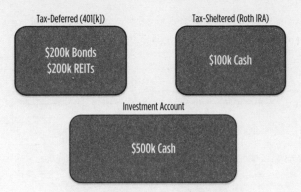

Stocks can sit in your regular investment account since they throw off tax-efficient qualified dividends.

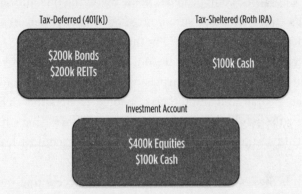

Finally, preferred shares throw off qualified dividends, so they're fine in the investment account, but you don't have enough cash in the regular investment account to buy all of it, so why don't you buy the remaining shares in the Roth IRA? Sure, they don't need to be in the Roth IRA, but no harm if they are.

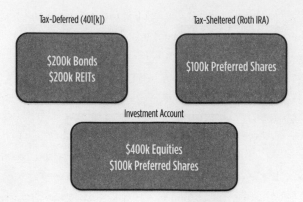

Tax-Deferred (401[k])

$200k Bonds
$200k REITs

Tax-Sheltered (Roth IRA)

$100k Preferred Shares

Investment Account

$400k Equities
$100k Preferred Shares

And there we have it! Your portfolio has now been tax-optimized. Under current rules, total tax bill: $0. Forever. That's all tax optimization is. It's not some complicated scheme involving offshore shell companies, it's simply making sure your money is invested in the right assets, and those assets are stored in the right accounts.

It's a game, and the rules are out in the open. The government *wants* you to play. The most surprising difference that I've found between rich people and middle-class people is that the rich understand the rules while the middle-class people don't. That's it. Once I realized this, I started asking myself, "What else could I learn from them?"

Which brings me to our next topic: how to access that money decades before the age threshold of fifty-nine and a half.

WITHDRAWING FROM YOUR TAX-DEFERRED ACCOUNTS

In our second sample portfolio on page 141, half of your money is in tax-deferred or tax-sheltered accounts, and unfortunately, you can't go out and buy dinner with a 401(k). Think of a 401(k) as an uncooked pot roast; if you eat it now, you'll probably die. First, you have to cook it—as in, withdraw money into an accessible account. But when you withdraw it, it gets taxed, and if you cook it too quickly, your pot roast gets burned and you have to hack half off to make it edible.

I'm . . . not a very good chef, is what I'm trying to say.

Anyhoo, the trick to getting your 401(k) money out is to cook it slowly. Remember how I said that the standard deduction would be a big piece of the puzzle? Here's where it comes into play. The standard deduction is the tax-free amount everyone qualifies for on their tax return. As of 2019, it's $12,200 per person, or $24,400 per married couple. (If your situation allows you to itemize deductions in excess of the standard deduction, go ahead and do that, but for the purposes of this chapter, we'll assume everyone uses the standard deduction.) If you were to, say, leave your job, your earned income would drop to $0. So, if you were to withdraw from your 401(k) an amount equal to your standard deduction, that amount would be tax-free! You could do this once a year, saving taxes on the way in and paying nothing on the way out!

For Americans, there's a 10 percent penalty if you withdraw before the age of fifty-nine and a half, but you can get around that by building what's called a Roth IRA conversion ladder. Here's how it works.

During your career, you will typically contribute to a 401(k) or similar plan that's run by your employer. You may end up with multiple plans under different employers.

After you quit a job, you'd call each of your 401(k) providers and ask to have your accounts merged into a single traditional IRA you control. The IRS allows this to protect people who leave their jobs on bad terms or when their company dissolves after they leave so they can still manage their own retirement funds. Most financial institutions will know how to do a 401(k) rollover, and this transfer is not taxed since you're consolidating your tax-deferred accounts into one place.

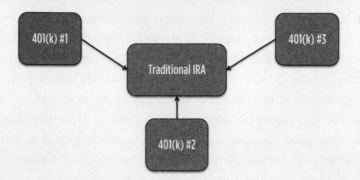

Next is a Roth IRA conversion, in which you take a chunk of money and transfer it from a traditional IRA into a Roth IRA. Since you're moving deductible contributions from a tax-deferred account to a tax-sheltered account, these Roth IRA conversions *are* taxable, so after you retire and your earned income drops to zero, you want to transfer your standard deduction and not a penny more.

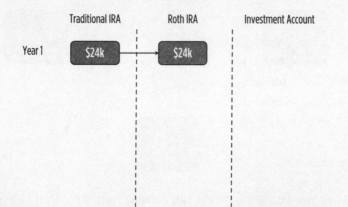

IRS rules state that you can withdraw IRA conversions tax-free and penalty-free five years after a conversion. So, every year, convert the amount of money equal to your standard deduction from your traditional IRA into your Roth IRA.

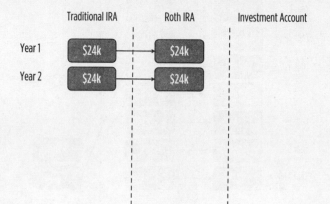

After five years, or more accurately on January 1 of year 6, you can withdraw that first conversion.

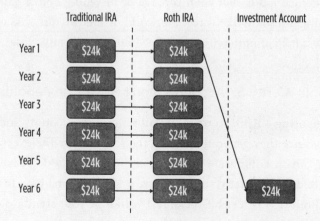

And so on and so on.

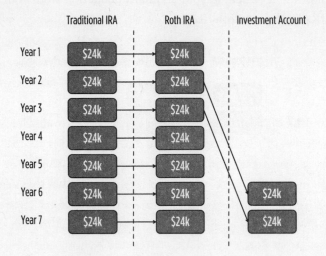

So, while there are limits to withdrawing from your 401(k), if you do leave your job earlier than the age of fifty-nine and a half to do something awesome like travel the world or follow your passion, you can access it by jumping through a few (only slightly annoying) hoops.

Loophole Alert! 457 Accounts Don't Have Age Penalties!

I've been using 401(k)s to represent all retirement accounts, including 403(b)s, since they generally play by the same rules. The exception is the 457, which is for state employees. These suckers don't have that early withdrawal penalty, so if you have a 457, you don't have to do any of this Roth IRA ladder business; just withdraw your standard deduction directly into your investment account.

CAPITAL GAINS HARVESTING

To round out this system, let's come back to capital gains. To recap, capital gains accrue when you sell an ETF unit at a higher price than what you paid for it. This only happens when you realize capital gains in a taxable account; sales inside a tax-deferred or tax-sheltered account aren't reported.

The great thing about capital gains is that you have absolute control over when and how much to realize in any given year, since capital gains only become taxable when a unit is sold. Rich people love capital gains because they can manage their sell orders so that they never pay taxes on them, through a process known as capital gains harvesting.

Here's how it works. If you're sitting on an ETF that's gone up in value, common sense would tell you not to sell it unless you need the money (or are rebalancing your portfolio, a process we talked about in chapter 11); if you sell, you'll realize a capital gain, and therefore have to pay tax. The risk to not realizing it is that, over time, the amount of unrealized capital gains will grow so much that you'll face a huge tax bill when you sell. (I know, I know: break out the tiny violin.)

Rich people (as usual) have found a way around this, though.

Remember that you can earn up to $78,750 as a married couple in combined dividend/capital gains income and pay a tax rate of 0 percent. So, if you have room in that 0 percent tax bracket, it makes sense to deliberately realize capital gains since you won't get taxed on them.

Let's say you have a $500,000 position in an equity ETF. At the end of the year, that ETF has increased to $600,000. Woohoo! Champagne time! Here's what your statement looks like:

Ticker	Units	Basis	Price	G/L
STK	100,000	$500,000	$600,000	$100,000

Basis is the price you acquired those units at. "Price" is the current market price, and "G/L" stands for "gain/loss." Right now, it's indicating you're sitting on an unrealized capital gain of $100,000.

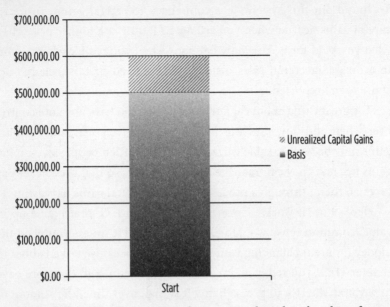

Now, this is fantastic. But it does mean that there's a bit of a tax bomb waiting for you. When the time comes to sell, you'll be hit with a $100,000 capital gain and have to pay some tax on it. But here's the thing. Capital gains are the most flexible of all income types because you can choose when and how much to incur. You can avoid that tax simply by timing your sell orders in a certain way. First, add up the taxable income you've already incurred this year. You did a Roth IRA conversion equal to your standard deduction of $24,000 per married couple. This equity ETF has been paying out 2 percent in qualified dividends over the year, so that's another $10,000. That means that of the $78,750 tax-free capital gains/dividend bracket, you've used up $34,000. That still leaves $78,750 − $34,000 = $44,750!

Do the math: a basis of $500,000 over 100,000 units means you bought these units for $5 per share. Now they're worth $6 per share.

That means each share carries $6 − $5 = $1 of unrealized capital gain. Therefore, you should sell $44,750 / $1 = 44,750 shares. This will realize exactly $44,750 of capital gains, which you can harvest for free.

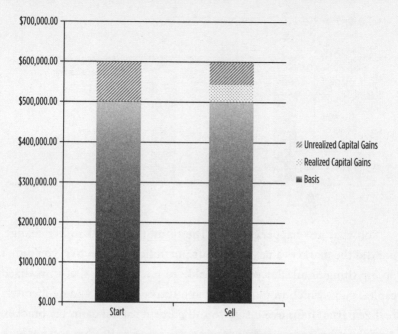

Then you'll immediately buy those units back for the current market price of $6 per share. Now this is what your statement looks like:

Ticker	Units	Basis	Price	G/L
STK	100,000	$544,750	$600,000	$55,250

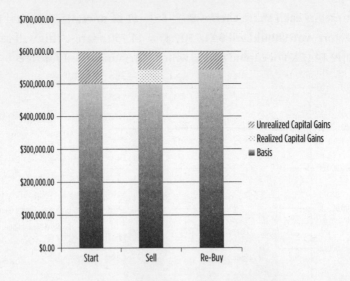

So, what just happened here? The number of units didn't change, nor did the market value. From your portfolio's perspective, you didn't do anything at all. But you were able to take part of that unrealized capital gain, which would have been a future tax bill, and deliberately realize part of it for free inside your 0 percent capital gains tax bracket. And then, by immediately rebuying the same units, you were able to restore your original portfolio, only now with a much lower unrealized capital gain. Do that a few times and after a couple of years, you'll be able to get your basis to catch up to the market value, making your capital gains tax bill $0 going forward.

So that's capital gains harvesting. If you're careful and do your math properly each year, you never have to pay capital gains tax again.

This scenario is pretty US-centric, and Canadian readers may be wondering how much applies to them. The short answer is, most of it. As of 2019, Canadian eligible dividend income is federally taxed by multiplying by 38 percent (known as the gross-up amount), adding that to your taxable income, and then multiplying that grossed-up amount by 15.02 percent to calculate a credit meant to offset taxes paid. The net effect of this is that an individual can earn up to $47,630 in dividends and pay no tax, so a married couple can earn up to $95,260 in eligible dividends tax-free.

Capital gains, however, are taxed differently. In Canada, there's no distinction between long-term and short-term capital gains, which is great, but realized capital gains are multiplied by the capital gain inclusion rate, 50 percent as of 2019, and that amount is added to your regular income.

In short: dividends are taxed about the same, and capital gains are taxed somewhat higher. To even out the score, Canadian tax-deferred accounts (e.g., the RRSP) don't have an age penalty for withdrawals. So, Canadians don't need to bother with that IRA conversion ladder business. They can withdraw their personal exemption (currently $12,069 per person, $24,138 per married couple) every year without the five-year waiting period.

The net effect is that Canadians can earn more tax-free dividends than Americans, but they have to share their meager personal exemptions between withdrawing from their RRSP and realizing capital gains tax-free. One tactic is to alternate. One year, use the personal exemption to melt down your RRSP. Next year, use it to realize capital gains. Year after that, go back to your RRSP. And so on. That's what I do.

WHAT ABOUT STATE/PROVINCIAL TAXES?

You may have noticed I've again done all my calculations using only federal tax rates. This time, I've left state/provincial taxes out because each state/province has different rules concerning dividends and capital gains. California, for example, treats dividend and capital gains tax as regular income, and has a marginal tax rate of 6 percent for a married couple reporting $78,750. Ontario, on the other hand, has a similar treatment of dividend income that results in no tax paid if no tax is paid at the federal level. And just to be different, Florida has no state income tax whatsoever.

The thing about being a regular worker is that you generally have to live where your employer is located. But if you game the system so you don't need a normal job, you won't have this problem! You can be anywhere. Rich people do the calculations for their state and decide if their tax burden makes it worth staying. Maybe you will decide that staying in California is worth a 6 percent tax on your dividends/capital gains. Or maybe moving to Florida sounds appealing. The point is, by designing your portfolio to avoid federal taxes, and designing your life to avoid state/provincial taxes, you may never have to pay a dollar in income tax ever again. Whether you choose to do it is up to you.

So rich people don't pay taxes, but now you won't have to either.

Again, it's all perfectly legal—no sneaky tricks, no shell companies. While I was working, I was paying an average tax rate of 25 percent, and I was happy it wasn't higher. But 0 percent? Never in a million years did I think it was possible. But it is.

CHAPTER 13 SUMMARY

- ▸ Employment income and interest income are taxed at the worst rates, while qualified dividends and capital gains are taxed much more favorably.

- ▸ Tax optimization is the process of putting your assets into the right accounts so you reduce (or eliminate) taxes post-retirement.

  - Put assets that pay interest or non-qualified dividends in your tax-deferred or tax-sheltered accounts.

  - Put assets that pay qualified dividends in your normal investment account.

- After you retire early, you can access the money in your 401(k) without paying a penalty by building a five-year Roth IRA conversion ladder.

  - First, consolidate all your 401(k) accounts into a traditional IRA.

  - Then perform a Roth IRA conversion equal to your standard deduction.

  - Keep doing this every year.

  - After five years, you'll be able to access the first converted amount penalty-free.

- Capital gains harvesting can be used to eliminate capital gains taxes.

  - Every year, realize as many capital gains as you can inside your 0 percent tax bracket by selling some ETF units.

  - Shortly thereafter, rebuy those units back to reset your cost basis.

Note: All advice outlined above was accurate at the time of writing. However, laws can change, which may render this advice suboptimal. Consult a certified public accountant before implementing anything.

— 14 —

THE MAGICAL NUMBER
THAT SAVED ME

From childhood up until age thirty, my life improved dramatically. After all, through grit and determination (and a healthy dose of fear), I had made it into the vaunted middle class as a computer engineer, where not only could I buy all the Cokes I'd ever wanted, my biggest problem was whether my breakfast muffins were organic and gluten-free.

But as Dad had taught me, anything that can go wrong *will* go wrong, and there isn't a damn thing you can do to stop it. One day, fate decided I hadn't *chi ku*'d enough and dropped a shit bomb. At work, an announcement was made that our department was being "restructured" due to budget cuts (despite the fact that the company had made two billion dollars that year). Familiar faces started disappearing, replaced with unfamiliar ones that more often than not were stationed in an Indian call center.

Despite having been a loyal employee for six years and getting promoted twice, I had to submit weekly reports with detailed examples to prove why I shouldn't immediately be fired, too. All of my colleagues were also hustling to prove why they shouldn't be on the chopping block. My best friend, as it turns out, didn't have the proof. Didn't matter that she'd been working eighty-hour weeks. Didn't matter that she had recently lost her mother to a brain aneurysm, her uncle to pancreatic cancer, and her grandmother to a heart attack.

The pink slip was waiting for her the day she got back from her grandmother's funeral.

Every day I wondered when the axe was going to fall. It was around this time that my boss went on disability leave. Turned out, there was a blood clot in his leg and the doctors said he might die if he didn't reduce his hours at work. A month later, he came back, acting like nothing had happened. The blood clot was still there, and he limped around with a cane, but he just worked even longer hours and screamed at us to do the same. Everyone was either on antidepressants or having regular meltdowns. One of my coworkers couldn't take it anymore and also went on disability leave.

Then I watched my mentor collapse and almost die at his desk.

That night, when I went home, I experienced my first panic attack. I also learned a new life lesson:

Money is worth bleeding for, but it's not worth dying for.

Growing up poor had given me the Scarcity Mind-set that helped me claw my way up to the middle class. But somewhere along the way the Scarcity Mind-set had run out of steam. I'd made it, right? No more stomach worms, no more fishing for toys in medical waste heaps, no more treating empty soda cans like the most precious thing in the world. I thought the whole point of getting a high-paying job was to be safe and happy. But I had done all the "right" things and people were *still* dying around me? What was the point of this money if all it meant was the shiniest coffin in the graveyard?

It was time for a change. It was time to stop the bleeding.

THE HOARDING MIND-SET

Looking at my mentor's empty chair the next day, I remembered a story I'd once read in the newspaper about a man who worked hard for decades so that he would be able to retire at sixty-five and travel the world like he always wanted. But he never ended up retiring because he was scared he didn't have enough money, so he kept working "just one more year"—year after year. Then his heart gave out, he died at his desk, and his kids had him cremated and ended up traveling around the world with his ashes in a tin can.

The article was supposed to be one of those "Awww, that's sweet. What nice kids to fulfill that man's dreams" human-interest stories, but when I read it, I didn't identify with the kids; I identified with the tin can.

As I've said, I remain grateful for growing up with a Scarcity Mind-set. It kept me alive. But now it wasn't doing what it was supposed to. It had turned into a Hoarding Mind-set.

The Scarcity Mind-set teaches you to sacrifice your time and your health for money, because money is life. And that works when all you care about is survival. But the problem with the Scarcity Mind-set is that it doesn't have an end goal. Once survival is no longer in jeopardy, there's no off switch. You continue to sacrifice needlessly, forever. It only ends once you use up all your life energy and die in a cubicle somewhere.

The Scarcity Mind-set trades life energy for survival. The Hoarding Mind-set trades life energy for nothing. I had seen it almost claim one victim, and I didn't want it to claim me as well.

I needed a way out.

To Start a Business

I knew there had to be another way of thinking about money—one that didn't end up with me in a tin can—and I began my quest to find it. Over the next few months, I researched like a madwoman. On the Internet, at the library, and in bookstores, I searched and searched for answers. At first, I thought the answer was, well, more money. Rich people don't have to worry about money, right? I devoured books like Tim Ferriss's *4-Hour Workweek* and Robert Kiyosaki's *Rich Dad Poor Dad*, concluding that the secret was starting a successful business. After all, the rich people on TV were all CEOs and entrepreneurs.

So, for a few years, I worked my nine-to-five job, and in the evenings I furiously built online business after business, hoping one of them would take off and save me from that tin can. I had a poster above my desk at home that read "TIME = MONEY" to motivate myself to keep pushing.

First, I tried side gigs. I had been reading a blog from a digital marketing expert who claimed to make $100,000 a month after starting a niche website and selling advertising space. All you had to do, he said, was follow his step-by-step approach to researching long-tail keywords, spamming articles on aggregator sites, and commenting on other people's blogs. The point of this was to create "backlinks"—links from all over the Internet that pointed back to your site. When you had enough backlinks, Google's ranking algorithm would rank you on the first page for that niche market.

Every day for months, I diligently followed all the steps. *$100,000-a-month affiliate income, here I come!* I even got some traction. The problem was, this marketer's site got popular, and once enough people were using his tactic it blew up. Google changed their algorithm. Failure number one.

Next, I tried selling stuff on Amazon. I'd read about people making six figures a year by buying heavily discounted items in bulk, listing them on Amazon, and turning a profit on the difference. The problem was I didn't live near an outlet and we were living on the top floor of a town house without much storage space. Shipping costs quickly added up, I couldn't move enough units, and I couldn't turn a profit. Failure number two.

I tried making an app. I kept reading about developers making the next Flappy Bird or whatever and getting buried in cash. That sounded like a decent fit. I am a computer engineer after all. My million-dollar idea was based on a book called *One Red Paperclip*, which told the story of how someone bartered their way from a single red paperclip through a series of increasingly valuable trades until they managed to get a house. I decided to build a trading marketplace called SwapIt.com. I registered the domain and roped Bryce into helping me code it, and within a few months, we were ready to launch.

Then we ran into something called a "two-market problem." People would go into the app but not find anything to trade. They wouldn't stick around. As a result, there was nothing to trade. It was a circular death spiral.

One day, I described my business to an entrepreneur friend over lunch. He gently asked, "How are you going to monetize an app in which no money ever changes hands?" I replied: "Crap. I don't know!" Failure number three.

Starting a successful business is insanely difficult. (Who knew?) According to Bloomberg, 90 percent of entrepreneurs fail within eighteen months, often simply due to bad luck or bad timing. The competition is fierce. It's all so discouraging that most people give up. When I did some research into the 10 percent who don't, I found out that they work psychotically hard: waking up at four o'clock every day, grinding for a few hours, going in to a desk job at seven o'clock, then dragging themselves home to keep pushing until they pass out. Plenty drill themselves into debt, losing their shirts and minds in the process. Even the ones who *do* make it have to continue working like dogs to keep the business from collapsing. Your competitors are always nipping at your heels.

I was trying to escape my horrible job, not trying to find a new way to kill myself. Plus, too many things were outside my control, which I hate. Becoming a "side-trepreneur" wasn't going to help me quit my day job, and I could give up years of my life with nothing to show for it.

One day, as I was staring at my failed app, I picked up a paperweight and threw it at the wall in frustration. That knocked my "TIME = MONEY" poster off the wall. It landed on the floor upside down, the glass in its frame shattered. It now read "MONEY = TIME."

Huh.

What if I was going about it backward? Instead of killing myself to accumulate more money, what if I found a way to use the money I had to buy back time?

And that's when I discovered the mind-set that would ultimately save me: the Freedom Mind-set.

THE FREEDOM MIND-SET

The Freedom Mind-set shifts your thinking, from money being the most important to *freedom* being the most important. Once your needs are taken care of, the next step shouldn't be *hoarding*. It should be *getting your time back*.

Instead of having your money sit in a bank account or going toward a jumbo mortgage, what if it was invested instead? Invested in such a way that it generated money continuously. You could harvest this "income" without ever depleting the principal.

What if the income was enough to cover your living expenses?

You'd never have to work again.

I mean, you *could* keep working if you wanted to, but if your boss told you to work sixteen-hour days and never see your family again?

You'd tell him to kindly F off!

And if he fired you? You'd get a nice juicy severance package, add it to your pile of money, and ride off into the sunset, cackling like a maniac.

Yeah, I thought. *I could get behind this. After all, I love telling people to F off!*

I took all my business books, shoved them under my bed, and turned my research toward a different topic: retirement.

Retirement planning is the process of making your money last after you leave work at sixty-five. I had never thought about it since I was nowhere near retirement age, but my curiosity was lit. How do retirement planners make your money last? Can these strategies be adapted for someone who isn't sixty-five?

As it turns out, yes. Yes, they can.

The beauty of it all boiled down to one magical number. The magical number that saved my life.

What Is the 4 Percent Rule?

The 4 Percent Rule, also known as the Rule of 25, comes from a study at Trinity University into retirement planning and economic theory.[1] The authors took price data from the stock and bond markets through all of recorded history. Pretending there was a retiree starting with a bucket of cash, they simulated what would happen if she withdrew a certain percentage of her portfolio every year, leaving the rest invested. They counted how many retirees made it to the end of their retirement with their cash intact, and how many ended up broke and dying alone in an alley surrounded by empty cat food canisters (okay, it wasn't quite that detailed).

Picture a man named Allen, who retired in 1975. Allen has $500,000, and he needs $50,000 to live each year. So, Allen's withdrawal rate is 10 percent. He invests his money into the stock market, only selling assets every January to fund his next year's living expenses. Does he make it? Or does he run out of money?

Now there's Betty, who retired in 1982. Betty has $650,000, but she only needs $26,000 each year to live. Her withdrawal rate is 4 percent. She also invests her money into the stock market and withdraws every year. Does she make it?

After hours and hours of calculator punching (or, more likely, whipping poor grad students into doing the work), the researchers came up with an answer. A withdrawal rate that had a 95 percent success rate. Meaning that out of the one hundred made-up retirees, ninety-five of them made it to the finish line without running out of money. Here's a picture of those hundred retirees (generated with the online tool at FIRECalc.com).

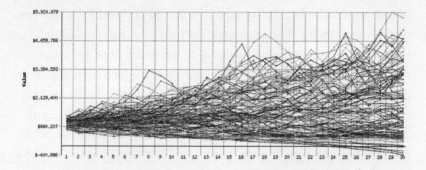

Each line is a made-up retiree starting at a different point in time. The solid line at the bottom is the threshold of failure where the retiree runs out of money. The vertical axis represents that person's retirement portfolio while withdrawing the equivalent of 4 percent of their starting value every year, adjusted for inflation. Any retirement that dips below the solid line at the bottom ran out of money, while if it stayed above they were A-OK. Nineteen out of twenty (95 percent) made it with their portfolio intact. In fact, most of them wound up with *more* money than they started with! Thus, the researchers determined 4 percent was a reasonable safe withdrawal rate, or SWR.

This means when 4 percent of your portfolio matches your living expenses, you have a 95 percent chance of making it thirty years without running out of money! At that point, you no longer need your job. You can flip off your boss, play his head like a bongo, and blast out on a rocket ship of glory!

When I read this, my head nearly exploded. To figure out the number I needed to retire early and quit my hateful job forever, I could simply take my yearly living expenses, multiply by twenty-five, and get my target portfolio size. (Dividing your living expenses by 4 percent is the same as multiplying them by twenty-five. That's why the 4 Percent Rule is also called the Rule of 25.)

This was a fantastic starting point, but it still wasn't perfect. This study was conducted for people retiring at sixty-five, who needed thirty years of funds. If I retired in my thirties, I'd need a much longer time frame. And what if I turned out to be one of those unlucky 5 percent whose retirement ran aground? Fortunately, I figured out that the thirty-year retirement can be adapted to a retirement of any length by using a process I call "Perpetual Re-retirement," which we'll discuss in chapter 17. And in chapter 15, we'll discuss the solution Bryce and I came up with to fix the 5 percent failure rate, called the Yield Shield.

Discovering the 4 Percent Rule was, without exaggeration, a lifesaver. It gave me a goal I could work toward. I didn't have to stay at a hateful job forever; there was an end in sight! I needed to multiply my expenses (which were around $40,000 per year) by twenty-five, giving me a target portfolio of $1,000,000. That would be enough to escape my cubicle prison and ride off into the sunset forever.

But a million dollars is not a small amount. With two engineering degrees, we started with a combined $125,000-per-year after-tax salary (don't be discouraged if your salary isn't anywhere near that level; you can still achieve financial independence and I'll show you how in chapter 21), and my Scarcity Mind-set made sure we saved a lot of it, but how long would it take us to get to our target portfolio size?

How Money = Time

Your time to retirement doesn't depend on how much you make. It depends on how much you save. This makes some intuitive sense. If someone nets a million bucks a year but they also spend a million bucks a year, they can never retire because they're 100 percent dependent on their job. Shut off the taps and they're done. They're not saving a dime. But if someone makes $40,000 a year and only spends $30,000, they're ahead of the game. The millionaire who looks great on paper has a savings rate of 0 percent, while the modestly earning person has a savings rate of 25 percent.

If we were to plot how long it takes to retire based on their savings rates, the chart would look like this.

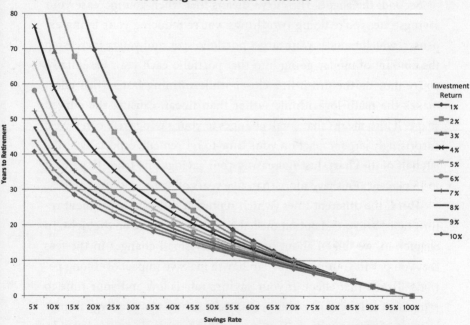

How Long Does It Take to Retire?

Now, I didn't just conjure this up from thin air. For the data wonks out there, the mathematical derivation for this chart is based on the 4 Percent Rule and can be found in appendix A.

Done? Great. Here's how this chart works. The horizontal axis is your savings rate—your after-tax pay minus expenses—ranging from 5 percent to 100 percent. The vertical axis is your time to retirement in years, assuming you're starting from scratch (i.e., with not a penny to your name). The curved lines are your retirement portfolio returns, ranging from 1 percent to 10 percent annualized.

Americans have an average savings rate of 5–10 percent.[2] You can see that if someone's investment portfolio returns an annualized average of 6–7 percent a year, their time to retirement is forty to fifty years. This is where the "normal" retirement age of sixty-five comes from.

There are a few interesting things about the chart. First, income is *nowhere* to be seen. It doesn't matter whether you make $50,000 a year or $500,000 a year; the only thing that matters is your *savings rate*.

Second, the shape. The curve means that when you increase your savings rate, you're doing two things: you're reducing your living expenses, which reduces your target portfolio size, and you're increasing the amount of money going into that portfolio each year. Essentially, you're moving the finish line closer while running faster. This effect makes the math logarithmic rather than linear, causing the curved shape. It also means that small changes to your savings rate can have a surprisingly large impact on your time to retirement, especially at the left half of the chart. Just increasing your savings rate from 10 percent to 15 percent can shave more than five years off your working career!

Third, the different lines (which represent different investment return rates) are spread out on the left and then converge on the right. In chapter 10, we talked about how relatively small changes in the fees that you pay in your portfolio can have a massive impact over long periods. This is that effect. If your savings rate is low and your time to retirement is long (forty-plus years), your returns have a large impact because of compounding. That means that for people on the left side, it's important that they manage their investments correctly.

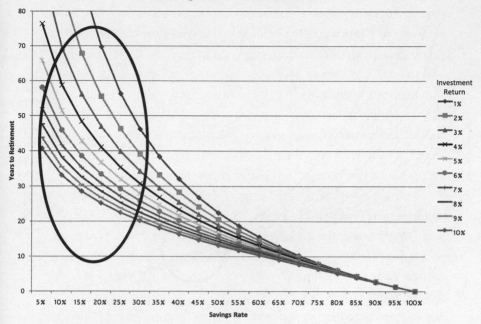

For these people, the difference between a 4 percent and a 6 percent annualized return on their investments could affect their retirement date by up to a decade. Conversely, for people on the right (the super savers), their performance doesn't have much impact on their retirement date. This is because their ability to save money is so powerful it overwhelms the comparatively meager returns.

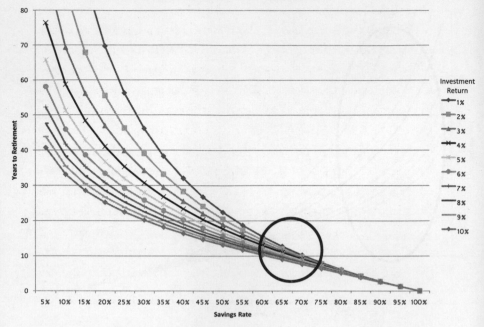

This is *crucial*. This is the math behind why past mistakes don't matter, which I wrote about in chapter 7. Even if you screwed up financially in the past, even if you're reading this in your forties or fifties without a penny to your name, you can still catch up if you supercharge your savings. From a starting net worth of $0, if you start saving 60 to 70 percent tomorrow, you'll still be able to retire in about ten years (I know that sounds like a lot, and it is, but we'll talk strategies in chapter 21). And because returns don't have as big of an effect at those rates, you could dump your money into a savings account and you'd *still* win.

Freedom

This is the Freedom Mind-set. Once survival is no longer at stake, money can buy you freedom—if you know how to save it. Once you get to your target portfolio size using the 4 Percent Rule, you don't have to work anymore. At this point you are financially independent. You never have to see the inside of a cubicle again.

When I discovered this, my head spun. I had a sneaking suspicion that I was closer to the right side of the chart than to the left. My Scarcity Mind-set had made me obsessed with saving money. I rarely shopped for clothes, and except for that short-lived purse binge, I didn't own luxury items. We had been living in a small one-bedroom apartment this entire time with the intent of saving for a down payment.

I spent the rest of that night poring over my spreadsheets, which I had created after I started working to track my spending in detail (there's that Scarcity Mind-set again). Bryce always thought that was overkill, but it meant that I could easily go back through the years and calculate our savings rate. Turns out it was 52 to 78 percent. Based on our combined after-tax salaries starting at $125,000 per year, we had managed to save $500,000 in just six years, which, thank God, we hadn't put into a house. (To see the year-by-year breakdown of our salaries and savings, go to appendix B.)

That meant when we started working, we had inadvertently been on a path to retire in nine years. Technically, we only had three more to go.

That evening when Bryce came home, I greeted him at the door by telling him:

"Hey, hon? I think we can retire in our thirties."

CHAPTER 14 SUMMARY

- ▸ The Scarcity Mind-set becomes a problem when you're no longer in poverty. Now it's a Hoarding Mind-set, which causes you to be needlessly fearful forever.

- ▸ The Freedom Mind-set is how you flip your thinking into realizing that money can buy you time.

- The 4 Percent Rule states that if your living expenses equal 4 percent of your investment portfolio, you will be able to retire and not outlive your money with 95 percent certainty over thirty years.

- The single biggest determinant of when you can retire is your savings rate, not your income.

PART 3

BECOMING WEALTHY

— 15 —

THE CASH CUSHION AND THE YIELD SHIELD

Just like that, I had gone from anticipating dying at my desk doing a job I hated to considering the possibility of no longer having to work for a living. The idea that it could be achievable in just three years rather than decades filled me with a giddy energy that had me floating around our apartment for weeks.

But it was all still theoretical. I had a stack of academic papers on my desk and a bunch of math scribbled on a whiteboard. In the early sixties, NASA also had a stack of academic papers and math scribbled on a whiteboard; turning that into a rocket that could land on the moon was an enormous challenge, one that took a full decade to get right.

According to my projections, our savings would hit our financial independence (or FI, as the cool kids call it) target in 2015, so I had until then to turn that whiteboard math into a rocket ship I felt safe enough to get into. To do that, I had to come up with answers to those annoying but all-important questions that kept me up at night when I wanted to be happily dreaming of walking into my boss's office and handing him my resignation.

What if the stock market tanks right as I retire?

What do I do with my life if I'm not working?

What do I do about health insurance?

What about kids?

My whiteboard addressed exactly none of these concerns. The really scary part was that my usual method of answering these questions no longer worked. Normally, when confronted with a problem I don't know how to solve, I look to see what other people have done—people I trust and think are smart—or books, blogs, and academic research. But there was nobody out there in my exact situation that I could copy from.

Now, don't get me wrong. There were plenty of people who retired decades earlier than normal. Some had built multimillion-dollar businesses. Others had financed their retirement with investment properties bought cheap during the Great Financial Crisis of 2008, which they now rented out. But I couldn't find any information about how a thirty-year-old retiree deals with kids or health insurance. There was no research on what to do if the stock market drops by 25 percent the day after retirement or how to find meaning outside of work. We were on our own.

It may not surprise you to hear that, once again, Bryce saved my butt.

I'm naturally conservative and risk-averse. I'm not a conformist (I refuse to follow the herd when I believe the herd is wrong, like when it comes to buying houses), but if something is scary or unknown, I will happily step aside and let someone else try it first. Coming from a totalitarian country, it's a survival instinct that kept my family and me alive.

Bryce is the opposite. He grew up climbing rocks and flying down ski slopes, and doing other activities I consider the realm of lunatics. He'll jump into a risky situation with full confidence that he'll somehow figure it out.

Optimist. Pessimist. We were the perfect team to pull this off.

When I posed each of these questions, Bryce would declare the situation "fine," if we "just follow the 4 Percent Rule and control our expenses."

To which I would respond, "Yeah, but what if we retire into a multi-year bear market?"

Which would send him scurrying back to the whiteboard.

Over time, however, I'm happy to report that we did, in fact, figure it out. It took three years, but we managed to come up with satisfying, flexible solutions that answered all my questions.

In the first part of this book, I described how the Scarcity Mind-set helped me avoid the big mistakes people make about money (choosing the wrong career, getting into debt, etc.). In the second part, I showed you how I adapted lessons from the wealthy to propel me from middle-class to rich. Now it's time to talk about the solutions that we came up with to solve the problems preventing people from leaving their jobs in their thirties. Three years later, not only have we *not* gone bankrupt, our net worth has *grown* to $1.3 million—despite our having to make a withdrawal during the 2015 oil crisis.

In short, we built a rocket ship.

THE BIG PROBLEM WITH THE 4 PERCENT RULE

The biggest problem with the 4 Percent Rule is that it's not a guarantee. In fact, the formal definition of the 4 Percent Rule states that withdrawing 4 percent of your starting portfolio each year, adjusted for inflation, yields a 95 percent success rate over thirty-year retirement periods.

That still means 5 percent of people who retire according to the 4 Percent Rule fail, meaning they run out of money at some point during their retirement.

It all comes down to luck. If you retire right before an economic boom, you might experience ten years of great stock market returns followed by five years of declining markets. But you would have made so much money during those first ten years you'd shrug off the losses. However, if you retire right before an economic bust, the picture changes dramatically. You'd watch your portfolio plummet while withdrawing from it for living expenses. This is the worst-case scenario. Unlike individual stocks, index funds won't go to zero, so when a drop happens, the correct thing to do is wait (or buy more). The absolute *wrong* thing to do is sell. But when you're retired, you have to sell at some point, which depletes your portfolio so much that when the rebound happens it can't recover. You end up being in the dreaded 5 percent club of broke-ass retirees.

The only difference in the two scenarios above is the order, or sequence, in which you get these returns. That's why in the world of financial planning this is called sequence-of-return risk. You can't predict the stock market's performance in any particular period, so do you just pray and hope that you're part of that 95 percent of retirees? Some people might be okay with those odds, but as a pessimist, I'm not.

To fix this problem, we developed a system made up of two parts: the Cash Cushion and the Yield Shield.

Again, the biggest danger in a stock market crash for an early retiree is having to sell when prices are plummeting. If you do that, you lock in your losses and you have fewer units available to pull you back up with the inevitable rebound. On paper, the strategy is quite simple: when you're down, don't sell. But that can be easier said than done. If you're still gainfully employed, no problem. Ignore the fearmongering headlines, don't sell, and, if possible, buy more. This is how we survived the stock market crash of 2008 without losing any money. But if you're retired and depending on portfolio withdrawals to pay for food, you don't have that option.

This is where the Cash Cushion comes in. The Cash Cushion is a pile of *cash* stored in a high-interest savings account. In the event of a stock market downturn, this cash can be used as a *cushion* (see what I did there?) so you don't have to rely on selling assets to pay for your living expenses. It's a reserve fund.

To figure out how big a Cash Cushion we needed, I went back and studied the amount of time it takes for a stock market to recover from a big crash. It turns out the median length is two years. During the Great Depression—the worst-case example—it took about five years after accounting for dividends. After the 2008 crash, it took two. So a five-year Cash Cushion should be sufficient to weather any storm.

If someone were trying to retire early with living expenses of $40,000 a year, you'd think the math would be straightforward, if daunting: $40,000 × 5 = $200,000. That's a big chunk of change to have at the ready.

Here's the good news: you actually need much less than that. This is because of the second part of this system, which I call the Yield Shield.

Every ETF has a yield—money handed over per unit of the ETF you own, typically every month or quarter. For bond ETFs, this is the monthly interest the underlying bonds pay. For equity ETFs, this money is coming from dividends the companies issue to their shareholders.

Your fund company will provide this value on each ETF as either a yield (given as a percentage) or a certain distribution amount per share. So, for example, an ETF trading at $18 per share that distributes $0.03 every month has a yield of:

$$\$0.03 \times 12 \, / \, \$18 = 2\%$$

Since each ETF has a yield, and your investment portfolio is made up of ETFs, your portfolio has a yield as well. This yield accumulates as your ETFs spin off distributions every month, and assuming you haven't set up your brokerage account to automatically reinvest those distributions, this yield will show up as spare cash. This gets generated regardless of whether the stock market is rising or falling. To harvest it, simply withdraw it into your checking account. The reason this is so valuable is because unlike the capital value of your portfolio, which goes up and down with every move on the stock market, the yield gets determined when you buy. Even if the overall portfolio later goes down in value, the yield it generates remains mostly unchanged (see appendix C for caveats). So if your portfolio yield on a million dollars is 3.5 percent or $35,000 and you hit a bad year that causes you to go down to $900,000, it's still yielding $35,000.

Remember, the danger of becoming one of the 5 percent of people who go broke during their retirement is at its highest if you sell assets in a down market. But if you simply harvest spare cash, you aren't selling anything. In other words, the dividends are safe to withdraw and spend.

Accounting for the portfolio yield (dividends + interest), your Cash Cushion would be:

$$Cash\ Cushion = (Annual\ Spending - Annual\ Yield) \\ \times Number\ of\ Years$$

Recall that this is the portfolio Bryce and I decided to use for our retirement journey:

Name	Allocation
Bonds	40%
Canadian Index	20%
US Index	20%
EAFE Index	20%

And here were the yields associated with each ETF, at the time:

Asset Type	Allocation	Yield
Bonds	40%	3%
Canadian Index	20%	2.5%
US Index	20%	1.75%
EAFE Index	20%	2.5%

This gave me a total portfolio yield of about 2.5 percent. So, for our retiree with annual spending of $40,000 and a portfolio size of $1,000,000 (calculated via the 4 Percent Rule), their Cash Cushion needs to be:

$$\$40,000-(\$1,000,000 \times 2.5\%) \times 5 = \$75,000$$

That's much lower than the $200,000 we thought they needed. But still, $75,000 is a lot of money to save on top of your FI amount. I wanted to see if we could do better.

And this brings me to a process I like to call raising the Yield Shield. Raising the Yield Shield is the process of *temporarily* pivoting your portfolio into higher-yielding assets. Note the key word "temporarily." Long-term, your investment portfolio should be a low-cost, index-tracking portfolio. Why? Because those are the conditions under which the Trinity study was conducted. If you stray too far, the 4 Percent Rule no longer applies. But creating a Yield Shield for the first five years of retirement can counteract the biggest problem with the 4 Percent Rule.

First, pick higher-yielding assets that are similar to the assets that are already in your portfolio. Then, strategically swap them out to increase your portfolio yield. This will have the effect of increasing your portfolio's volatility, and I'll explain why, but what we're doing here is taking on higher volatility for higher yield.

In those rare 5 percent of cases where portfolios fail, they fail because of the first five years. That danger zone is when you need to make sure you don't have to sell assets in a down market to pay for living expenses. So, put up your Yield Shield for five years. When you make it out intact, you can be confident that you're in the 95 percent of retirees who will make it.

So which higher-yielding assets make up our Yield Shield?

Preferred Shares

The first are preferred shares, a hybrid of a stock and a bond. They are traded on the stock market along with other shares, but unlike common stock they don't come with voting rights, meaning they're not a vehicle of ownership like common stock is. In fact, companies issue preferred shares as a way of raising money, much like they do bonds. But unlike bonds, preferred shares are lower on the totem pole when it comes to getting paid in the event of a default. If the company doesn't have enough cash, dividends on common shares get dropped first, then preferred shares, and only after that, bonds. So, in financial distress, those "preferred" shareholders get paid after bonds but before common shareholders.

In exchange for this downside, preferred shares offer a much higher yield. While an equity index might have a yield of 2 percent, preferred shares tend to pay 4 to 6 percent. They are more volatile than bonds but less volatile than stocks, so they are a way to increase yield without massively spiking volatility. Another upside is that unlike bonds, which pay interest, preferred shares pay qualified dividends. This means preferred shares are favorably taxed, as we talked about in chapter 13.

I've advised against buying individual stocks, and this goes for preferred shares. Preferred shares are complicated to own individually. Even issues from the same company can behave differently. Some are cumulative, some are noncumulative, some are convertible to common stock, some aren't, some are fixed-rate, and some float with prevailing interest rates. It's beyond the scope of the text to define all of the terms here, but I advocate owning preferred shares in an index ETF, the same way I own stocks. That way, you can own the entire market without having to pore over the details of each individual issue.

For reference, here are a few ETFs that invest in the preferred share indexes:

Name	Country	Ticker
iShares S & P/TSX North American Preferred Stock Index	Canada	XPF
iShares US Preferred Stock	USA	PFF
PowerShares Preferred Portfolio	USA	PGX

Full disclosure: the fund I owned while establishing the Yield Shield was XPF. The other funds are US analogues, and as always please consult a licensed financial adviser before making individual purchases.

Real Estate Investment Trusts

Now, given my feelings on housing, you may be surprised to learn that I do in fact own real estate. Just not the way most people do.

Real estate investment trusts, or REITs, are corporations that own and manage real estate, but they're not sitting on it with the hopes of selling at a higher price. They own and manage *investment* real estate: office buildings, shopping malls, nursing homes, apartment complexes, etc. REITs buy up these properties, find tenants, and hire people to manage the day-to-day upkeep. Every month, they collect rent and pass the profit to their shareholders.

Because REITs were created to provide income to their shareholders, their yield is higher than what the stock market can offer. Plus, I admit it's somewhat fun owning REITs. Because REITs own so many commercial buildings in the United States and Canada, you can look up the individual properties and you'll probably find your favorite shopping malls or movie theaters, or even the building you work in. If you own the REIT, you own a piece of those buildings!

And as with preferred shares, it's possible to own REITs in an index, so you can own the entire sector rather than having to sift through individual offerings. Here are a few REIT ETFs for your reference:

Name	Country	Ticker
iShares S & P/TSX Capped REIT Index	Canada	XRE
iShares Core US REIT	USA	USRT

Full disclosure: The fund I owned was XRE.

Corporate Bonds

As the name would imply, corporate bonds are similar to government bonds but issued by a company rather than a country. Like preferred shares, corporate bonds are issued to raise money, but on the hierarchical pecking order of debt, bonds are first in line. If a company has cash available, bonds are paid first, then preferred shares, then, after that, dividends on common stock. For that reason, corporate bonds are considered safer than preferred shares but riskier than government bonds. After all, it's easier for a corporation to run out of money than the government. Since corporate bonds are more volatile than government bonds, they pay a higher yield, by around 1 to 2 percent.

Here's where we make a distinction between corporate bonds and so-called high-yield bonds. Ratings agencies like Moody's and Standard & Poor's evaluate each corporate bond issue based on the company's financial health and assign it a letter grade. A is great, B is okay, and C is sucky, just like in high school. AA is even better than A, and AAA is as high as you can go—basically risk-free. The term "corporate bonds" indicates bonds that are "investment grade," or have a rating of BBB– or higher (using the Standard & Poor's scale). Anything below that is considered a "high-yield" bond, or less politely, a "junk" bond.

I've owned junk bonds and they are exceptionally volatile. They pay a juicy yield over government bonds, but *man*, do they swing in value. They typically include companies in sectors like air travel, oil and mining, and tech, so while their yield is sweet, their prices swing like equities, so ultimately I don't recommend them. Stick with investment-grade stuff.

Here are some ETFs that track this segment of the market:

Name	Country	Ticker
Vanguard Total Corporate Bond	USA	VTC
iShares Canadian Corporate Bond	Canada	XCB

Full disclosure: The fund I owned was XCB.

Dividend Stocks

And finally, there are dividend stocks. Dividend stocks are common stocks that pay a higher-than-normal dividend. Typically, these are large, successful, established companies in saturated markets without much room to grow. Think Johnson & Johnson or Coca-Cola.

In young, high-growth companies like tech startups, any income usually gets reinvested in expanding the business, hiring more people, and building more factories. But mature companies like Coca-Cola often run into the problem of having more money than they know what to do with. So rather than invest in something risky and speculative, they tend to distribute that money back to their shareholders.

You want to be one of those shareholders.

Here are some ETFs that track this segment of the market:

Name	Country	Ticker
Vanguard High Dividend Yield	USA	VYM
iShares Canadian Select Dividend	Canada	XDV
iShares International Select Dividend	International	IDV

Full disclosure: The fund I owned was XDV.

Putting It All Together

Those are the four pillars of the Yield Shield. Now it's time to put it all together. Take each pillar, match it to the part of your portfolio it's most similar to, and swap it out for a higher-yielding version. This increases portfolio volatility, yes. But it also makes you less vulnerable to that volatility. Even if my overall portfolio value swings more, because I get paid a steady yield in the form of spare cash every month, I don't need to sell assets to pay for living expenses. This has a big effect on my early retirement plan.

Remember that the entire point of this exercise is to reduce the risk of being part of the 5 percent of people whose retirement plan fails. Swapping out part of your portfolio for higher-yielding assets increases your Yield Shield. And that, in turn, decreases how much of a Cash Cushion you need. Remember the formula:

$$Cash\ Cushion = (Annual\ Spending - Annual\ Yield) \\ \times Number\ of\ Years$$

This is the portfolio I started out with:

Asset Type	Allocation	Yield
Bonds	40%	3%
Canadian Index	20%	2.5%
US Index	20%	1.75%
EAFE Index	20%	2.5%

After creating my Yield Shield, this is what my portfolio looked like:

Asset Type	Allocation	Yield
Bonds	**40%**	**4.4%**
Government Bonds	10%	3%
Corporate Bonds	10%	3.5%
Preferred Shares	20%	5.6%
Canadian Index	**20%**	**4.4%**
TSX	5%	2.5%
Dividend Stocks	5%	3.5%
REITs	10%	5.75%
US Index	**20%**	**1.75%**
EAFE Index	**20%**	**2.5%**
Total	**100%**	**3.5%**

Asset Type	Allocation	Yield
Bonds	**40%**	**4.3%**
Government Bonds	10%	3.0%
Corporate Bonds	10%	3.3%
Preferred Shares	20%	5.5%

American Index	30%	2.88%
S&P 500	15%	1.8%
REITs	10%	4.4%
Dividend Stocks	5%	3.1%
EAFE Index	30%	2.7%
Total		3.4%

These figures were correct at the time I created my Yield Shield; yours may vary.

Notice the new portfolio yield (on the Canadian portfolio): 3.5 percent! Let's see what that does to the size of my Cash Cushion:

$$Cash\ Cushion = (\$40,000 - \$35,000) \times 5 = \$25,000$$

By temporarily shifting my assets, my Cash Cushion dropped from $200,000 to just $25,000. For more details about the Yield Shield portfolio and how it performed in 2008, see appendix C.

Between Bryce and me, we calculated a combined cost of living of $40,000, and therefore an FI number of $1,000,000.

A million dollars sounds like an insane amount of money—especially to me. But because I chose a career with a good POT score, because my Scarcity Mind-set helped me optimize costs, and because (and I can't stress this enough) we didn't buy an overpriced house, after just nine years of working we were about to cross this threshold.

One day, Bryce called me at work to tell me he had made a reservation at a fancy restaurant for a special occasion. I had no idea what this occasion was. It wasn't my birthday, and it wasn't our anniversary, but given that it was my favorite restaurant, I played along.

After the meal was over, Bryce handed me sheets of paper. They were our bank statements. A sticky note on the front read "TOTAL" over a number scrawled in Magic Marker.

I gaped at that number, then looked up at him.

"Is this for real?"

Bryce grinned, then held up a glass of champagne. "Congratulations, millionaire."

CHAPTER 15 SUMMARY

- ▸ Following the 4 Percent Rule still gives you a 5 percent chance of running out of money, due to a phenomenon known as sequence-of-return risk.

- ▸ Your backup plan is to use the Cash Cushion and the Yield Shield.

  - • Cash Cushion: A reserve fund held in a savings account that you can use to avoid doing a full portfolio withdrawal during down years.

  - • Yield Shield: A combination of dividends and interest being paid by your ETFs that is delivered as cash without selling any assets.

- ▸ The Yield Shield can be raised by pivoting some of your assets into higher-yielding assets, such as . . .

  - • Preferred shares

  - • Real estate investment trusts (REITs)

  - • Corporate bonds

  - • Dividend stocks

- ▸ The size of the Cash Cushion is determined using the following formula:

  - • Cash Cushion = (Annual Spending – Annual Yield) × Number of Years

— 16 —

GETTING PAID TO TRAVEL

"You're quitting with no job lined up?"

"Travel the world? How the hell are you going to pay for it?"

"Why would you quit? Don't you like working here?"

My colleagues didn't know the real reason I was quitting—I was officially retiring at the tender age of thirty-one. The story I told was that I was your stereotypical millennial going on a gap year to "find myself." Everyone bought it.

I had done the math a hundred times, knowing that using the 4 Percent Rule, our million-dollar portfolio would cover our $40,000-per-year expenses, and with the Yield Shield and Cash Cushion in place, we had a plan that could weather any storm. Except I hadn't accounted for the storm raging inside my head. The math was giving me the green light, but I was *terrified*.

My dad had taught me the value of *chi ku*. He had taught me that a good education and a good job were as valuable as my life. Was I letting him down? Making a huge mistake?

Painstakingly, I'd put together my rocket ship, piece by piece. And now, after almost a decade, it was ready to blast off into space. *What if*

I don't have enough? Am I making a big mistake? What if the whole thing blows up?

Those thoughts haunted me for months. They haunted me as we gave notice to our landlord. They haunted me as we sold most of our stuff and minimized our possessions into two backpacks. They haunted me right up until we boarded our flight to begin our one-year victory lap around the world. As we buckled in and the safety video flashed onto our in-flight screens, my only thoughts were: *Are my dreams finally coming true? Or is this going to turn into a lifetime of regrets?*

FALLING IN LOVE WITH TRAVEL

If you had told me as a child that I'd go from the top of a medical waste heap to the top of the Swiss Alps, I'd have said that you were nuts. But standing on Fürenalp in Engelberg, gawking at the snow-capped mountains, the obscenely green grass, and the adorably mooing cows, I realized my dreams *were* coming true. I giggled like an idiot and ran toward a trampoline we (weirdly) found at the peak. Bouncing around, feeling the wind in my hair, the sun on my face, and singing "The Sound of Music," I felt like I was on top of the world—which I guess I sort of was.

I didn't think anything could top hiking in the Alps, but the life-changing experiences just kept piling up, each one better than the last. I scaled the cliffs of Santorini while gazing at the impossibly blue Aegean Sea. I biked alongside the canals of Amsterdam. I breathed in the salty smell of the sea in Howth and experienced culinary heaven in the form of Kobe beef in Osaka. I steamed away a decade of stress in a Seoul bathhouse, and I received my PADI scuba certification in Koh Tao, after conquering my debilitating fear of water.

In short, I fell in love with travel. The idea that traveling for a year would get it out of my system turned out to be a lie. For a decade of nose-to-the-grindstone work, time had been worthless. Punch in, punch out, go home, rinse, repeat. The year before I retired, I took two pictures on my phone. For the *entire year*. That's all the memories that were worth keeping.

The year after I retired, my phone ran out of memory from all the photos. Every day felt fresh and new. I had finally tasted freedom, and I didn't want it to end. So it was with a great deal of trepidation that I boarded that flight back home after our year of traveling the world.

Lying in my old bed, which had been transplanted to Bryce's mom's house, I felt like a bird in a cage, staring at the sky. I tossed and turned from the jet lag. Then I took out my laptop, where I had cataloged every dollar, euro, and yen spent on our journey. I tapped away quietly, trying not to wake Bryce as I added everything up.

"Holy shit," I said too loudly.

"What?" Bryce mumbled. "Something wrong?"

I ignored him. I checked and rechecked every number and every formula over and over. *This can't be right. There's no way.*

"What?" He sat up, fumbling for his glasses in the dark. "Did we screw up? Did we spend too much?"

I shook my head.

"Then what?"

I pointed at the screen, at our total: $40,150.

We had managed to travel the world for the same cost as staying at home.

Let that sink in. We had visited twenty countries on three continents. We had flown the entire circumference of the globe. We had done something very few people on Earth have the privilege of doing. And it cost as much as staying in one place.

Bryce was wide awake all of a sudden. The gears were turning in his head, just as they were in mine.

"You realize what this means, don't you?" he asked.

I nodded. I knew.

We could travel the world—forever.

COST OF TRAVELING THE WORLD

Countries visited: 20 (the USA, England, Scotland, Ireland, the Netherlands, Denmark, Belgium, Germany, Switzerland, Austria, the Czech Republic, Hungary, Greece, Japan, South Korea, Singapore, Malaysia, Thailand, Vietnam, Cambodia)

Region	Duration	Monthly Cost (USD)	Monthly Cost (CAD)
North America	1 month	$2,441	$3,174
UK	1 month	$3,962	$5,150
Western Europe	1 month	$3,515	$4,569
Eastern Europe	1 month	$2,657	$3,454
Asia	2 months	$3,243 + $2,376	$4,216 + $3,089
Southeast Asia	6 months	$2,031 + $2,057 + $2,038 + $1,836 + $1,674 + $1,703	$2,640 + $2,675 + $2,649 + $2,387 + $2,176 + $2,214
Total	12 months	$29,533 USD/year	$38,393 CAD/year

Adding in $875 CAD per person per year × 2 = $1,750 CAD for travel insurance, it ended up costing us $30,879 USD or $40,143 CAD per year.

The lie we've been sold is that traveling is expensive. But by splitting the year between expensive regions (like the UK, Western Europe, and Japan) and inexpensive ones (like Southeast Asia), our daily costs averaged only $42 USD or $55 CAD per person per day. We stayed in Airbnbs and hotels, sometimes going out to eat, sometimes cooking. We even managed to sneak in splurges like fresh oysters and lobsters in Boston, a four-day scuba-diving certification course in Thailand ($250 USD per person, accommodations included), scuba diving in Cambodia ($80 USD per person for two dives), hiking in the

Swiss Alps ($87 USD per person), and Kobe beef ($48 USD per person) in Japan!

Here are our costs broken down by region and category:

NORTH AMERICA

Category	Cost in USD/ Month/Couple	Cost in CAD/ Month/Couple	Comments
Accommodations	$760	$987.65	
Food	$1,453	$1,889.40	28% spent on groceries, 72% on eating out
Transportation	$162	$211.32	Includes taxes paid on flights bought with frequent-flyer miles
Activities	$0	$0	Our biggest activity? Pigging out.
Clothing/Toiletries/ Data/Etc.	$66	$86.10	
Total	$2,441	$3,174.47	

UK

Category	Cost in USD/ Month/Couple	Cost in CAD/ Month/Couple	Comments
Accommodations	$1,827	$2,375	
Food	$944	$1,227	46% spent on groceries, 54% on eating out
Transportation	$664	$863.41	Includes flights from regional airlines like Ryanair and EasyJet
Activities	$455	$592	
Clothing/Toiletries/ Data/Etc.	$71	$92.59	
Total	$3,961	$5,150	

WESTERN EUROPE

Category	Cost in USD/ Month/Couple	Cost in CAD/ Month/Couple	Comments
Accommodations	$1,685.38	$2,191	
Food	$954.32	$1,240.62	34% groceries, 66% eating out
Transportation	$584.49	$759.84	Includes local flights and buses to get around
Activities	$179.99	$233.99	
Clothing/Toiletries/ Data/Etc.	$110.42	$143.55	
Total	$3,514.60	$4,569	

EASTERN EUROPE

Category	Cost in USD/ Month/Couple	Cost in CAD/ Month/Couple	Comments
Accommodations	$1,217.69	$1,583	
Food	$987.80	$1,284.14	37% groceries, 63% eating out
Transportation	$288.46	$375	
Activities	$130.77	$170	
Clothing/Toiletries/ Data/Etc.	$32.20	$41.86	
Total	$2,656.92	$3,454	

ASIA (Expenses for Japan)

Category	Cost in USD/ Month/Couple	Cost in CAD/ Month/Couple	Comments
Accommodations	$1,335.38	$1,736	
Food	$1,136.77	$1,477.80	26% groceries, 73% eating out
Transportation	$532.91	$692.78	Includes taxes on flights paid for with points, low-cost airline tickets, and local trains
Activities	$193.74	$251.86	
Clothing/Toiletries/ Data/Etc.	$44.28	$57.56	
Total	$3,243.08	$4,216	

SOUTHEAST ASIA (Expenses for Vietnam)

Category	Cost in USD/ Month/Couple	Cost in CAD/ Month/Couple	Comments
Accommodations	$591.93	$769.51	
Food	$516.97	$672.06	20% groceries, 80% eating out
Transportation	$451.28	$586.67	
Activities	$191.13	$248.47	
Clothing/Toiletries/ Data/Etc.	$84.53	$109.89	Including visa entry fees
Total	$1,835.84	$2,386.60	

We kept costs reasonable by adding Southeast Asia to our itinerary. Not only does it have fantastic weather, it has fantastic prices too. In Chiang Mai, Thailand, for example, we rented a brand-new one-bedroom condo with gym, sauna, and pool. It cost $470 per month. An entire tableful of freshly steamed seafood (yes, "tableful" is a unit of measurement) was $12 per person. A plate of chicken pad thai? $1.25. And an hour-long oil massage? $10, tip included.

The prospect of leaving Thailand became excruciating after I realized you could live like a queen on $12,000 to $15,000 a year, and this pattern of getting a four-star lifestyle for a one-star price continued to blow us away in Vietnam, Malaysia, and Cambodia.

So if you're planning a world trip and find it difficult to balance your budget, add Southeast Asia into the mix. The more time you spend there, the less chance you'll break your budget. Remember how we talked about bonds' smoothing out the ride in your portfolio? Well, Southeast Asia is like the bonds of your travel portfolio; it evens out your costs. And you could do the same thing with other lower-cost places, like Mexico, Central America, South America, Eastern Europe, or Portugal.

It's been three years since we quit our jobs to travel the world, and I'm happy to report that every day is still new, exciting, and full of adventure. Plus, now that we're experienced nomads, our travel costs have gone down even further. Last year, we only spent $36,000 CAD for the whole year! And since our portfolio paid us $40,000, even though we no longer have an income, we got *paid $4,000* to travel the world!

What was I so afraid of again?

TRAVEL HACKING

Another trick that helps keep costs down is known as "travel hacking." If you accumulate enough frequent-flyer miles, you can use them toward flights and hotels, hacking your way to free travel! Normally, this is a luxury reserved for businesspeople, entrepreneurs, flight attendants, or anyone who flies a significant number of times a year. But you can do it even if you've never set foot on a plane before. All you need is good credit and a spreadsheet.

The trick is to apply for credit cards with big sign-up bonuses, match the required spending, then cancel the cards. Wait for three to six months and do it again. For example, the Chase Sapphire Preferred card offers 60,000 points if you spend $4,000 within the first three months, and waives the annual fee for the first year. That's worth over $750 of free travel! So, if you and your spouse apply for this card and meet the required minimum spending, you can both travel to Europe or Asia for free. In addition to the sign-up bonuses, many credit cards offer other goodies like no foreign transaction fees, auto rental insurance, and entrance to airport lounges that offer free food and drinks—just make sure you're not so busy stuffing your face that you miss your flight (like we almost did).

One note before you go nuts with applications: let me tell you about the 5/24 Rule. As the name implies, to be approved by Chase, you must not have applied for more than five personal credit cards across all banks in the last twenty-four months.

Before we left for our victory lap around the world, we applied for enough credit cards to rack up 200,000 points each. As a result, we were able fly the long-haul routes and pay only the $80 to $100 in taxes. This ended up saving us around $6,000 per year. If we'd had to pay that amount out of pocket, we would've needed $6,000 × 25 = $150,000 more in our portfolio. Yikes! Travel hacking saved us from having to work an extra two years. Which is good, because I wouldn't have been able to stop myself from firing my boss for that long.

Even if you're not planning on becoming nomadic like us, you can save big bucks during your vacations, too. Just make sure you're using credit cards responsibly. Do not attempt travel hacking if you have existing debt (see chapter 5), and *only* take out new cards if you know you'll be able to pay the balance in full every month.

If you can travel-hack and are American, you're in luck! You have an insane amount of options. Check out TravelCards.CardRatings .com to find the best reward cards. Canadians, meanwhile, can find the best options (like our favorite, the American Express Gold rewards card that comes with a 25,000-point sign-on bonus) at CanadianTravel Hacking.com.

AIRBNB

Another trick we've learned to keep our costs down is using Airbnb. Between Airbnb and travel hacking, we saved around $18,000 a year. You get to experience living like a local, plus your own kitchen and access to a washing machine. Unlike staying at a hotel, where you're stuck watching your waistline expand and your wallet shrink, Airbnb lets you feel at home. I've discovered all sorts of hidden gems (like the best place for a steak sandwich in Lisbon and the best dessert in Chiang Mai) by asking my Airbnb host for their recommendations.

TRAVEL INSURANCE AND EXPAT INSURANCE

"Massive heart attack," "ICU," "Might not make it."

These are words you never ever want to hear, especially when you're halfway across the world from home. We were in Thailand and Bryce had just drifted off to sleep when he got a call from his mom. His grandmother was in the ICU and doctors gave her days, if not hours, to live. After he hung up, we booked the next flight home, started packing, and canceled all our upcoming reservations.

When you get bad news while traveling, the last thing you need is the financial stress of buying last-minute flights and forfeiting hotel costs. This is why we bought travel insurance before we left. Not only would it cover medical emergencies up to $1 million each, trip cancellation, and trip interruption (in the case of political unrest or natural disasters), it also covered the cost of flying home and flight/hotel cancellation costs in the event of a family member's illness or death. The company we choose, World Nomads, ended up being helpful and reliable, processing our claim of $3,000 efficiently and making the cost of insurance worth every penny ($1,750).

Whether you're planning a vacation abroad or a nomadic life like ours, make sure your credit card benefits include international medical insurance, or buy travel insurance separately. Few things can derail your retirement quite like an unexpected medical emergency.

If you're going to buy travel insurance, you *must* be covered by insurance in your home country. This is because the travel insurance assumes that you can be repatriated if necessary. That being said, even if you don't have insurance back at home, all is not lost. You can still buy expat insurance, which is something we'll talk about in chapter 18.

VISAS

One of our readers' most frequently asked questions is, "What do you do about visas?"

During our first year of travel, we relied mostly on tourist visas, staying in Europe for the allocated ninety-day period before flying to Asia. In Vietnam and Cambodia, we applied for e-visas online, paid the processing fees, and printed them out before arrival. In Thailand, we got a thirty-day tourist visa automatically at the airport, which we chose to renew because we loved the country so much. Overall, the process was efficient and painless.

Now that we're more experienced travelers, we've also discovered that even in Europe, if you want to stay longer than the allotted ninety days for tourists, you have options. Wealth visas, like the non-lucrative visa for Spain, D7 for Portugal, and the German freelancer's visa, allow you to stay longer, and some even give you access to the national health care system.

If you're interested in moving to any of those countries long-term, here are some more details about each:

Spain

The Spanish non-lucrative visa, or "wealth visa," gives foreigners the option to live in Spain by providing proof of fixed monthly income, in the form of a pension or investments. If you're receiving at least 2,200 euros per month, plus 550 euros per month for each family member, you can stay in Spain for one year with the option to renew.

Portugal

The D7 visa gives foreigners the right to live in Portugal by demonstrating an annual income of 8,120 euros in pensions, rented real estate, or investments. The holder can then obtain a residence permit for one year, which can be renewed for successive periods of two years. After five years, it can be converted into a permanent residence. And the best part? As a resident, you get access to the National Health Service, plus a European Union passport.

Germany

Germany is one of the few countries that give artists, freelancers, or self-employed people residency with the freelance, or *"Freiberufler,"* visa. You will need to prove you can support yourself with your freelance work.

Before we started traveling, we had no idea we even had the option to stay long-term in Europe. If you're American or Canadian, you have a golden passport that you can use to obtain residency or extended tourist stays without too much hassle. And if you ever decide to become a nomad like us, know that you can stay overseas for the long run.

USING TRAVEL TO RETIRE EARLIER

We've all been brainwashed to believe that we have to move to a big city, get a well-paying job, and then work until age sixty-five. That advice from our parents' generation, though well meaning, is outdated. Not only does travel give you the benefit of cutting your expenses after retirement, it can also help you reach financial independence faster.

It's easier than ever for people to work remotely, without ever stepping foot into an office. This has the downside of enabling outsourcing (which is what happened at my office) but the upside of location independence. It's time to consider outsourcing yourself.

If you can find a way to work remotely, you can take advantage of something called "geographic arbitrage," which means earning money from a country with a strong currency and spending it in a country with a weak currency—for example, earning US dollars working online while living in a country that uses pesos, baht, or kroner. If you make $2,000 a month as a virtual assistant, that yearly income of $24,000 leaves you without a lot of options in the States. But if you were working remotely from Oaxaca, Mexico, where you could live in a nice apartment and eat out most days on $1,000 a month, you'd *still* be able to save almost 50 percent of your salary without breaking a sweat! Even better, that means you could become financially independent in fifteen or so years (see chapter 14 for the math) with a conservative 6 percent yearly return.

This is exactly what our reader Colby is doing. After getting fed up with earning minimum wage as a car salesman in Canada, he moved to South Korea to become an English teacher. Even though his salary is only $30,000 per year, because his rent and flight costs are compensated by the school, and his tax rate is only 3 percent, he manages to save $20,000 a year, a savings rate of 67 percent. While his friends back home are struggling to save just 10 percent of their $50,000-per-year salaries, he's knocking it out of the park. He has a flexible schedule, which allows him to travel throughout Asia. And— drumroll, please—he's only ten to twelve years from financial independence.

Don't believe the lies. Travel isn't expensive. It can even *save* you money and help you retire early.

CHAPTER 16 SUMMARY

- ▸ The costs of traveling the world can be surprisingly low.

- ▸ For one year, we spent only $40,000.

- ▸ By alternating the time spent in higher-cost locations like Western Europe with time in lower-cost places like Eastern Europe and Southeast Asia, it's possible to "design" a travel budget.

- ▸ Useful techniques to keep travel costs down:

  - Travel Hacking: Using credit card signups to accumulate points for flights.

  - Airbnb: Much cheaper than hotels, plus they often come with a kitchen so you can cook your own food and live like a local rather than a tourist.

- ▸ Make sure you get travel insurance!

— 17 —

BUCKETS AND BACKUPS

During our first year of retirement, Bryce and I learned two important lessons: One, traveling the world could cost *less* than living in a high-cost city. Two, our retirement portfolio was surprisingly resilient.

When we quit our jobs, we assumed that the worst of the economic crisis was behind us. But then the oil crash happened. For those of you who weren't glued to the *Wall Street Journal* in 2015, that was the year the word "fracking" popped up all over the news. The United States had embarked on a mission to increase its domestic oil production to become less dependent on oil imports from the Middle East. Fracking made this possible. The Middle East (and specifically Saudi Arabia) didn't like that. So, they attempted to flood the market with cheap oil, sending the price of a barrel of crude from above $100 down to the mid-$30s. The idea was to make oil so cheap that it would drive the frackers out of business.

It didn't work. What it *did* do was crash the stock markets. The Canadian stock market, due to its large energy component, got hit particularly hard, so in year one of our retirement, our portfolio's rate of return went negative.

Remember: the 5 percent of portfolios that fail are those unlucky cases where the person retires right at the beginning of a market crash. And even though we had a Yield Shield and Cash Cushion to withstand something like this, it was like hearing a rattling in our rocket ship just as we were being launched into space. We were like, "Man, this thing *better* work like we designed it . . ." Since you're reading this book, you're probably not surprised to hear that it *did* work. All the puzzle pieces did what they were supposed to do, when they were supposed to, and as of the time of this writing, our portfolio is higher than when we first flew to Europe. Let's see how this works in practice.

THE BUCKET SYSTEM

To start, let me introduce the Bucket System. The Bucket System simply means arranging your money into different accounts, or "buckets," based on what that money's job is. You probably already do this in your normal day-to-day life: you have a checking account where you keep the money you need for groceries, a savings account for your emergency fund, and savings accounts for retirement.

Once you actually make it to retirement, though, your buckets are going to be a little different. Here's how we arranged ours.

Cash
Cushion

Portfolio

Current Year
Spending

QUIT LIKE A MILLIONAIRE

The Portfolio bucket is where the majority of our money is held, invested in the low-cost index ETFs we described in chapter 10. Current-Year Spending is where we keep money we're planning on spending that year. And finally, the Cash Cushion is the five-year reserve we described in chapter 15. Categorizing your different financial needs this way allows you to decouple your day-to-day spending from the day-to-day gyrations of the stock market. You don't want to be caught in a situation where a temporary dip in the S & P 500 causes your rent check to bounce.

Now, just to be clear, a "bucket" is not necessarily the same thing as an "account." A bucket can have one or more accounts. The Portfolio bucket, for example, will typically have:

1. A joint investment account

2. Your tax-deferred retirement account (traditional IRA, 401(k), or RRSP)

3. Your tax-sheltered retirement account (Roth IRA or TFSA)

4. Your spouse's tax-deferred retirement account

5. Your spouse's tax-sheltered retirement account

The Cash Cushion and Current-Year Spending buckets can be separated into two different checking/savings accounts, or lumped into a single high-interest savings account. We opted for the latter, but it's up to you. Both are fine.

At the beginning of each year, the Portfolio's job is to fund the Current-Year Spending bucket. So, every January 1, do the following, *in order.*

The first step is to gather all the cash generated in your portfolio over the previous year via the Yield Shield and consolidate it in your joint investment account. Americans have to build a five-year Roth IRA conversion ladder as described in chapter 13, while Canadians can simply call up their RRSP provider and ask them to do a withdrawal. Recall that if you withdraw only the amount of your personal exemption, that withdrawal will be tax-free (as discussed on chapter 13). TFSA withdrawals can be done at any time tax-free.

Once your Yield Shield cash has been gathered in the joint investment account, you need to decide what to do next. The Yield Shield typically generates enough money to cover most, but not all, of your Current-Year Spending, so you have to figure out where the difference is going to come from. If your overall portfolio has gone up in value, the solution is simple: take the ETFs that have risen the most and sell enough units to cover the difference.

Once the cash has been gathered in your joint investment account, call up your brokerage and do a withdrawal. This is *not* a taxable event, since you're just moving money between two *after-tax* accounts. Once the money arrives in your checking/savings account, you're done for the year.

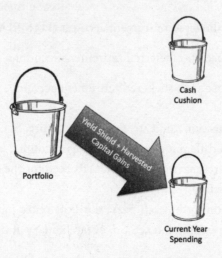

If your portfolio happens to be sitting at a loss, however, the last thing you want to do is sell. Here's where the Cash Cushion comes into play. After withdrawing your Yield Shield portion for the year, make up the difference by using one year of your Cash Cushion reserve fund.

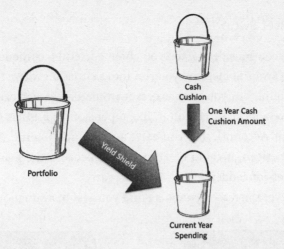

Remember that if you do this, you will reduce your Cash Cushion's reserve by one year, but you will have avoided selling in a market downturn. And because your portfolio is made up of low-fee index ETFs, it will always recover if you wait long enough. Over any fifteen-year window, the S & P 500 has never lost money in the history of the stock market. Once that recovery happens, remember to replenish your Cash Cushion so you're ready to handle the next market dip.

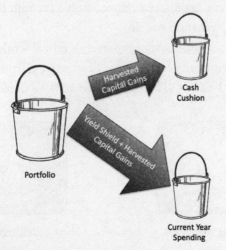

Cash-Asset Swap

Before we continue, let me tell you about a useful technique called the cash-asset swap. Sometimes you run into a situation where there's cash in an account, but you can't access it immediately. For example, you might have a locked-in account, like a pension or a LIRA (Locked-in Retirement Account), that you can't access until a certain age. Or, if you're American, it could be your 401(k), because the five-year Roth IRA conversion ladder takes, well, five years.

Whatever the reason, you may find yourself in a situation like this:

Accessible Account

$5,000 Cash

Inaccessible
Account

You have some cash in some inaccessible account like a traditional IRA or a LIRA. What do you do?

You perform a cash-asset swap. Here's how it works. First, pick an ETF that exists in both accounts. For illustrative purposes, I'm going to make up an ETF called STK that's priced at $10 a share.

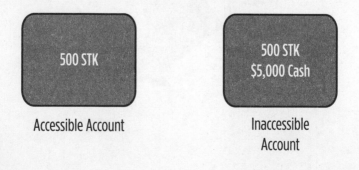

500 STK

Accessible Account

500 STK
$5,000 Cash

Inaccessible
Account

Then you calculate how many units of this ETF will equal the amount of cash you want to get out from your inaccessible account. In this case, we want to move $5,000, so this would be $5000 / $10 = 500 shares.

Log in to your brokerage account and place two orders: a sell order for five hundred shares in the accessible account and a buy order for the same five hundred shares in the inaccessible account. If your brokerage allows it, specify the exact price of $10 you'd like this order to be filled at.

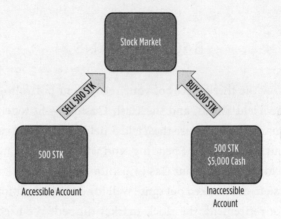

If the orders go out at the same time, what should happen is that the stock market will match up your buy and sell orders with each other. Essentially, you'll be "buying" this ETF from yourself.

Once the trade executes, the situation looks like this.

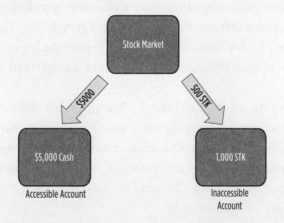

Voilà! You now have access to the cash you wanted, and because you bought and sold the same amount of shares, you haven't changed your overall portfolio's allocation. You've essentially accessed your locked-in cash using the stock market as the middleman. Neat, huh?

While it's easiest if you can do this with the same ETF, you can still do it with two different ETFs; you just need to calculate the right amount of each ETF based on its respective price.

BACKUP PLANS

So that's how the three pieces of your retirement portfolio—the stock market, the Yield Shield, and the Cash Cushion—fit together. When the stock market goes up, use the Yield Shield and harvest capital gains to fund your Current-Year Spending, and when the stock market dips, use the Yield Shield and your Cash Cushion.

This system has worked out quite well for us. As I mentioned, in our first year of retirement, the stock market dipped. We used the Yield Shield and one year from our Cash Cushion to fund year two. By the second year, the market had recovered and even advanced, so we harvested some capital gains and used that to fund year three. And in the third year, our portfolio was particularly robust, gaining 10 percent, so we used those gains to fund year four, while also replenishing our Cash Cushion. Since we retired, our net worth has grown from $1 million to $1.3 million. And with our Cash Cushion replenished, we are ready to face the next market correction, with more money than we started with!

Once we started meeting other early retirees, we realized there are even more ways to prevent your retirement from failing. Incorporating these ideas into our strategy has created a system that's even more resilient, even in the event of a sustained stock market crash that burns through your entire Cash Cushion. We call this "Buckets and Backups," because alliteration rocks.

There are no guarantees in this world, so you need to have many backup plans. If one fails, move to the next.

Backup Plan #1: Yield Shield

In a bear market, don't forget that even when your portfolio drops you're still getting paid dividends and interest. This income shields you from selling shares and is Backup Plan #1.

Backup Plan #2: Cash Cushion

Backup Plan #2 is to implement the Cash Cushion withdrawal we just described. If you've hit a particularly bad multiyear crash that completely depletes your Cash Cushion, move on to #3.

Backup Plan #3: Travel More

It may seem counterintuitive to use travel as a backup plan, but as we discovered, if you live like a local and not as a tourist, traveling the world can cost less than living in one place. Use this to your advantage.

In chapter 16, I demonstrated that by shifting the amount of time spent in each part of the world, you can design your yearly budget to hit a certain target. If you had a string of bad years and your Cash Cushion ran out, under normal circumstances you'd be forced to reduce your spending to stay within your Yield Shield. But by spending more time in low-cost regions like Mexico, Portugal, Eastern Europe, and Southeast Asia, you could accomplish this with *zero* impact on your lifestyle. Heck, you could even consider it an upgrade. Would you rather cut down on eating out or spend more of your year lying on a beach in Thailand?

One of the amazing things about Backup Plan #3 is that it skirts a fundamental rule in finance, which is that more spending equals more comfort, while less spending equals less comfort. If we were to spend a year in Southeast Asia, our spending would drop from $40,000 to about $24,000. And since our Yield Shield gives us $35,000 a year even in a bear market, we wouldn't have to sell any assets *and* we'd have extra cash at the end of the year.

That's why we have a saying we like to repeat to ourselves whenever the stock market takes a nosedive: *If shit hits the fan, we're going to Thailand.*

(I know that many of you are probably thinking, *Easy for you to say! You don't have kids!* We'll cover the topic of retiring early with kids in chapter 19.)

Backup Plan #4: The Side Hustle

Cost cutting and geographic arbitrage are great tools, but if you want to stay where you are without changing your lifestyle, you have another option: a side hustle!

I know, I know; another finance book advising you to "start a business!" as if it's just that easy. I tried it myself, and I failed—multiple times! The big difference with starting a side hustle *after* you've retired is that your bar for success is much lower. If you quit your job to crochet hoodies for cats and only make $5,000 in a year, you'd consider that an abject failure. You gave up a salary for this?! But after retirement, $5,000 would be a rousing success. That's enough to replace your Cash Cushion withdrawal. Your portfolio yield plus your side hustle earnings should be enough to fund your Current-Year Spending. Since your Yield Shield is doing most of the heavy lifting, small earnings can have a massive effect on your post-retirement finances.

I have yet to meet an early retiree who has *not* made money since saying good-bye to the nine-to-five. It's part of our DNA. People who manage to amass the wealth required to retire tend to be smart, driven, and creative. After the first six months of decompressing, boredom sets in. There are only so many hours of Netflix you can watch. We'll discuss this effect in chapter 20, but briefly, when early retirees decide to be productive, whether it's with a passion or a hobby, they make money.

Heck, writing was the passion I chose to pursue after I retired. I'd wanted to be a writer ever since I was that eight-year-old girl staring in wonder at the bookshelves of my local library. One day, I promised myself, my name would be on one of these shelves.

Strange how things work out.

Backup Plan #5: Return to Work Part-Time

There's a big weapon you've built up over your career: your skill set. By virtue of working in an industry long enough to amass the funds you need to retire, you've gained important skills that you shouldn't discount just because you're no longer in that field. Those skills can be remonetized. Maybe you return to your job part-time or do some consulting on the side. Some early retirees we've met in our travels have careers that require a minimum number of hours to maintain their license, like nursing or real estate agents. The simple act of complying with these rules acts as a natural backup plan.

CLOSING THE LOOP

Way back in engineering school, I learned the difference between an open-loop and a closed-loop control system. Without boring you with the details of control theory, the difference between an open-loop and a closed-loop control system is a bullet versus a missile. A bullet's path is determined by the person aiming the gun and environmental factors like wind and gravity. Once the bullet leaves the chamber, it has no ability to correct its trajectory midflight. If the target moves, the bullet will miss.

A missile, on the other hand, has the ability to change its path. If the target moves, its sensors will detect the change, and its thrusters will point at the target's new position. In control theory, this system has what's known as a feedback loop, where it detects alterations in the environment and reacts accordingly. Because of this, missiles are more reliable than bullets since they self-correct.

Control theory makes the guidance systems of missiles and rockets possible, and is one of the core building blocks in what we call rocket science.

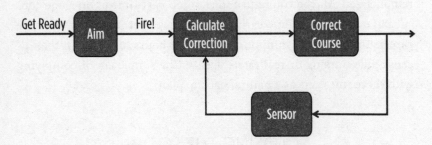

So, what does this have to do with retirement? Well, basing your retirement solely on the 4 Percent Rule is an open-loop system.

QUIT LIKE A MILLIONAIRE

You save twenty-five times your annual spending, pull the trigger, and rely on the math at the time the bullet left the chamber. If that math changes significantly (e.g., your expenses increase or your portfolio gets hammered), you are going to run into trouble. The final piece of the puzzle in designing a stable retirement is to turn this open loop into a self-correcting closed-loop system. And for that we need a sensor, like the one on the head of a missile, that tracks our trajectory.

Fortunately, we have a sensor handy, one that you've already seen in action in chapter 14: FIRECalc. FIRECalc runs a simulation across all historical scenarios and determines how often a retirement succeeds and how often a retirement fails.

But just because you used that calculator at the beginning of your retirement doesn't mean that you can't use it again. In fact, at the beginning of each year, you should take your current portfolio and next year's projected spending and plug it into FIRECalc to reflect your updated situation. This way, the success rate calculated by FIRECalc can be used as an overall "health" score of your retirement. This also tells you which backup plans you need to execute. Let's say you started off with a $1,000,000 portfolio and $40,000 in annual spending. FIRECalc tells you that there's a 95 percent success rate for your situation, or a 95 percent "health" score.

Next year, though, the stock market is down and your portfolio value drops by 5 percent. You've spent $40,000, and your portfolio of $960,000 is down 5 percent to $912,000. Fortunately, Backup Plan #1, the Yield Shield, has added an additional $35,000, resulting in a balance of $947,000.

Let's plug the numbers into FIRECalc to see if you're in trouble. A $947,000 portfolio with $40,000 annual spending results in a 93 percent success rate. And while 93 percent ain't bad, it's not 95 percent.

So, what can you do to get back to 95 percent? First, execute Backup Plan #2: the Cash Cushion. In this case, that means transferring $5,000 from your reserve fund, increasing your portfolio size to $952,000. But according to FIRECalc, your success rate is still 93 percent.

It's time to try Backup Plan #3: Travel More. If you spend more time in a low-cost region like Eastern Europe or Southeast Asia, you can easily bring your annual costs of $40,000 down to $38,000. Ding ding ding! This brings your success rate back up to 95 percent. In fact, if you stick with geographic arbitrage and bring your annual costs down to $37,000, your portfolio "health" rises to 97 percent.

If you think of retirement as a missile flying toward a target, you have used FIRECalc as its sensor to tell you whether you're on track or starting to fly off course. That information suggests which backup plans to execute. Next year, plug your updated numbers into FIRECalc and see whether your retirement has gotten back on track, or whether further corrections are needed.

Essentially, you have turned early retirement from an open-loop system into a closed-loop system.

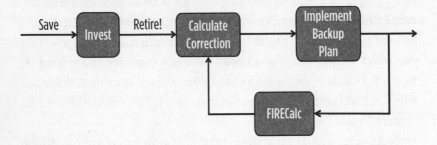

Perpetual Re-retirement

Closing the loop, which I call Perpetual Re-retirement, also gets around a limitation of the Trinity study. The 4 Percent Rule is based on a thirty-year retirement period. But in case you haven't noticed, early retirees have a much longer retirement time frame! There are precisely *no* studies out there that cover what happens if you stop working before sixty-five. Perpetual Re-retirement rather elegantly solves that problem. Every time you plug your numbers into FIRE-Calc, you are calculating your success rate for a thirty-year retirement starting *now*.

By using Perpetual Re-retirement to evaluate your retirement health each and every year, not only will you be able to see and correct for any stock market drops, but you'll be able to adapt the findings of the Trinity study for a retirement that lasts as long as you want, all using tools that are available to you for free.

It ain't rocket science.

No, wait, actually it *is*.

CHAPTER 17 SUMMARY

► To manage your portfolio in retirement, arrange your money into three buckets:

- Portfolio: This holds the investment portfolio you're going to live on.

- Current-Year Spending: This holds the cash you intend to spend for the year.

- Cash Cushion: This holds your reserve fund in a savings account.

At the beginning of each year, fund the Current-Year Spending bucket:

- First, transfer the cash generated by your Yield Shield.

- If your portfolio is sitting on a gain, sell off some ETFs to make up the difference.

- If your portfolio is sitting at a loss, make up the difference using your Cash Cushion.

- Remember to replenish your Cash Cushion when markets have recovered.

- Have multiple backup plans you can implement in case of an extended market downturn:

  - Backup Plan #1: Use your Yield Shield.

  - Backup Plan #2: Use your Cash Cushion.

  - Backup Plan #3: Use geographic arbitrage to reduce your living expenses.

  - Backup Plan #4: Start a side hustle.

  - Backup Plan #5: Temporarily return to work part-time.

- Every year, measure the overall health of your early retirement plan by plugging your current assets and expected spending back into FIRECalc ("Perpetual Re-retirement").

  - This makes the Trinity study valid for retirements longer than thirty years since each time you do this, you are creating a new thirty-year retirement scenario.

— 18 —

INFLATION, INSURANCE, AND HEALTH CARE: SCARY THINGS THAT AREN'T THAT SCARY

As of the time of this writing, Bryce and I have been retired and traveling for three years with no plans to stop. One of the most interesting parts of our journey has been the subtle reaction shift from friends and family back home.

In the first year, they thought we were "getting it out of our system."

In the second year, they figured we'd realize our horrible mistake and come back.

But after the third year, their skepticism turned into genuine curiosity. We were traveling, we were happy, and we hadn't run out of money. Instead, our net worth had gone *up*.

"What's your secret?" they asked.

The answer was there the whole time (and we'd pretty much been shouting it from the rooftops): travel. In the last chapter, we showed how geographic arbitrage can help control your living costs during a market downturn. But we were shocked by how elegantly traveling fixes other major financial problems.

So in this chapter, I'd like to address three Very Scary Things™

people stress about that basically become nonissues when they retire and travel the world: inflation, insurance, and health care.

INFLATION

Inflation is a complicated beast and countless books have been written that explore all the technical aspects of how it works. Since I don't want you to die of boredom, I'm not going to go through it here. Just know that inflation is, in a nutshell, how much your cost of living increases from year to year. You notice inflation when you go into Starbucks and grumble at the price of a cup of coffee—up $0.25 from a year ago—and when your grandparents show you an old department store catalog with lawn mowers on sale for $5.

Inflation is the bane of retirement planners everywhere. Traditional retirement planning means investing heavily in equities when a person is young, then shifting into fixed-income assets like bonds over time. Once the person hits sixty-five, the majority of their portfolio is in bonds, and the danger is a spike in inflation after retirement, in which case their fixed income won't keep up with the cost of living.

My investing strategy avoids this situation entirely. I've achieved income stability not by shifting into fixed income but by using a combination of the Yield Shield, the Cash Cushion, and Buckets and Back-ups. My portfolio never flips into a majority-fixed-income allocation. And because I'll stay invested in equities throughout retirement, my portfolio is naturally hedged against inflation. This is because companies sell goods to people, and when people pay more money for their goods (like that cup of coffee) because of inflation, that company is making more money. All else being equal, inflation is reflected in that company's earnings, which are reflected in an increased share price, which is reflected in your portfolio. By investing in equities, your portfolio grows *with* inflation.

There's another interesting thing I've noticed about inflation: it changes depending on where you are. The inflation reported by the United States only applies to the United States. It's completely independent from the inflation experienced in Portugal, South Africa, Hong Kong, or Japan. This even happens from state to state. The inflation numbers the central bank reports are a national average, so some states have above-average inflation and some below. Just because the cost of living is rampaging in San Francisco doesn't mean it's happening in Des Moines.

This simple realization has a huge impact on retirement planning. Because you're no longer tied to a particular city by your job, inflation doesn't just happen to you based on factors beyond your control. Instead, inflation becomes something you can control. Your current city's cost of living going up too fast for your liking? Spend the next year exploring Eastern Europe! Or if that's too extreme, spend time in another city or state whose inflation is a fraction of yours.

It's another facet of geographic arbitrage, and it has a profound impact on your finances. The 4 Percent Rule means that taking out 4 percent of your portfolio, *inflation-adjusted each year*, for a thirty-year period will result in a 95 percent success rate. It assumes you increase your spending with the inflation rate. If you can sidestep that adjustment, your likelihood of success goes up dramatically. In fact, since we started traveling, our personal inflation rate has been flat or slightly negative each year. As we've gotten the hang of it, we're spending *less* money each year in retirement than the year before.

By using the Yield Shield and Cash Cushion to avoid selling in a down market, and traveling to control inflation, three years later, our retirement health has grown from a 95 percent success rate . . . to 100 percent.

INSURANCE

Insurance is another thing that scares the pants off people, and I completely understand why. The entire industry is based on fear, with the most pessimistic sales pitch you could ever craft: "You'd better buy this insurance, because who knows? Some unfortunate thing could happen, and if you don't have this coverage you'll be screwed."

These people must be fun at parties.

In this section, I'll discuss the three most common types of insurance: homeowner's, car, and life. Health insurance is its own monster that we will discuss in the next section.

Homeowner's Insurance

If you own a home, you need homeowner's insurance. Since a house is the largest part of many people's net worth, one electrical fire, flood, or tornado could decimate your wealth, so not insuring it is asking for the universe to school your ass.

As we mentioned in chapter 9, homeowner's insurance, on average, costs 0.5 percent of your home's value each year. When your policy renews annually, be sure to shop around to get the best possible deal, but aside from that the only two ways to eliminate this cost are to go uninsured (don't recommend) or to not own an expensive home in the first place and rent instead (do recommend).

Renting makes home insurance a moot point.

Car Insurance

Car insurance is even more mandatory, since it's illegal to drive without insurance. So, you can't avoid it. There are tricks to lower the cost, though. Getting an antitheft device in your car can lower premiums. Dropping comprehensive coverage for older cars that have already depreciated can also make sense. Getting your insurance through your employer or alumni association is also a good idea. However, the best way to reduce your car insurance cost is to *not own a car*. Again, travel makes this decision easy, because if you're jet-setting around Europe you don't need one.

That being said, sometimes a car really is essential for survival, especially in small towns where public transportation isn't great. The good news is that small towns also tend to have low housing costs. So, I like to tell people who write to me that if you're finding yourself drowning because of high homeownership costs *and* high car expenses, you're doing it wrong. Either own a home that's cheaper and farther from work or get rid of the car and spend more to be close to everything. Don't do both!

Another solution is to use car-sharing services. You reserve a car for a certain time slot, go to a predesignated lot near your house, grab the keys, and you've got yourself a ride! This gives you access to a car to haul groceries without the cost of buying it, maintaining it, filling it with gas, and insuring it. The one we used while we were working saved us $8,000 a year because our costs averaged only $40 a month. Zipcar is the biggest car-sharing service in North America, but there are dozens popping up all over the place.

Life Insurance

Life insurance is another expense people get confused about. I don't blame them. Term life, whole life, universal life—there are so many policy types and complicated riders it makes you want to jump off a cliff. (But if you did *that*, your family would be screwed, since, you know, you don't have life insurance.) The worst thing to do if you're trying to clarify your needs is to ask an insurance salesman. Just like when I went to the bank to ask about investment accounts, the answer to "Which life insurance should I buy?" will be "The most expensive one I can sell you." But not buying life insurance seems irresponsible, especially if you have kids and you're the primary breadwinner. So, what most folks do is procrastinate, sigh heavily, and finally trundle into their closest bank branch and get saddled with an incomprehensible policy costing them hundreds of dollars a month. My readers do this all the time.

Here's the industry's big secret they don't want you to know: *If you retire early, you don't need life insurance.*

The purpose of buying life insurance is to make sure your family is taken care of in case you get run over by an ice-cream truck, by providing them with enough money that they can survive without you. In other words, it's supposed to cover their living expenses if something were to happen to you.

You know what else does that? Your portfolio. Becoming financially independent means you've built up sufficient assets and invested them properly to passively generate enough income so that you don't have to work anymore. That does the exact same job as life insurance. Your portfolio is the breadwinner, whether you're there or not.

This insight breaks down the entire life insurance industry into a simple math problem.

Using the 4 Percent Rule, figure out how much you need to retire. Then, count up how much money you have.

How Much You Need − How Much You Have =
Your Life Insurance Benefit

Say my current living expenses are $40,000. According to the 4 Percent Rule, I need $40,000 × 25 = $1,000,000 to retire. I currently have $100,000. So, the life insurance benefit I need to buy is $1,000,000 − $100,000 = $900,000.

This is how much your family will need to become financially independent if you unexpectedly kick the bucket. And because you've calculated a point in the future at which you won't need life insurance anymore, most of those policies become unnecessary. The only thing you'll need is term life insurance—a policy you buy for a specific amount of time (the "term"), say, five years. If you buy a five-year term life policy, it covers you for exactly five years. After that, you have to renew or purchase a new one. And how much coverage you need is determined by the formula above. Term life insurance is the cheapest type of life insurance you can buy. This is because the insurance company is calculating the odds of your dying within the term of the policy, which are typically low. The other policy types are designed to cover your whole life, so by definition, they assume you will die at some point in the contract. In other words, under a whole life or universal life policy, the insurance company will pay out eventually. For a term life policy, probably not. That's why it's less expensive. As of the time of this writing, a term life policy for $900,000 can be purchased for between $15 and $30 a month. Compare that to the hundreds of dollars a month for the other types of life insurance.

Also, if you're going to make a run for FI, it makes sense to get as short a term as you can from your insurance company and renew each year. Even though life insurance costs increase as you get older, the amount of coverage you need actually gets smaller as you get closer and closer to your FI target. The gap of $900,000 becomes $800,000, which becomes $700,000, and so on. As your benefit needs shrink, your already-cheap life insurance premiums also shrink, until eventually you become financially independent and retire. At which point you can safely wave good-bye to the life insurance industry and never have to deal with those sharks again.

HEALTH CARE

Hoo boy. Buckle in and watch as I demolish the idea that paying for health care is necessarily scary. First of all, if you're reading this and thinking, *Health care? Why would that be scary?* then you're probably not American. Health care (or, more specifically, health insurance) in the United States is expensive. Americans spend nearly twice as much as other high-income nations, despite having shorter average life-spans, higher infant mortality, and higher obesity rates.[1] And the risks of going uninsured are massive. In fact, the number one cause of personal bankruptcy in America is medical debt. Finally, since most Americans get their health insurance through their job, the natural question is, "If I leave my job, won't I lose my health insurance?"

The answer is no. You can still have health insurance, and you'll probably be able to get it far cheaper than when you were working. Here are all the different ways you can reduce your health insurance costs after you retire.

Obamacare (ACA)

Obamacare, or the Patient Protection and Affordable Care Act, is your first and best line of defense against rising health care costs in retirement. This is because Obamacare ties the amount you pay for insurance to your income. The less you make, the less you pay. And it does this through federal subsidies. Every year the federal government publishes a number it determines as the federal poverty level, or FPL. Based on your income as a percentage of the FPL, you may qualify for a federal subsidy that helps pay for part or all of your health insurance premium.

While working, you likely don't qualify for assistance since your income is too high (400 percent of the FPL is the maximum you can earn and still receive subsidies) or your employer already offers health insurance benefits, but after you retire, your employment income drops to zero. And because of that, you may be surprised to see your health care costs shrink to almost nothing!

Note that the ACA determines your subsidy based on your MAGI (modified adjusted gross income), which includes Roth IRA conversions, qualified dividends, and harvested long-term capital gains. To order to qualify for ACA subsidies, pay special attention to avoid exceeding 400 percent of the FPL while combining the strategies mentioned earlier to minimize taxes.

Moving to a Different State

One big caveat to Obamacare is that you need to live in the right state. When the ACA became law in 2010, part of it relied on expanding funding to Medicaid, the health insurance program covering low-income families administered by each state. The idea was that the Obamacare-related subsidies would take care of people from 138 percent to 400 percent of the FPL, while Medicaid would take care of the 0 percent to 137 percent range. Under this system, everybody would have access to health insurance regardless of income.

Unfortunately, not all states cooperated. Some states chose *not* to expand Medicaid, which created a very dangerous situation known as the "Medicaid gap." In states where Medicaid was not expanded, it's possible for your income to be too high for Medicaid but too low for Obamacare subsidies to kick in, leaving you to pay the whole premium yourself. Out of fifty states (plus the District of Columbia), thirty-three have expanded Medicaid while eighteen haven't. Check your state's Medicaid site to see which type of state you're in. If you live in the latter, I would recommend moving to one that did expand Medicaid. You don't want to run into a situation where a health problem completely destroys your retirement plan. Wherever you decide to retire, if it's within the United States, make sure Medicaid was expanded there.

You may also consider relocating to take advantage of the wide range of health insurance costs from state to state. As of 2016, the cost of health insurance premiums in a low-cost state like New Mexico was *half* the price of premiums in a high-cost state like New York![2]

High-Deductible Catastrophic Care Plans

Now, as much as I'd like to say, "Just rely on Obamacare," and be done with it, the current political climate has not been friendly toward the ACA. So, while I hope that it sticks around in some shape or form, it's a good idea to review what early retirees did pre-ACA, in case America's health care system reverts.

Before 2010, the health insurance market was much less regulated. Limitations on coverage for preexisting conditions meant that if you got sick and the insurance auditor found so much as a yeast infection in your past you hadn't reported, you could get thrown off the policy and risk bankruptcy. Yikes!

In an environment like that, what is a young, healthy early retiree we'll call Pete to do? Like everyone else, Pete wants to insure away the risk of bankruptcy for the minimum cost, but he also has the advantage of having a large net worth. Because Pete can afford to pay for doctors' visits out of pocket, and even cover the occasional emergency, his policy should have the following features:

- Coverage only for catastrophic emergencies with a high coverage limit ($500,000–$1,000,000)

- A defined maximum out-of-pocket expense limit ($10,000–$20,000)

- A high deductible

- Compatibility with a Health Savings Account (or HSA)

This is known as a high-deductible health plan, or HDHP. This means that Pete pays for his health care most of the time and the insurance kicks in only if he (or someone in his family) suffers an unforeseen, catastrophic medical expense that could potentially bankrupt him. And because of how unlikely this is, the premium for such a policy is affordable (e.g., the one that blogger Mr. Money Mustache used is $237 USD per month with a $10,000 deductible for a family of three).

An HSA is a type of investment account that's used for health expenses. Unlike a 401(k), it's not tied to your employer, so you can open one at any bank or brokerage account. Here's how an HSA works (as of 2019):

- To be eligible, your health insurance plan must have a deductible of at least $1,350, or $2,700 for a family.

- You can contribute up to $3,500 per year, or $7,000 for a family.

- Your contributions are pretax, similar to a 401(k) or a traditional IRA, meaning that you will get a tax deduction.

- Investment growth is tax-free.

- You can withdraw your money tax-free for qualified medical expenses.

So an HSA combines the best of the 401(k) and the Roth IRA, in that it allows tax-deductible contributions, tax-free growth, and tax-free withdrawals, but only for medical expenses.

HDHP + HSA plans existed before the ACA, and still exist today under Obamacare. This gives us reasonable certainty that even if the ACA were repealed, the HDHP + HSA solution that early retirees used before Obamacare existed would still be a viable solution. We're only including this policy in case America reverts to its pre-Obamacare health care system.

Expat Insurance

But now I'd like to talk about *my* solution. Meaning, this is what *we* do for health insurance. It may surprise many readers that we have to do anything at all. After all, we are Canadian. Aren't we supposed to have a gold-plated government-run single-payer health care system at our disposal?

Surprisingly, no! Canadians are only eligible for our gold-plated government-run single-payer health care system if they *live in Canada*. Once we left Ontario for more than two years, we lost our health insurance. That's right. We were faced with the same flop-sweat-inducing terror of being uninsured as our American friends.

So what did I do? The same thing you would have done. I Googled. Turns out, there's a whole world of insurance for people like us. It's called expat insurance, and it provides policies for people who leave their home country and aren't eligible for their new country's health care system. Because health care costs differ by country, there are two geographical zones when it comes to expat insurance coverage: the USA, and everywhere else. Seriously. These are your choices. "The USA," and "the world except the USA." There's one price for Americans and another for everyone else. And that second price is significantly lower.

We recently purchased a year's worth of expat insurance from IM-Global, up to $1,000,000 in coverage with a deductible of $2,500. The cost was $156 a month. For the two of us. I don't know what you're paying for health insurance if you're currently living in the United States, but I'm guessing it's more than that.

If you're American, this fact may fill you with rage, as it should. But a far more interesting question is: what if I retire outside my country? Because if you did that, you wouldn't have to worry about health care costs anymore. Here's a snippet from the policy I have:

"As part of that commitment, our company offers a Medical Concierge program, an unparalleled service that saves you on out-of-pocket medical expenses. *We also offer a cash incentive and to waive 50% of your deductible* for choosing to receive treatment from some of the best medical facilities *outside the U.S.*" (emphasis added).

That's right. This insurance company will *pay* you to receive treatment outside the United States.

Turns out, health care isn't that scary after all. And the solution to that annoying problem is—you guessed it—geographic arbitrage.

However, if you want to retire in the United States (for family reasons, for example), you still have the option of using the ACA. Even if that goes away, you can use a high-deductible catastrophic plan and money in your HSA.

CHAPTER 18 SUMMARY

- ▸ Inflation doesn't affect you when you travel because inflation is a per-country effect. By switching countries you sidestep inflation.

- ▸ Insurance is also not a major factor after retirement.

  - • Homeowner's and car insurance are not necessary if you don't own a home or a car.

  - • Life insurance is no longer necessary after you retire since your portfolio will take care of your family's living expenses without you.

  - • Health insurance is handled by the ACA. Once you retire, your income will drop and you'll become eligible for federal subsidies (but be careful not to exceed 400 percent of the FPL when combining tax-minimization strategies).

  - • If you're American and retire abroad, expat insurance is less expensive than domestic insurance plans.

— 19 —

WHAT ABOUT KIDS?

"You're selfish for not having kids."

"You couldn't do this with a family."

"Once you have children, this whole plan won't work."

I've lost count of how many times I've been accused of being self-centered and/or a terrible person, as well as had everything I say dismissed because I don't have kids and therefore "don't understand what it's like." Historically, my response to those people has been something along the lines of, "Fuck off, I don't judge you for your reproductive decisions so don't judge me for mine."

That being said, I've come to understand why people say things like this to us. They are worried that because they've decided to have kids (which, as we all know, are super expensive), FIRE (Financial Independence Retire Early) doesn't apply to them and therefore they'll never be able to quit their job and travel the world—or even just pay off their mortgage. These people are, by the way, wrong. Having kids does not exclude you from implementing my approach and living your best, most liberated life.

I'm acutely aware that there's nothing as irritating to parents as someone without children giving parenting advice. That's why I decided to reach out to some people with bona fide expertise. The first part of this chapter, which deals with the true cost of having kids, is a collaboration with Pete Adeney from the blog MrMoneyMustache .com, Jeremy Jacobson from the blog GoCurryCracker.com and Justin McCurry from RootofGood.com. All three are fellow finance bloggers whom I respect tremendously and who have become financially independent and retired early—with kids (Justin has three of them!).

The second part of this chapter deals with how to travel with school-age kids, so I collaborated with two people who have successfully done it: Jennifer Sutherland-Miller, an education consultant from the blog EdventureProject.com, and Lainie Liberti, a leader in the movement of mobile educators known as world schoolers.

Ready to start busting some myths? I know I am.

THE REAL COST OF KIDS

In 2015, the USDA reported that it costs, on average, $233,610 to raise a child to the age of eighteen in America. But that's not the whole story. The problem is, the media often relays this number like a price tag. If we dig deeper, we'll see holes in the methodology.

The first clue is that the USDA reports different numbers based on how much a family earns. In 2015, the national average annual cost per child was $12,306 if the family earned less than $59,200, but that cost doubled to $25,108 if the family earned more than $107,400.[1] The reason for this disparity is that much of that cost is variable—based on choice rather than necessity. Higher-earning families tend to choose to spend more on their kids and that's why their per-child costs are higher. It's possible to raise a child on far less by making savvier choices.

Western capitalist societies operate under the assumption that if you want a good life, you have to spend a lot of money. I've discovered that this isn't true. Travel and location-independent living, for example, reduce your costs while increasing your quality of life. A similar assumption exists in child-rearing: in order for a kid to grow up happy and healthy, you have to spend a lot of money.

What if the opposite were true? What if it were possible to raise a child for far below average, while at the same time giving them a high quality of life?

I reached out to early retirees doing exactly that. The Jacobsons, the McCurrys, and Pete Adeney (aka Mr. Money Mustache) are friends we met through the FIRE community who retired in their thirties with kids. Jeremy travels the world with his son and wife. Justin has three kids and lives with his family in Raleigh, North Carolina. Pete has a son and lives in Longmont, Colorado. I wanted to learn about their experiences, how much it costs, and the kind of life they're able to give their families. Their answers were surprising, to say the least.

The USDA breaks down the cost of child-rearing into seven categories: housing, food, child care, transportation, health care, clothing, and miscellaneous. Let's see how our early-retired parents deal with each.

Housing

As always, housing is the biggest category, taking up 29 percent of total expenses, or $67,746.90 per child until the age of eighteen. This means housing costs an extra $313 per month per child. It's also the category I approach with the most skepticism. The USDA reports that these expenses include mortgage payments, property taxes, insurance, home maintenance, etc. In other words, home ownership costs. These increased costs are driven by the fact that many couples rent while they're childless and then decide to buy a home when they have a child. So the additional housing costs are driven by the dramatically higher costs of owning a home rather than renting.

According to Justin, he paid just $18,000 for an additional six hundred square feet of living space to accommodate his three kids in Raleigh. That added approximately $1,500 per year, or $500 per year per kid. Extrapolated over eighteen years, that's a total of $15,000 per kid. Jeremy, an American expat and self-proclaimed "renter for life," rents a one-bedroom apartment in Taiwan for $1,323 per month and co-sleeps. However, when the kid gets older and needs his own bedroom, Jeremy plans to move to a two-bedroom rental, which would add about $350 to their monthly living expenses. He is spending around the 2015 USDA average. Pete thinks the cost of kids depends on where and how you choose to live. He lives in expensive Colorado, where an extra bedroom adds approximately 200 square feet to a house, translating to $60,000 increase in housing prices. At his 4 percent mortgage rate, this means an increase of $200/month or $2,400/year. He thinks the USDA estimate is high but not exorbitant. To keep housing costs down, Pete says, "You can always live in a smaller house, start with a serious fixer-upper, and learn to do your own high-end renovations in order to more than offset any housing costs."

Food

Food is the next-biggest item, taking up 18 percent of total per-child expenses, or $42,049.80. Because this is over eighteen years, this equals about $200 per child each month.

You would think food is the most difficult cost to optimize away, but all three of our early-retired parents report dramatically lower costs than what the USDA predicts. Justin says that by taking advantage of discount stores like Aldi, Lidl, and Walmart Supercenters, his total grocery bill per kid amounts to only about $100 per month, or half of what the USDA predicted. Pete estimates a frugal family cooking plan (using Costco-style bulk groceries) costs only $4.00/person per day or about $122/person per month. Even though that total seems low, Pete has never compromised on quality or his health, because as a self-proclaimed "lifelong health and fitness nut," he only buys fresh, natural ingredients—never junk food, desserts, or sodas. However, if you're someone who can't live without Friday take-outs and/or buying groceries from Whole Foods, it's easy to quadruple his estimate.

Child Care

You hear it over and over again: child care is expensive! Day care and preschool consistently rank as one of the biggest line items in new parents' budgets, especially if they live in major cities. According to the USDA, child care costs eat up 16 percent of the cost of raising kids, or $37,377.60, and you can't *not* have this, right? After all, someone has to watch the kid when the parents are at work.

Here's the thing that Justin, Jeremy, and Pete reminded us about: if you retire, you actually don't need day care or preschool anymore. This cost drops to zero, since you no longer have to go to work. Pete recommends getting your spending, living, and work situations sorted out *before* starting a family.

Transportation

Transportation makes up 15 percent of the cost of raising a kid, or $35,041.50, and this one is especially baffling. But when you dig into what the USDA considers transport costs, the reasoning becomes obvious. According to them, this covers car payments, gas, insurance, maintenance, and repairs. In other words, it supposes a family buys a car just to drive the baby around. If you want to do that, fine, but let's not pretend a shiny new station wagon is a necessity. Used vehicles, car sharing, public transportation, and biking are options other early retirees have used to bring down their kid transportation costs. Amazingly, the USDA also includes the cost of buying the kid their own car when they turn sixteen as a necessary expense! No wonder this category is so high!

My experts confirmed that this number is bogus. Justin did all the things the USDA assumed: he bought a bigger car to accommodate his larger family, and he even plans to buy his daughter her own car when she turns sixteen, which the siblings can share once they are old enough

to drive. But their used minivan cost just $8,000, and gas and mainte-
nance work out to roughly $300 per year. He'll buy a used car for their
daughter for around $5,000, plus $2,000 a year for gas and extra insurance. All told, Justin is expecting to spend around $14,000 on their
family's two cars.

Jeremy, a car-free bike enthusiast, scoffed at my question, saying his
so-called transportation costs totaled something like $150—for a
stroller. He does not intend to buy his son a car, since he doesn't feel the
need to own one either. He prefers to take public transit and bike
around Taipei with his son. Pete estimates it costs around 50 cents per
mile, on average, to drive, but you can cut this cost in half by driving a
fuel-efficient hatchback, bought used with cash. You can cut this even
further by designing your life to require less driving. Walking, cycling,
or using a scooter are the preferred methods Pete's son, Simon, uses to
get to school. Pete strategically chose a home within a mile of Simon's
school to avoid the need to drive. When I asked Pete whether he was
planning to buy his son a car, he said, "Nobody's going to ruin this
great situation by buying this boy a car when he's a teenager—what
kind of cruel punishment is that?"

Health Care

Again with the health care. Yes, health care in America is expensive, but
as we discussed in chapter 18, it doesn't have to be. In retirement, those
costs plummet due to the ACA, and even if they don't, there's always the
option of traveling and relying on expat insurance. The USDA reports the
average cost of health care for a child to be $1,500 a year, but adding a
dependent to an expat insurance policy with worldwide coverage outside
the United States is just $400. Jeremy travels the world with his family
and pays less than $100/month for travel insurance for the entire family.

Justin has an even better solution. According to him, the ACA actually costs *less* as you have *more* kids due to how the federal subsidies

are calculated. A couple with no kids, for example, would pay $3,200 per year at an adjusted gross income of $40,000 per year (the cost threshold they would have to hit before getting the subsidy). The same couple with three kids would see their health insurance costs drop to $1,400 per year—a savings of $1,800 per year.

Kids can actually *save* you money in health insurance costs. Who knew? If you're not eligible for ACA subsidies in retirement because you make a high income like Pete, he believes adding a child to your insurance policy increases the monthly cost by about $100 per month. His son recently broke his arm while playing in the park and Pete ended up with a $5,000 out-of-pocket expense. The good news is that his income earned in retirement can be used to cover this cost.

Clothing

The USDA projects $18,000 of clothing costs per child, which is hilarious since I don't even spend that much on clothing for myself. Justin spends $1,000 a year to clothe his family of five, total, or $3,600 per kid for eighteen years. Jeremy joked that he's barely spent $18,000 on clothing in his life. Pete says the secret to clothing your kids is that there is a never-ending stream of hand-me-downs from other older parents, just "begging to be given away" so the parents can feel better when their kids grow out of everything. The only exception are shoes, which Pete prefers buying new. Even then, he estimates the cost of clothing Simon to be only $500 per year, half of the USDA's estimate.

Miscellaneous

"Miscellaneous" includes personal care expenses (haircuts, toothbrushes), entertainment (portable media players, sports equipment, televisions, computers), and reading materials (nonschool books, magazines). This is just 8 percent of the total projected costs, and at $18,000 over eighteen years, not that unreasonable compared to the other categories. In fact, our experts agreed with that estimate, having spent between $9,000 and $18,000 themselves.

Total

So according to the USDA, having a kid costs $233,610. This is what our experts' actual costs have been: Justin's total is around $2,600 per kid per year, or $46,800 total, less than a quarter of the USDA estimate. As he pointed out, if he were to factor in the tax credits he gets back from the government, his net cost is closer to $500 per child. In fact, Jeremy reported that after taxes, he actually made a profit from his kid! Pete estimates the cost of raising a kid to be $8,340 per year or $100,080 total, less than half the USDA estimate.

So there you have it, from three financially independent parents who have kids on their own—by being strategic with your spending and not making hugely wasteful decisions, the cost of raising kids can vary wildly, from half of the USDA estimate all the way down to a quarter, depending on where you live.

Justin, Jeremy, and Pete all write fantastic, detailed blogs that break down all of these expenses, and they can be found at RootofGood.com, GoCurryCracker.com, and MrMoneyMustache.com, respectively. Check them out if you want to know more.

TRAVELING THE WORLD WITH SCHOOL-AGE KIDS

Now that we've busted a few myths on how much it costs to raise kids, let's deal with the other elephant in the room: education. Traveling with little ones might be well and good when they're infants or toddlers, but once you need to enroll them in school, you'll have to stop traveling, right?

Honestly, we thought so too. Like everyone else, we believed that all fun stops once you have kids, which is part of what prompted us to travel the world in the first place. Better get it out of our system before we have to settle down. We were shocked to discover this isn't true! There's an entire community of people who have bucked this convention and not only continue to travel but raise their kids on the road.

We were staying in Tulum, Mexico, a few years ago and in between diving in cenotes and playing with sea turtles, we got to know the other guests at our Airbnb. One of them was a mother from Australia traveling with her son.

"Wow, it's so great you two are traveling together," I told her. "So, his school let you take him out in the middle of the school year?"

"No," she replied. "He doesn't go to a traditional school. We're world schoolers."

I blinked. "Come again?"

Meet the world schoolers. The world is their classroom. While the catchy name can be traced back to around 2012, the practice itself seems to have originated in the early 2000s, when a community of alternative education advocates began comingling with the so-called digital nomad crowd—location-independent travelers who work remotely online. They began experimenting with ways to adapt nontraditional education methods to a nomadic lifestyle, and world schooling was born.

This first wave of world-schooled kids has recently come of age, attracting media attention over the fact that rather than being weird, antisocial, and poorly adjusted people, these young adults are intelligent, sociable, entrepreneurial, and in many ways better developed than their traditionally schooled counterparts.

I reached out to the leaders of this movement to learn more. By combining what they've done with nomadic education with what we've done on financial independence and early retirement, we can find innovative answers to the problem of how to retire and travel with school-age kids.

Lainie Liberti, cofounder of the We Are Worldschoolers Facebook group, and Jennifer Sutherland-Miller, alternative education consultant and founder of the blog EdventureProject.com, were gracious enough to provide their valuable input here. Both have brought up their own children in a world-schooling environment and now help other families do the same.

Doesn't world schooling cause social problems in kids since they don't have a stable community?

Apparently, this is the first question anyone in the world-schooling community gets asked. Everyone's always wondering: does world schooling make kids weird and antisocial?

The answer is, of course, no. In the past, moving around and changing schools every few years may have interfered with a kid's ability to make and maintain friendships, but these days it's so easy to connect with people online that it's not a significant problem. World schoolers have their own community that continuously organizes meet-ups all over. The kids use these events to mingle and form friendships and use social media to stay in touch. Some groups of families even travel together for a period of time—in an RV or a caravan around the United States or Australia, for example.

In many ways, world schooling provides an elegant solution to the social problems that traditionally schooled kids deal with on a day-to-day basis. World-schooled kids can choose their social circle, and their parents are deeply involved in their education. Thus, gangs, bullying, cliques, and online harassment are far less of a problem. Parent and child have control over who they spend time with because the family is not locked into one area or school zone.

To take an extreme example, think about how much fear and frustration surrounds the issue of school shootings in America. Now try to apply the idea of a school shooting to a family of world schoolers who do most of their education online.

Doesn't really work, does it? World schooling is a perfect defense against school shootings since there's no physical school to shoot.

How does world schooling work?

This is a big and complicated question since there's no one "correct" way to world school, so we'll try to introduce the core concepts to give you a taste.

World-schooling styles range from student-driven "unschooling"— similar to the Montessori approach—to a more traditional classroom-based style known as "classical." In between are methods such as Charlotte Mason, which emphasizes the environment and storytelling over dry textbooks, and third-culture kid, or TCK, which emphasizes cultural immersion and international schools. However, all methods have one thing in common: the world is a student's most active learning tool.

For example, rather than learning about the Vietnam War in a textbook, a world schooler might travel to Vietnam to visit the sites where major battles took place and interview people who participated in the war. They learn languages by immersing themselves in other cultures and speaking to locals. They learn math by calculating exchange rates, geography by climbing the mountains they study, and astronomy by navigating with the stars.

In short, world schoolers learn by doing, rather than by sitting in a classroom.

How are assignments graded and marked?

If you went to a school like mine, you're familiar with the experience of taking a test, having it marked, and being handed back a grade or score. In world schooling, it works a bit differently. Keeping in mind that there are many different styles, generally assignments and tests aren't designed to be assigned a numerical score. Rather, they're intended to ensure that the student learns the content.

So when an assignment or test is completed by a student, rather than their performance being used as a metric to compare their worthiness against the rest of the class, their correct answers are applauded while their incorrect answers are used as teaching tools and learning experiences. Rather than punishing students for answering incorrectly, parents use the test to guide the student's learning experience and fill in any knowledge gaps they have. They can take the test as many times as they like to solidify their knowledge.

What if you don't have any teaching experience?

To a curious parent, world schooling might sound interesting, but the idea of taking on your child's education is daunting, especially if you don't have any teaching background. And to be honest, a large part of the world-schooling parent community does have some kind of teaching background. That's because the movement can be traced back to the early 2000s, when there was little certainty that these ideas would work. So of course, the early adopters were specifically trained in education. They had the skills (and courage) necessary to guide their kids through a brand-new path of learning and come out thriving.

Twenty years later, those early adopters have seen their kids successfully integrate into the postsecondary school system and are explaining just how they did it. They're writing blogs and publishing books, and their movement has grown from just two hundred people to more than fifty thousand.

It's always been my approach: You don't have to trailblaze. Others have already done it. Just copy their moves!

Can world-schooled students get back into the traditional school system?

People are taught the "waterfall" model of schooling, where they believe that a child's performance in grade one determines their admission to grade two, which determines their admission to grade three, and so on. Any screwup at any point in the waterfall cascades downward, disrupting their kid's education and their life, until they're rejected from Harvard and living under a bridge.

But the truth is, kids experience schooling disruptions all the time. Sometimes a family needs to relocate because of a job. Sometimes a family relocates across borders (like mine did when we immigrated to Canada). Sometimes a family's home country doesn't even have schools that are recognized by their host country, like in refugee or asylum situations.

We long ago figured out ways to incorporate students who come from a nonstandard educational background into the traditional school system. What this means is that world schooling is not a one-way decision. If you try it and realize it's not for you (or your child), you can reenter the traditional school system at any time. All you have to do is go through the same process a transfer student moving into a new city would go through.

How do they apply for college/university?

College and university admission officers are increasingly looking for applicants with unique experiences. After all, there are only so many applications from straight-A students in debate club they can read in a day. As a result, none of the world-schooled kids we spoke to had any problems getting into higher ed. Hannah Miller (world-schooled daughter of Jennifer Sutherland-Miller), for example, enrolled in Oregon State University's Ecampus program and then transferred to Queen's University in Kingston, Ontario, to study geography, when she was ready to put roots down.

Colleges are looking for students who can successfully complete their programs, and what better way to measure that than to see students complete a college-level class before they get to college? Enrolling your child in an online Advanced Placement (AP) class is a popular approach because AP classes could potentially award college credits or enable your child to skip college intro classes. Even in the high school down the street, AP classes are considered a great way to stand out, and doing well in an AP class from, say, the highlands of Guatemala would erase any doubts about the efficacy of world schooling. After all, results speak for themselves.

Remember, there's always the option of transferring your child back into traditional school for the final few years of high school. That way, they would apply to university like everyone else.

Does the government recognize world schooling?

Absolutely. Just not by that name. No government currently recognizes the term "world schooling," but they do recognize homeschooling, and the same well-established rules and regulations that govern home-schooling apply to world schooling, too. Some states require you to register and check in every year with progress reports and standard-ized testing results. Other states are hands-off. Others even pay you a subsidy, since you're not taking up a spot in the state school system.

As long as homeschooling is allowed and recognized, world school-ing will be allowed as well. Make sure you're in compliance with any rules and regulations that apply in your state or province of residence, and you're good to go.

Where do I go to get started?

This was just a brief introduction to early retirement with kids and the world-schooling approach. Each of our experts, namely Pete Adeney, Justin McCurry, Jeremy Jacobson, Jennifer Sutherland-Miller, and Lainie Liberti, could fill tomes with the breadth and depth of their knowledge on the specific topic they're experts in. Fortunately for you, all of them have, writing extensively in their blogs and Facebook group about how to retire with kids or educate those kids on the road. To learn more, start by going to their websites, listed on the following page.

- ▸ Kids don't have to be as expensive as people make them out to be.

  - Also, many expenses, like day care, drop away once you retire.

  - Pete Adeney retired in Colorado with his son. Justin McCurry retired in North Carolina with three kids. Jeremy Jacobson retired and now lives nomadically with his son. All three raised kids on a fraction of the cost that normal parents pay.

  - Check out their blogs MrMoneyMustache.com, RootofGood .com, and GoCurryCracker.com for more details.

- ▸ There's also a group of parents that travel permanently with their kids and educate them on the road, called the world schoolers.

  - Check out the blog EdventureProject.com or the Facebook group www.facebook.com/groups/worldschoolers for more details.

Resources

EdventureProject.com

Facebook.com/worldschoolers

GoCurryCracker.com

MrMoneyMustache.com

RootofGood.com

— **20** —

THE DARK SIDE
OF EARLY RETIREMENT

"Remind me again why we did this to ourselves?" White-knuckling the armrest, I stared out the window, willing the plane to stop shaking. Somewhere between Dallas and Quito, we had hit a patch of turbulence. I desperately wanted to hear the captain over the speakers telling us everything was going to be fine, but the speakers stayed silent.

You'd think that after twenty-three flights in one year, I'd have gotten used to "rough air" (the airline industry's favorite euphemism). Nope. I closed my eyes, dizzy and nauseated, as the plane bounced up and down, spilling drinks all over the cabin.

Deep breath in. Deep breath out. I can do this . . .

Five hours later, getting my first breathtaking glimpse of Quito, a city of cloud forests nine thousand feet above sea level, the terrifying ride faded quickly in my memory.

Fear tends to consume our minds, blurring our thinking until nothing else matters. Reality is often less scary. (Not that that helps. Logically, I knew that being up in that vibrating 747 was safer than driving to work every day, but it didn't stop me from feeling the fear.) When we get e-mails from readers on the verge of retiring, all they can talk about is a phenomenon called the "Wall of Fear," coined by Pete

Adeney, aka Mr. Money Mustache. Instead of feeling excited, they worry about all the things that could go wrong.

I don't blame them. I also faced the Wall of Fear right before we retired. After being in the Matrix for almost a decade, it's easy for us to "become" our jobs. Our identity and social circle are so wrapped up in work that giving it up—even if it's stressful, even if you hate it—creates an identity crisis.

This is One More Year Syndrome. Sufferers of this condition believe that even though their portfolios have crossed the 4 percent threshold, their Cash Cushion and their Yield Shield are in place, and their rocket ship is ready for liftoff, if they work just *one more year*, that'll make things even safer. Inevitably, after that year, they think, *Sure, my portfolio is bigger, but it'll be even* better *if I work one more year . . .* , and the cycle continues. They never make the leap.

That's okay. You shouldn't ignore your fear. That would be like trying to sleep through a rock concert. Ignoring it won't make it go away. Fear is useful. Without it, our ancestors would've turned into mammoth chow a long time ago. Fear is necessary for survival. But the point of life isn't to hide under your bed and never take any risks. The point of life is taking the leap but bringing a parachute—just in case.

To scale the Wall of Fear, we need to conquer the most common concerns we hear about early retirement:

1. Running out of money

2. Loss of community

3. Loss of identity

RUNNING OUT OF MONEY

The easiest way to run out of money is to deplete your portfolio during the first five years by selling into a down market. This is known as "sequence-of-return risk," and we discussed it—as well as strategies on how to deal with it, such as the Yield Shield and Cash Cushion—in chapter 15. Another way to run out of money is with unexpected health care costs, which is absolutely a risk if you're American. In chapter 18 we talked about how early retirement and location independence make paying for health care easy in chapter 18. Or you could run into inflation and unexpected child care costs, which we discussed in chapters 18 and 19.

Our experience, after being retired for three years and having gone through a market crash in year one, has taught us that the fear of running out of money is overblown. Not only has our net worth grown by $300,000, our expenses continue to drop. We're safer and richer than when we left.

So you don't need to fear running out of money. But what about running out of friends?

LOSS OF COMMUNITY

When you're working, your colleagues are your social circle. If you retire, won't you be lonely and sad, watching Netflix in your underwear while your friends are all at work? If you start traveling, won't you leave all your friends and family behind? Might you lose friends who are jealous or angry since you've chosen a different path?

These are all legitimate questions. And judging by the thousands of angry comments that flood in whenever we're profiled somewhere, you won't have a shortage of haters, either. But I find the haters more amusing than malicious. Your pizza-night friends don't want you to cut out carbs. Your unemployed friends don't want you to get a job and not be available for daytime hangs. And your working friends don't want you to retire. Haters gonna hate because you make them question their lives.

Wading through the mud of online vitriol taught us that when people get angry about your choices, it isn't about you. It's about them. The psychology is just so transparent that it's practically a badge of honor.

When you break the system, it forces them to take a long hard look at themselves. The confident ones will be happy for you. The unhappy ones will blame you for invalidating their own path.

After we went public with our story with a spot on CBC (the Canadian Broadcasting Corporation) that has since been viewed over four million times, one family member started ducking my calls. My mom's response was, "So what? You don't even have a house." My dad said, "You don't have enough. Get back to work." Even the math didn't help sway him. These are emotional reactions, not logical ones.

The good news is that this chill didn't last. After three years of happily living our lives, we've found that most of that rejection has morphed into curiosity. The same family member who avoided us has recently started asking for financial advice. My dad recently told me, "I'm proud of you," for the first time in my life. I thought getting a book published with Penguin was hard, but compared to getting acceptance from my impossible-to-please parents, it was a picnic.

The longer you're retired, the more confident you become. And if you lose friends by choosing a different path, those friendships weren't worth keeping in the first place.

Your New Community

Over the years, we've said good-bye to a number of frenemies. It's a bummer in the moment, but that kind of toxicity will only hold you back. Genuine friends are the type of people you want in your life. And one of the biggest advantages of retiring has been getting to know new genuine friends all over the world. When we were working, we rarely had the time or headspace to venture out and meet people. With so little support, no wonder it was scary to retire. Since then, our minds have been opened.

In 2017, I was invited for the first time to speak at the Chautauqua retreat, which meets each year all over the world. That year, it was in the UK. A weeklong gathering founded by JL Collins, one of the leaders of the financial independence movement, Chautauqua challenges you to think outside the box, provides practical and emotional support in meeting your financial goals, and connects you to an international tribe of genuine friends. We ended up having one of the best weeks of our lives. And the main reason can be summarized in one sentence:

"You're my people."

Everyone we met was curious, open-minded, and caring, and they never judged us. We learned from this experience that, by far, the best relationships are with people who love you for you. They don't try to shove you into a box you don't fit into. Finding people who truly get you is what Chautauqua is all about. Since then, we've reunited with these newfound buddies all over the world.

Whether you are looking for camaraderie on your path to financial independence or are near retirement and hoping to find your community, you can find genuine friends at any of these conferences and meet-ups:

Chautauqua: FIChautauqua.com

Mr. Money Mustache Meetups: MrMoneyMustache.com/meetups

ChooseFi Facebook group: Facebook.com/ChooseFi

CampFI meet-ups: Choosefi.com/CampFI

LOSS OF IDENTITY

The line snaked around the conference hall, made up of people whispering with excitement, some bouncing on the balls of their feet in anticipation.

Who is that line for? I wondered.

I craned my neck to see the table at the front, trying to guess which author they were all waiting for. The table was empty, save for a stack of books. Each had a red cover, a cartoon girl on the front, and the title spelled out in big white letters: *Little Miss Evil.*

Holy shit! That's my book! They were waiting for me!

Standing in the autographing area at BookExpo America in New York City, I couldn't believe that after seven years in the writing trenches, I'd made it. Bryce and I were newly minted authors and there was a whole line of people waiting for a signed copy of *Little Miss Evil*, our children's novel.

Remember how I said in chapter 4, "Don't follow your passion (yet)"? Well, I've been saving that "yet" for now. Once you've become financially independent, you are finally free to follow your passion, whatever that may be. Achieving your dream is the greatest feeling in the world—when you don't have to worry about surviving on cans of cat food. Because that's exactly what would've happened if I had pursued my passion before becoming financially independent. Get rich, *then* follow your dreams. Get the order wrong and you're in big trouble.

How do I know this? Because even though there was a long line of people at my book signing, the check that I received for seven years of struggle and rejection was a few thousand bucks. That's before subtracting taxes and all the money I spent on writing classes, books, and critiques.

Don't get me wrong. I was prouder of that check than any of the fat paychecks I made as an engineer, but if I had to rely on it to live, I would've been stressed out of my mind! Because I waited until I became financially independent first, I could enjoy the moment without worrying about where my next payout was coming from.

I say "Don't follow your passion (yet)" and encourage the POT score approach because, out of the three biggest fears shared by our readers when it comes to following their dreams—

1. What if I'm not good enough?

2. What if my passion doesn't make enough money?

3. What if there's too much competition?

—the fear of not being good enough is the main one holding them back.

I don't blame them. Failure is terrifying, and I know this from personal experience. Before I got that book published, I'd amassed hundreds of rejections from literary agents and publishers. It was a frustrating, even gut-wrenching, experience, but now I know it's all part of the process. In order to develop a skill, you will fail repeatedly—until you are good enough. While you're busy face-planting, you won't earn a single cent. Again, this would've been fine if I had a trust fund, but I didn't; I had to get a good-paying job and work on writing on the side, while building a robust investment portfolio, to feel like I could (literally) afford to delve into my creative side. Once I became financially independent, I could write full-time even though the royalty checks couldn't support me.

Some people get lucky and their passion happens to be in a lucrative field. If that's you, fantastic. The rest of us have to find another way. You will fail, too. And it will hurt. But if you build a portfolio that pays your expenses first, those failures will hurt only emotionally, not financially. After all, it's really hard to keep those creative juices flowing when you're worried about keeping the lights on.

After becoming an author, I quickly realized the sheer amount of competition out there. Nielsen BookScan reports that of the 1.2 million books it tracks, only 25,000—barely more than 2 percent—have sold more than 5,000 copies. *Publishers Weekly* reports that the average book sells only *500 copies*. And this is out of the writers who got published! For each of those lucky ones, there are thousands of writers still struggling to find a publisher. That's why I like to think of financial independence as a suit of armor. It protects you from those common worries I listed earlier, because it allows you to follow your dreams without needing to make a single cent. You've become financially *invincible*.

Many of our readers worry that they're going to lose their identity in retirement, but what actually happens is you have the chance to build a *better* identity. Have a childhood dream you've been too afraid to pursue? Now's the time to go for it. And if that dream doesn't earn you a dime? Who cares! Your portfolio will pay for your living expenses, so you can forge ahead without fear. We volunteer for a nonprofit called We Need Diverse Books, an advocacy group dedicated to diversifying children's literature. It feels great to not have to choose between helping others and paying the bills. If you've always suspected you have the mind of an entrepreneur, no sweat. With your expenses covered, you can keep failing and learning without worrying about losing your shirt.

Lose one identity, build a better one.

Becoming financially independent doesn't have to be about quitting your hateful job and traveling the world. It's about having choices. If you love your work, by all means, keep working. "FIRE" stands for "Financial Independence Retire Early," but the "RE" part is optional. Only the "FI" part is necessary to forge the armor that will keep you protected if a job you love goes away or turns bad. FI means you always have choices.

Becoming financially independent is about designing the life you want. Once you've built a portfolio large enough that 4 percent of it covers your expenses each year, work is an option, not a mandate. If you want to fully retire like us and travel the world, do that. If you like your job, continue working with a more flexible schedule. If you want to spend more time with your kids, family, friends, or pets, you can do that too.

There will always be worries when you go against the norm. But just like the perceived danger during a turbulent plane ride, they're mostly in your head. After you walk away from the plane unscathed, you'll wonder, *What the heck was I so afraid of?*

Three years after saying good-bye to our cubicle prisons, we can't help but wonder why we were so terrified to jump. I love our new identities and I have no regrets about losing the old cranky, overworked ones. And if you become financially independent, you won't either.

— 21 —

YOU DON'T NEED A MILLION TO BREAK FREE

A frequently asked question from our readers is "You guys had six-figure engineering salaries. I don't. Can I still retire early?"

I get why they're skeptical. In the FIRE community, early retirees generally had high-paying jobs like engineer, lawyer, or accountant, at which they could squirrel money away to pay off any debt and build a healthy portfolio. And it's true that you get a head start if you chose a field with higher salaries. So, does that mean if you didn't choose one of these higher-paying fields you're doomed to work until you die? Are you screwed?

Nope. Even if you have an average salary, you can still retire early. And here's the math to prove it:

Say you have a married couple, earning the combined US median family income of $62,175 per year.[1] Using an average tax rate of 15.2 percent,[2] after taxes they net $52,724.40. By optimizing their spending—living in a small space or moving to a less expensive city, cooking at home, using car-sharing services like Zipcar—they manage to live on $40,000 per year, which is how much we lived on in expensive Toronto and how much my friend and early retiree Justin McCurry currently lives on with three kids in Raleigh, North Carolina. That means they can put $12,724.40 per year into their portfolio. This gives them a 24 percent after-tax savings rate, and according to the 4 Percent Rule, it means they'll need $40,000 × 25 = $1,000,000 to become financially independent. At a conservative return of 6 percent per year on average (inflation-adjusted), by the magic of investing and compounding they'll have a million in thirty years.

Here's the breakdown:

Year	Starting Balance	Annual Contribution	Return (6%)	Total
1	$0.00	$12,724.00	$0.00	$12,724.00
2	$12,724.00	$12,724.00	$763.44	$26,211.44
3	$26,211.44	$12,724.00	$1,572.69	$40,508.13
4	$40,508.13	$12,724.00	$2,430.49	$55,662.62
5	$55,662.62	$12,724.00	$3,339.76	$71,726.38
6	$71,726.38	$12,724.00	$4,303.58	$88,753.96
7	$88,753.96	$12,724.00	$5,325.24	$106,803.20
8	$106,803.20	$12,724.00	$6,408.19	$125,935.39
9	$125,935.39	$12,724.00	$7,556.12	$146,215.51
10	$146,215.51	$12,724.00	$8,772.93	$167,712.44
11	$167,712.44	$12,724.00	$10,062.75	$190,499.19
12	$190,499.19	$12,724.00	$11,429.95	$214,653.14
13	$214,653.14	$12,724.00	$12,879.19	$240,256.33
14	$240,256.33	$12,724.00	$14,415.38	$267,395.71
15	$267,395.71	$12,724.00	$16,043.74	$296,163.45

Year	Starting Balance	Annual Contribution	Return (6%)	Total
16	$296,163.45	$12,724.00	$17,769.81	$326,657.26
17	$326,657.26	$12,724.00	$19,599.44	$358,980.70
18	$358,980.70	$12,724.00	$21,538.84	$393,243.54
19	$393,243.54	$12,724.00	$23,594.61	$429,562.15
20	$429,562.15	$12,724.00	$25,773.73	$468,059.88
21	$468,059.88	$12,724.00	$28,083.59	$508,867.47
22	$508,867.47	$12,724.00	$30,532.05	$552,123.52
23	$552,123.52	$12,724.00	$33,127.41	$597,974.93
24	$597,974.93	$12,724.00	$35,878.50	$646,577.43
25	$646,577.43	$12,724.00	$38,794.65	$698,096.08
26	$698,096.08	$12,724.00	$41,885.76	$752,705.84
27	$752,705.84	$12,724.00	$45,162.35	$810,592.19
28	$810,592.19	$12,724.00	$48,635.53	$871,951.72
29	$871,951.72	$12,724.00	$52,317.10	$936,992.82
30	$936,992.82	$12,724.00	$56,219.57	$1,005,936.39

In this example, we are assuming the absolute worst-case scenario, that our couple aren't ambitious and don't get any promotions or switch jobs to boost their salaries. If they did, the timeline would naturally be shorter. Note that all figures are real, inflation-adjusted dollars, meaning that behind the scenes, it's assumed that both your salary and savings rate are growing with inflation. For more details on how these tables are constructed, please refer to appendix D.

So, even though they don't have six-figure salaries, by saving and investing as much as they can, they will be able to retire in thirty years.

Assuming they started working at age twenty-four, they would retire at fifty-four—eleven years earlier than the retirement age of sixty-five.

Our couple will manage to retire earlier than normal, but they can do better. If they are able to increase their salaries (by using the POT score and going back to school, getting promotions, jumping to higher-paying jobs, etc.), they could fast-track their time to retirement.

This is exactly what reader Brandon did to increase his salary from $24,000 per year to $110,000 per year. No one in his family had ever gone to college, so for twelve years Brandon worked in a factory making only $7.50 per hour. But by investing in himself and going back to school to get a degree in international business and management information systems, Brandon quadrupled his salary.

Sometimes you don't even need to go back to school. You can seek out a new job. Remember Colby, the expat English teacher in South Korea making $30,000 per year (chapter 16)? He recently switched jobs to teach English in Shenzhen, China, and doubled his salary. Not only is he able to save and invest $40,000 per year, he's helped other readers find jobs teaching English overseas as well, proving to them it's possible to increase your salary while enjoying a life of travel.

In Iceland, we met Rob and Robin Charlton, an American couple who retired at forty-three. Robin's first job was a travel agent, earning a painfully low $14,000 per year. But because she switched careers to become a nurse and he continued to work as a technical writer, their combined pretax salary went up to $89,000 per year. As a result, they were able to save and invest more, allowing them to retire in fifteen years with a portfolio of $926,000! They've been traveling the world since 2007 and are writing about their adventures on WhereWeBe.com.

But what if you don't want to wait fifteen to thirty years? There are a few ways to get there sooner than expected, some of which may sound familiar: SideFIRE, PartialFI, and geographic arbitrage.

SIDEFIRE

Financial independence is a suit of armor: by shielding you from running out of money, it allows you to fearlessly follow your dreams. That shield is useful even if you're not 100 percent financially independent. For example, if you've always dreamed of becoming a writer but couldn't support yourself on a writer's salary (which is pretty common), by making $20,000 per year as a freelance writer, you've reduced your required portfolio size by $20,000 × 25 = $500,000.

This is what we like to call SideFIRE. By having a side hustle in "retirement," you don't have to become fully FI before reaping most of the benefits. You can build the life of your dreams using the power of a side hustle and have your portfolio supplement your living expenses. In the example I just gave, your portfolio would cover half of your $40,000-per-year expenses and your side-hustle income would cover the other half. By developing a side hustle while you're working, you essentially kill three birds with one stone: you increase your savings rate by making more money, develop a new skill, *and* reduce the size of the portfolio needed to escape your nine-to-five.

Returning to the example of the couple earning a median family income of $62,175 per year before taxes, if they manage to earn $20,000 a year with a part-time job or side hustle after leaving their jobs, they would only need $40,000 − $20,000 = $20,000 per year in passive income from their portfolio. Using the 4 Percent Rule, that means they would only need $20,000 × 25 = $500,000 to achieve SideFIRE.

If they save 24 percent of their after-tax income, here's what the math looks like:

Year	Starting Balance	Annual Contribution	Return (6%)	Total
1	$0.00	$12,724.00	$0.00	$12,724.00
2	$12,724.00	$12,724.00	$763.44	$26,211.44
3	$26,211.44	$12,724.00	$1,572.69	$40,508.13
4	$40,508.13	$12,724.00	$2,430.49	$55,662.62
5	$55,662.62	$12,724.00	$3,339.76	$71,726.38
6	$71,726.38	$12,724.00	$4,303.58	$88,753.96
7	$88,753.96	$12,724.00	$5,325.24	$106,803.20
8	$106,803.20	$12,724.00	$6,408.19	$125,935.39
9	$125,935.39	$12,724.00	$7,556.12	$146,215.51
10	$146,215.51	$12,724.00	$8,772.93	$167,712.44
11	$167,712.44	$12,724.00	$10,062.75	$190,499.19
12	$190,499.19	$12,724.00	$11,429.95	$214,653.14
13	$214,653.14	$12,724.00	$12,879.19	$240,256.33
14	$240,256.33	$12,724.00	$14,415.38	$267,395.71
15	$267,395.71	$12,724.00	$16,043.74	$296,163.45
16	$296,163.45	$12,724.00	$17,769.81	$326,657.26
17	$326,657.26	$12,724.00	$19,599.44	$358,980.70
18	$358,980.70	$12,724.00	$21,538.84	$393,243.54
19	$393,243.54	$12,724.00	$23,594.61	$429,562.15
20	$429,562.15	$12,724.00	$25,773.73	$468,059.88
21	$468,059.88	$12,724.00	$28,083.59	$508,867.47

By working on a side hustle to generate $20,000 a year, the couple can shave nine years off their time to financial independence. Remember how I said even when I succeeded in becoming a novelist, the pay was still not enough to live on? Five thousand to $10,000 per year sounds like chump change if you're trying to live on it, *but* if you have achieved SideFIRE and this is your supplemental income, it becomes significant. That's $5,000 of passive income you don't have to generate. According to the 4 Percent Rule, that means you can decrease the portfolio you need to escape from your job by a whopping $125,000. Think about how much time it would take for you to save that much money.

This is why side hustles, by themselves, are not super useful for your financial freedom, but coupled with a portfolio spinning off passive income, they can make all the difference in the world. And if your side hustle has to do with your passion, it's a triple win, because it decreases the size of the portfolio you need, lets you follow that passion, *and* generates additional income. You don't need a million to break free. You simply need a portfolio big enough to supplement the income you're making in retirement.

Check out Grant Sabatier's book *Financial Freedom* and Chris Guillebeau's *The $100 Startup* for ideas on how to make money on side hustles.

PARTIAL FI

What if you're not interested in a side hustle? What if you actually enjoy your job but just need more flexibility? What if you just want more time to spend time with family and friends? Say hello to Partial FI! When you are fully FI, the passive income from your portfolio must be enough to cover your expenses. But if you have the option to decrease your hours to part-time or become a contractor with the option to take mini-retirements or sabbaticals, Partial FI will allow you that flexibility and freedom. Some careers that require a certain number of hours to maintain your license, like nursing, are especially well suited to this path.

Say you make the median family income. By stepping down to part-time or accepting only a six-month contract, you would earn a pretax salary of around $31,000 per year. But because you're in a low tax bracket, your after-tax take-home pay would be around $28,000. If your annual spending is $40,000, you would only need $12,000 to bridge the gap in your expenses. This would require a portfolio size of $12,000 × 25 = $300,000 to generate that passive income. As we mentioned in chapter 13, like a couple in the 15 percent tax bracket, you would get 0 percent tax on qualified dividends and capital gains, meaning you can withdraw this income each year tax-free.

Year	Starting Balance	Annual Contribution	Return (6%)	Total
1	$0.00	$12,724.00	$0.00	$12,724.00
2	$12,724.00	$12,724.00	$763.44	$26,211.44
3	$26,211.44	$12,724.00	$1,572.69	$40,508.13
4	$40,508.13	$12,724.00	$2,430.49	$55,662.62
5	$55,662.62	$12,724.00	$3,339.76	$71,726.38
6	$71,726.38	$12,724.00	$4,303.58	$88,753.96
7	$88,753.96	$12,724.00	$5,325.24	$106,803.20
8	$106,803.20	$12,724.00	$6,408.19	$125,935.39
9	$125,935.39	$12,724.00	$7,556.12	$146,215.51
10	$146,215.51	$12,724.00	$8,772.93	$167,712.44
11	$167,712.44	$12,724.00	$10,062.75	$190,499.19
12	$190,499.19	$12,724.00	$11,429.95	$214,653.14
13	$214,653.14	$12,724.00	$12,879.19	$240,256.33
14	$240,256.33	$12,724.00	$14,415.38	$267,395.71
15	$267,395.71	$12,724.00	$16,043.74	$296,163.45

To reach Partial FI, it would take this couple a little over fifteen years!

You can still gain freedom and flexibility with part-time work or semiretirement in just over a decade, even if you start with zero net worth and have an average income.

GEOGRAPHIC ARBITRAGE

Side hustle not your thing? Can't or don't want to go down to part-time? No sweat. You can still achieve financial freedom with geographic arbitrage. Geographic arbitrage is the idea that you can earn income in a country with a strong currency (like the United States) but retire in a country with a weak currency (like Mexico, Vietnam, Malaysia, Thailand, or Poland). That means you can become financially free decades earlier than your cohort back at home, even if you don't have a high income.

If the idea of spending your days sitting on a beach in Thailand, eating tacos in a *zocalo* in Mexico, or hiking in the Tatra Mountains in Poland appeals to you, geographic arbitrage might be your ticket—as it was for our friends Steve and Elaine, our Airbnb hosts in Vietnam, who were originally from Australia. When I asked them why they had made the move, they told me: "We realized we could keep struggling and falling behind in Australia or move to Vietnam and already be ahead."

The choice was easy, according to Steve, who showed me the scary open-heart-surgery scar in the middle of his chest. After a massive heart attack, Steve realized that working in his stressful IT job wasn't worth dying for. He and Elaine decided to take the leap with their retirement savings. They now enjoy a relaxed pace of life and Steve's health is better than ever. Elaine gives back to her new community by running an orphanage that has already fostered twenty-two children.

While traveling in Vietnam and Thailand, we realized that due to the advantageous exchange rate, you can live a luxurious life there for as little as $1,130 USD per month, or $13,560 USD per year. Since the average salary in Vietnam is around $150 USD per month, this is an exorbitant amount by local standards. In order to raise $13,560 per year in passive income, you'd need a portfolio size of $13,560 × 25 = $339,000.

With a median salary of $62,175 a year and putting away $12,724 a year, you'd reach geographic arbitrage FI in:

Year	Starting Balance	Annual Contribution	Return (6%)	Total
1	$0.00	$12,724.00	$0.00	$12,724.00
2	$12,724.00	$12,724.00	$763.44	$26,211.44
3	$26,211.44	$12,724.00	$1,572.69	$40,508.13
4	$40,508.13	$12,724.00	$2,430.49	$55,662.62
5	$55,662.62	$12,724.00	$3,339.76	$71,726.38
6	$71,726.38	$12,724.00	$4,303.58	$88,753.96
7	$88,753.96	$12,724.00	$5,325.24	$106,803.20
8	$106,803.20	$12,724.00	$6,408.19	$125,935.39
9	$125,935.39	$12,724.00	$7,556.12	$146,215.51
10	$146,215.51	$12,724.00	$8,772.93	$167,712.44
11	$167,712.44	$12,724.00	$10,062.75	$190,499.19
12	$190,499.19	$12,724.00	$11,429.95	$214,653.14
13	$214,653.14	$12,724.00	$12,879.19	$240,256.33
14	$240,256.33	$12,724.00	$14,415.38	$267,395.71
15	$267,395.71	$12,724.00	$16,043.74	$296,163.45
16	$296,163.45	$12,724.00	$17,769.81	$326,657.26
17	$326,657.26	$12,724.00	$19,599.44	$358,980.70

Sixteen and a half years! And if you're willing to combine the ideas of geographic arbitrage and SideFIRE working as a digital nomad or teaching English overseas, by earning as little as $10,000 per year, you'd shorten your time even more, with a required portfolio of $13,560 − $10,000 = $3,560 × 25 = $89,000 within:

Year	Starting Balance	Annual Contribution	Return (6%)	Total
1	$0.00	$12,724.00	$0.00	$12,724.00
2	$12,724.00	$12,724.00	$763.44	$26,211.44
3	$26,211.44	$12,724.00	$1,572.69	$40,508.13
4	$40,508.13	$12,724.00	$2,430.49	$55,662.62
5	$55,662.62	$12,724.00	$3,339.76	$71,726.38
6	$71,726.38	$12,724.00	$4,303.58	$88,753.96

Six years!

As you can see, even if you earn an average salary you can still achieve financial freedom with SideFIRE, Partial FI, or geographic arbitrage. You don't need to become engineers like us—our readers come from various backgrounds, like teaching, nursing, the postal service, the military, owning a small business, etc. They write in to us daily, asking to have their finances analyzed. And after diving into countless reader cases, I've discovered that the power of this method comes from translating what most people don't understand (money) into something everyone understands: time.

Questions like "Should I go back to school for my PhD?" or "Should I move to Alaska to teach?" or "Should I buy a house?" become manageable when we can break down the scenario into "If you do X, your time to retirement gets stretched out by Y years." This crystallizes the choice by framing it in terms of how much time they are willing to trade for it. Even though this entire book seems like it's about money, it isn't. This book is about time.

Don't ask yourself, "How should I spend my *money*?" Ask yourself, "How should I spend my *time*?" Specifically, "How much time am I willing to spend working for someone else?"

If you honestly answer that, then money decisions become clear.

CHAPTER 21 SUMMARY

- ▸ If you build up a side hustle pursuing a passion project, you can retire with much less.

  - • A side hustle earning just $10,000 a year means your target portfolio requirement drops by $250,000.

- ▸ Continuing to work part-time can also have this effect.

- ▸ Retiring in a low-cost location can also drastically reduce the amount of money you need to save.

— 22 —

GO YOUR OWN WAY

Anybody who's ever set foot into the personal finance section of a bookstore or library knows what it's like to feel overwhelmed or confused. God knows I did. There are so many people writing about money it makes your head spin. But it's not the sheer volume that's the problem; it's the conflicting advice. Some say you have to start a business, some claim the secret is real estate, and others advocate picking individual stocks. All that contradictory information can spin you into "analysis paralysis." With so many possible directions, you're afraid of picking the wrong one, so you freeze and do nothing.

Looking back at my own path to becoming a millionaire, as well as hearing stories from others who have made this journey, I realized that all those books aren't necessarily wrong. They conflict because there are multiple ways to make money.

Here's how the world of personal finance works:

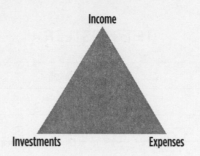

Income

Investments   Expenses

On the corners are income, expenses, and investments, represent-
ing the three forces of finance: money coming in (income), money going out (expenses), and money generated from money (investments). If
all three corners represent the average US income (according to the
2015 census) of $50,000 to $70,000, an average savings rate of 7.5 percent (according to the US Federal Reserve), and an average annual
long-term investment return of 6 percent after adjusting for inflation
(according to the S & P 500's historical performance), your finances
will be, by definition, average. Someone with average finances can expect to live a decent middle-class lifestyle, work for forty-some years,
and retire at the age of sixty-five with the help of Social Security.

People who manage to break out and become millionaires at a
young age, however, tend to be average (or slightly above average) on
two of these corners and exceptionally good on the third. This means
there are three types of millionaires. And every finance book (and, by
extension, every finance author) can be classified as one of these three
types. Even though they end up at the same destination, the methods
are different, and at times contradictory. In his bestselling book *Rich
Dad, Poor Dad*, Robert Kiyosaki famously claims that saving money is
for suckers like his Poor Dad: "If you want to be wealthy and financially secure, working hard and saving money will not get you there."

I, of course, know that the exact opposite is true: working hard
and saving money will absolutely get you there. That doesn't mean
he's wrong, though. His advice is correct given the type of millionaire he is.

THE HUSTLER

Income	Exceptional
Savings	Average
Investments	Average

The Hustler's source of wealth comes from their ability to earn money. Hustlers tend to gravitate toward entrepreneurial activities, correctly recognizing that trading time for money has a natural ceiling on how much you can earn. You only have so many hours a day, so tying your earnings to time limits your potential. If you become an entrepreneur, on the other hand, there is no upper limit on your earnings, so these people tend to work for themselves. Steve Jobs, Elon Musk, and Mark Zuckerberg are examples of successful Hustlers.

Hustlers see the world as endlessly full of opportunities to make money, and if given the chance they will talk your ear off about their next venture (or ventures). They tend not to put much emphasis on controlling their spending, as they view money as an infinitely renewable resource. After all, if they run out of money, they can make more!

Hustlers also tend to be very comfortable with risk and are willing to bet everything if they believe in a business they're creating. This tendency to risk it all is the source of much of their success—but also their failures. Elon Musk, after selling PayPal to eBay, at one point had over $200 million in cash. He invested all of it in Tesla, and in a divorce filing in 2010 was forced to publicly admit he was broke.

From $200 million to broke. It boggles my mind how anyone can spend that amount in a lifetime.

Tesla, of course, became a global phenomenon and a household name, but that's how risk-seeking Hustlers can be. Even with enough money to say good-bye to work forever, they will still risk everything for the next thrill.

- ▸ Robert Kiyosaki

- ▸ Tim Ferriss

- ▸ Steve Jobs

THE INVESTOR

Income	Average
Savings	Average
Investments	Exceptional

The Investor is an expert at turning money into even more money. When I do financial projections, I usually use 6 percent as a conservative estimate of the long-term performance of a 60/40 indexed portfolio, but an Investor would look at that number and scoff. *Six percent? That's it?* These guys aren't impressed unless an investment is making more than 20 percent.

What the Investor invests in can vary widely. Some pick stocks. Others buy real estate. Still others find some esoteric commodity like baseball cards or fine art. However, successful Investors are quick to point out what they do is not gambling. Gambling relies on luck. Investing relies on skill. As such, Investors know their field inside and out and have the skills needed to spot a good investment that others can't.

Like Hustlers, Investors don't tend to spend much time watching their spending. And like Hustlers, they tend to, by necessity, be extremely comfortable with risk. Additionally, successful Investors are skilled at using debt and leverage to maximize their returns. Taking on debt is a bad move for most people, but to an Investor, it is a way to invest with other people's money. A skilled investor who knows how to use debt properly can use it to *reduce* risk.

The most dangerous thing about the Investor pathway is that it's easy to delude yourself into thinking you've got the skills, when any initial wins could be just due to luck. Consistently successful Investors are exceedingly rare. As I mentioned in chapter 10, only 15 percent of active fund managers on Wall Street manage to beat the market in any given year.

NOTABLE INVESTORS

- ▸ Benjamin Graham
- ▸ Warren Buffett
- ▸ John Bogle

THE OPTIMIZER

Income	Average
Savings	Exceptional
Investments	Average

Optimizers make their fortune by obsessively controlling their spending. Optimizers tend to have regular jobs, making decent but not insane salaries, and for the most part lead normal lives.

What's abnormal is how much time and effort they spend on tracking and accounting for every penny they spend. When a cashier asks, "Would you like your receipt?" the answer is *always* yes. That receipt gets stuffed into a folder, which then gets entered onto a spreadsheet, which then gets sliced and diced and analyzed as if it's an alien microbe that holds the secret to immortality.

If you haven't guessed yet, I am a proud Optimizer.

We Optimizers get supremely annoyed when we are labeled as

"cheap" or seen as living a miserly life. Optimizers aren't cheap; we are experts at optimizing value. We have an encyclopedic database of prices in our heads, and we know how to get that bag of groceries for half the price. We are, in short, masters at getting the same (or better) life experiences as everyone else but at a fraction of the cost. Hell, Bryce and I have been traveling continuously for three years now, and our portfolio has gone *up* instead of down. Does that sound like deprivation to you?

We Optimizers do have our weaknesses, however. For one, we tend to be extremely risk-averse. This prevents us from starting businesses, following our dreams, or doing many things that might make us happy but would require us to take a risk that might mean losing money. That fear of loss is why I'm prone to panic attacks, like during the 2008 stock market crash or after my coworker almost died at his desk.

That fear of loss also makes it difficult for Optimizers to invest. We get so scared when our portfolios drop in value that we experience an almost irresistible urge to hide our money under our mattress. Now that I've withstood and survived not one but two market crashes, I'm confident enough to trust that temporary market dips are just temporary, but the truth is that when I executed my first buy order, I was terrified. Conquering that fear was the hardest thing I've ever done (including getting through an engineering program that I sucked at), but if I hadn't conquered it, I wouldn't be where I am today.

If you're also an Optimizer, I hope this book helped you understand why you're the way you are, and why that's totally awesome.

NOTABLE OPTIMIZERS

- Me

- Mr. Money Mustache, aka Pete Adeney

- JL Collins

DIFFERENT STROKES FOR DIFFERENT FOLKS

Since we've retired and started traveling the world, we've become friends with self-made millionaires of all three types, and one of the most interesting things we've noticed is that not only are there multiple ways to get there, the folks who pull it off do so because they know their own strengths and weaknesses and are able to match them to their approach.

As an Optimizer, I could never have taken another pathway to wealth, because my tolerance for risk is too low and my fear of debt is too high. As I mentioned, I *tried* to get rich by becoming an entrepreneur, and I failed every time. Looking back, I realize now that my phobia of losing money prevented me from properly investing in each venture, and my aversion to debt prevented me from seeking financing. Only since I've become financially independent and stopped having to worry about my gas bill have I been able to work as a writer.

Similarly, if an Investor or Hustler had tried to work normal jobs, ruthlessly track their spending, and build a portfolio of low-cost index funds, they would have lost interest and never made it.

The key to getting rich is to know your personality, know what you're good at and bad at, and pick the approach that fits you best.

THE MAGIC OF REPRODUCIBILITY

That being said, not all paths are created equal. I've noticed that the most common type of millionaire, by far, is the Optimizer. This is because unlike the other approaches, the Optimizer's is mathematically reproducible. I can tell you exactly what I did, and if you copy my moves, you will wind up a millionaire, too. That's not true for the Hustler or Investor.

If you read that Steve Jobs biography and attempt to copy everything he did, well, sorry, Apple already exists. Similarly, if you go after all of Warren Buffett's stock picks, you won't reap similar wealth because those stocks are no longer available at the same price as when he bought them. Hustlers and Investors have to discover their own unique path to riches that nobody else has taken—and once they do, it'll never be an option in exactly that same way again. Optimizers, on the other hand, can all do essentially the same thing and it'll work each time. That's the power of reproducibility. I can give away my secrets and they will work for you, too.

THE POWER OF POVERTY

Another striking thing I've noticed is that among millionaires, my story of clawing my way up from poverty is not unusual. In fact, it's quite common. But growing up that way manifests itself in different ways for each of us. For me, poverty gave me creativity, resilience, adaptability, and perseverance. For others, it inspired them to reach for the stars in ways their parents never could have dreamed of. And for others, it gave them a fear of being without that they never want to experience again. Any which way, though, poverty gave us the spark that drove us to do whatever it took to break out.

The only difference between us is that I don't mind talking openly about the shittier parts of my childhood. Most people prefer not to, either because they're ashamed or because they don't look back on that time fondly. Either way, dig deeper and it becomes clear that these people didn't make it *despite* their growing up poor, they made it *because* of it. I'm proud of it. I'm proud of the lessons it taught me, and I believe that it gave me many of the skills I used to get to where I am today. I wasn't born with a silver spoon in my mouth, and neither were many other self-made millionaires. That's not weakness. That's strength.

If any part of my story sounds familiar, you're not alone. Don't let anyone tell you you'll never be rich. I didn't, and here I am.

FINAL THOUGHTS

If you understand money, life is incredibly easy. If you don't understand money, like the vast majority of people, life is incredibly hard.

But money is not this big complicated thing that requires a genius-level IQ to understand. Instead, it's a series of simple lessons that, individually, are not difficult to grasp, but when you put them together they become a superpower.

I didn't understand money for the longest time, but once I did life became something I could control rather than something that happened to me. Money went from something I worried about constantly to something that gives me the freedom to do whatever I want. Not only do I never worry about money anymore, it just keeps growing on its own while I scuba-dive in the Galápagos!

I want you to understand your money as well, so you don't stress out about it anymore. I don't want the act of opening your credit card statement or bank account to fill you with dread, or the threat of a job loss to induce a panic attack. I want your life to be easy, like mine.

I guess here is where we say good-bye, for now at least. My journey from poverty to millionaire wasn't straightforward or easy, but it's reproducible, and that's what matters. You can do what I did, you can accomplish what I accomplished, and all you have to do is copy my moves. I didn't create the next Snapchat; I didn't bet on Amazon when it was $10. All I did was work hard and never take a dollar for granted, and I turned our above-average-but-not-unreasonably-so salary into a million dollars and retired at thirty-one.

If you understand money, life is incredibly easy. If you don't understand money, life is incredibly hard.

Now that you've read this book, you understand money. And as a result, your life will get easier.

Thank you for reading.

APPENDIX A
(CHAPTER 14)

Here is how we went from the 4 Percent Rule to the charts in chapter 14. To recap, the 4 Percent Rule states that you can safely retire for a thirty-year period with 95 percent certainty once your living expenses equal 4 percent of your portfolio.

$$0.04 \times P = E$$

P is your portfolio size and E is your annual expenses. Let's now express E in terms of your savings rate (S) and your income (I).

$$0.04 \times P = I \times (1 - S)$$

Now we express your portfolio in terms of how much of your income you save for N years, assuming that money is invested in a portfolio returning an annualized gain of r. In the field of economics and finance, this formula is referred to as the future value of an ordinary annuity, though you may recognize it from high school algebra as a slightly modified formula for the closed-form solution of a geometric series—and you thought everything you learned in school was useless!

$$0.04 \times I \times S \left[\frac{(1+r)^N - 1}{r} \right] = I \times (1 - S)$$

Now (like in that algebra class), we solve for N.

$$\left[\frac{(1+r)^N - 1}{r} \right] = 25 \times \frac{(1-S)}{S}$$

$$(1+r)^N = 25 \times \frac{(1-S)}{S} \times r + 1$$

$$N \times \log(1+r) = \log \left[25 \times \frac{1-S}{S} + 1 \right]$$

$$N = \frac{\log \left[25 \times \frac{(1-S)}{S} + 1 \right]}{\log(1+r)}$$

Phew! We have expressed N as a function of two variables: the savings rate, S, and the portfolio's annualized rate of return, r.

By plugging this formula into an Excel spreadsheet, we generate the charts shown in chapter 15 by sweeping the variable S between 5 percent and 100 percent, as well as sweeping the variable r between 1 percent and 10 percent.

MATH IS AWESOME! Never forget that.

APPENDIX B
(CHAPTER 14)

In the interest of transparency, I'm showing you the exact dollar figures behind our climb to millionaire status. There are a lot of numbers and charts that don't make for compelling storytelling, so I put them in this appendix rather than the main chapters. This section is completely optional and is mostly for all you weirdos who get turned on by graphs.

It should also be noted that while everything I've written about did happen, for dramatic reasons it may not have happened on the exact timeline I gave. Here I've clarified what happened when.

2006 (JUNE TO DECEMBER)

Bryce and I graduated from the University of Waterloo with computer engineering degrees in June 2006 with no debt since I worked internship jobs throughout school to pay tuition and living costs. We were able to leverage our internships into full-time offers at graduation, as software developers. Because of this, we hit the ground running and earned a combined total of $66,500 for half the year. This sounds high, but remember there were two of us, and this correlated with the average salaries of the field we both chose using the POT score (whether we realized it or not) I discussed in chapter 4. It should also be noted that as new grads making real money for the first time, we didn't watch our spending. We ate out every other day and went to bars and clubs most weekends. My brief purse addiction outlined in chapter 7 happened here. But even though we blew through a whopping $5,333.33 a month in spending, we still managed to save 52 percent of our after-tax income.

Monthly Spending

Category	Cost Per Month	Comments
Rent	$1,500	Because we weren't married yet, we were stupidly living in two separate places, each apartment costing us $700 and $800 per month, respectively.
Food/Entertainment	$2,700	
Transportation/Misc.	$300	
Vacation	$833.33	This is an average monthly number but more accurately we spent $5,000 each on vacation packages to the Caribbean to celebrate our graduation.
Total	$5,333.33	

End-of-the-Year Balance Sheet

Category	Amount
Combined after-tax income	$66,500
Spending	$32,000

Category	Amount
Savings	$34,500
Savings rate	52%
Net worth	$34,500

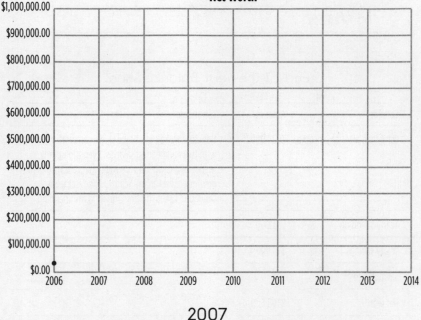

2007

This was our first full year of employment. With two engineering sala-ries and my Scarcity Mind-set, we were able to put away 59 percent in savings despite living in Toronto, one of the most expensive cities in Canada.

Monthly Spending

Category	Cost Per Month
Rent	$1,500
Food/Entertainment	$2,200
Transportation/Misc.	$300
Vacation	$250
Total for 2 people	$4,250

End-of-the-Year Balance Sheet

Category	Amount	Comments
Combined after-tax income	$125,000	Now that we're out of school, we can work a full year with two engineering salaries. Even though my friends and coworkers are making it rain with their newfound wealth, my Scarcity Mind-set from childhood keeps me from inflating my spending.
Yearly spending	$51,000	
Yearly savings	$74,000	
Savings rate	59%	
Net worth	$108,500	

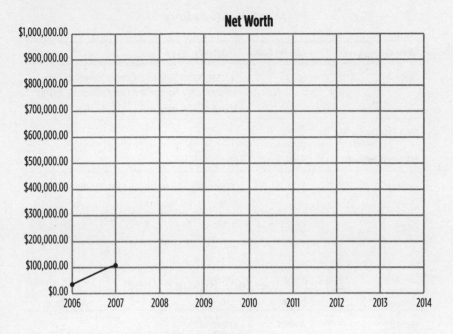

Net Worth

2008

With stable jobs and a net worth of $100,000, we realize we should probably act like adults and start investing, thinking, *What could possibly go wrong?*

Everything, apparently.

The 2008 stock market crash described in chapter 11 happens and our shiny new portfolio plummets by $58,000 in the first year. Fan-freaking-tastic.

Luckily, our growing savings rate and our index and rebalancing strategy save us from selling everything at a loss. But as you can see, our net worth barely moves despite both of us getting promotions and saving a combined $84,400 that year. Thanks a lot, 2008!

Monthly Spending

Category	Cost Per Month	Comments
Rent	$800	A scary incident happens at my apartment, so for safety reasons I decide to move in with Bryce and our combined rent halves from $1,500 to $800.
Food/Entertainment	$2,200	
Transportation/Misc.	$300	
Vacation	$583.33	We spend $7,000 on two vacations throughout the year.
Total	$3,883.33	

End-of-the-Year Balance Sheet

Category	Amount	Comments
Combined after-tax income	$131,000	We both get promotions at work but unfortunately, we just started investing in a portfolio, which is now crashing.
Yearly spending	$46,600	Luckily, we make the decision to move in together and halve our rent, which ends up cutting our costs.
Yearly savings	$84,400	
Savings rate	64%	With our portfolio down 30%, our growing savings rate is our only saving grace.
Investment gains/losses	−30%	The stock market crash causes our new portfolio to plummet. I spend a good part of the year in a panic.
Net worth	$134,900	

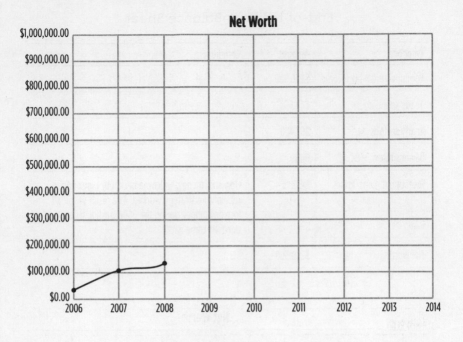

Net Worth

2009

This year is a testament to our index and rebalancing strategy. Because we didn't panic and sell at the bottom, instead shoveling money into our portfolio as everything crashed, we recovered by the end of 2009.

Monthly Spending

Category	Cost Per Month	Comments
Rent	$800	
Food/Entertainment	$2,200	
Transportation/Misc.	$300	
Vacation	$750	$9,000 for the year. Yes, we love our vacations.
Total for 2 people	$4,050	

End-of-the-Year Balance Sheet

Category	Amount	Comments
Combined after-tax income	$136,000	
Yearly spending	$48,600	
Yearly savings	$87,400	
Savings rate	64%	
Investment gains/losses	+43%	Holy shit, money, welcome back! Our index and rebalancing strategy worked! As a result we didn't lose any money during the 2008 crash and our portfolio came back.
Net worth	$280,300	

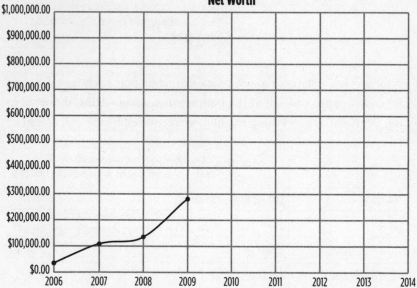

Net Worth

2010

Even though our portfolio has fully recovered from 2008, we make the biggest mistake of our investing lives this year. Because Bryce and I get married, we decide to save up for a house, as described in chapter 9, and as a result, we pull our money out of the market, missing out on two years of investment gains in the bull market. Luckily, our savings rate remains steady and a promotion and bonus help our net worth grow to hedge against inflation.

Monthly Spending

Category	Cost Per Month	Comments
Rent	$800	
Food/Entertainment	$1,700	We reduce our food and alcohol spending by $500 easily by cooking more instead of eating out, and ditching bars.
Transportation/Misc.	$300	
Vacation	$154.17	Our vacation costs are significantly reduced, but that's only because we got married and decided to spend on our wedding and honeymoon instead.
Wedding/Honeymoon	$833.33	$10,000 total for the year includes dress, suit, makeup, photographer, and honeymoon trip to Aruba. The reception costs were covered by cash gifts from guests.
Total	$3,787.50	Even though we splurged on an island destination wedding, our budget stayed reasonable because we cut back on eating out and going to bars. Worth it!

End-of-the-Year Balance Sheet

Category	Amount	Comments
Combined after-tax income	$145,400	I get my second promotion at work and a bonus at the end of the year, boosting our combined salaries.
Yearly spending	$45,450	
Yearly savings	$99,950	
Savings rate	69%	
Investment gains/losses	0%	We make the biggest investing mistake of our lives by exiting the market after we got our money back in 2008. In order to save money to buy a house now that we're married, we missed out on two years of bull-market investment gains.
Net worth	$380,250	

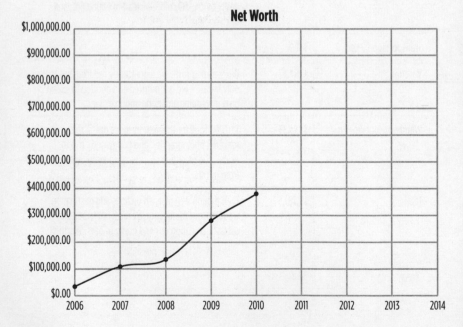

Net Worth

2011

This is the year that work takes a massive downturn for me. My friends are getting laid off and my whole department is forced to work longer hours than usual. We are also asked to justify our jobs by providing weekly reports on how we are allocating our time. Fun is had by no one.

Monthly Spending

Category	Cost Per Month	Comments
Rent	$800	
Food/Entertainment	$1,700	
Transportation/Misc.	$300	
Vacation	$583.33	$7,000 over the year for two vacations, one on a cruise, the other to Orlando.
Total	$3,383.33	

End-of-the-Year Balance Sheet

Category	Amount	Comments
Combined after-tax income	$167,500	Bryce gets a second promotion. Work is getting hellish for me, with lots of overtime, but at least our salary goes up.
Yearly spending	$40,600	With my work getting more stressful by the day and rumors of upcoming layoffs, I decide to optimize our spending as much as possible.
Yearly savings	$126,900	
Savings rate	76%	

Category	Amount	Comments
Investment gains/losses	0%	We're still staying out of the market and missing out on gains. But luckily our salaries are higher and our spending hasn't changed.
Net worth	$507,150	

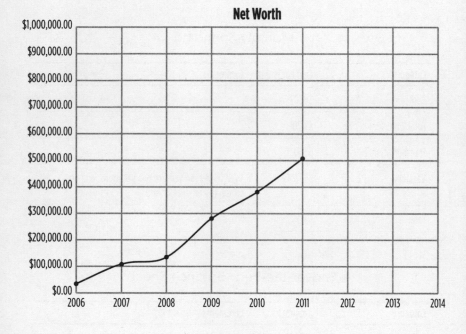

2012

Since work is getting stressful and the housing market in Toronto is looking more like a Ponzi scheme every day, I start to go into hyper tracking mode and break down our costs in even finer detail. This helps me identify and cut all the fat from our budget. This has the effect of pushing our savings rate to 78 percent, the highest it's ever been.

At this point, we discover FIRE (Financial Independence Retire

Early) and run the math to find that we are just three to five years from retirement if we invest our savings instead of using it to buy a house. Would I rather retire in my early thirties or own a house and continue stressing at work to pay it off? The choice is obvious.

Monthly Spending

Category	Cost Per Month
Rent	$800
Food	$1,100
Entertainment	$45
Bills/Transportation	$200
Gym	$100
Clothing	$30
Household/Gadgets	$50
Gifts/Donations	$175
Vacation	$583
Total for 2 people	$3,083

End-of-the-Year Balance Sheet

Category	Amount	Comments
Combined after-tax income	$168,680	
Yearly spending	$37,000	
Yearly savings	$131,680	
Savings rate	78%	

Category	Amount	Comments
Investment gains/losses	3.4%	We only started investing in the middle of the year, so we ended up missing part of the bull run again, ending up with only half the gains we would've gotten if we had invested the full year.
Net worth	$655,830	

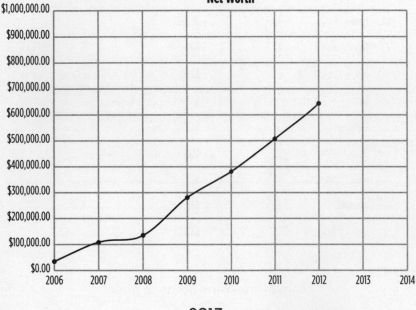

Net Worth

2013

I'm relieved we discovered FIRE the year before, because 2013 is the year my job really goes downhill. Not only am I working lots of overtime and so stressed I can't sleep, my earnings go down due to budget cuts in my department. Good thing we decided to get back into the stock market, as our rampaging portfolio makes up for it and saves my sanity. This year is what we describe in chapter 14. We are now just two years from retirement.

Monthly Spending

Category	Cost Per Month	Comments
Rent	$850	Our landlord suddenly realizes he forgot to raise our rent and bumps it up.
Food	$800	I get better at optimizing and bring our food costs down to $800 by planning meals better and buying groceries from Chinatown.
Entertainment	$40	
Bills/Transportation	$250	
Gym	$75	
Clothing	$3	I lose all interest in buying clothing because I've found my new love: writing. Bryce and I spend most of our evenings and weekends trying to get a children's novel published instead of consuming.
Household/Gadgets	$150	
Gifts/Donations	$150	
Vacation	$467	
Total	$2,785	

End-of-the-Year Balance Sheet

Category	Amount	Comments
Combined after-tax income	$155,000	My earnings go down as my entire department gets their bonuses cut despite all of us working overtime and losing sleep from stress.
Yearly spending	$33,416	
Yearly savings	$121,584	
Savings rate	78%	
Investment gains/losses	8.39%	
Net worth	$832,414	

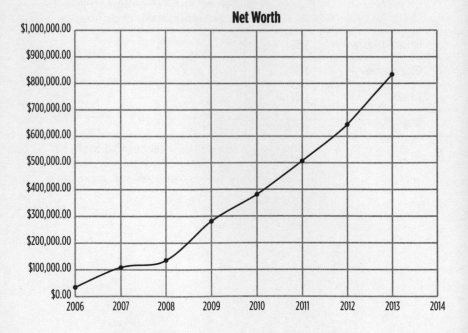

Net Worth

2014

We finish the race and become financially independent at the end of the year! At thirty-one years old, I can retire because my portfolio is spinning enough passive income to cover our expenses! We're *free*!

Monthly Spending

Category	Cost Per Month	Comments
Rent	$850	
Food	$750	
Entertainment	$100	
Bills/Transportation	$250	
Gym	$75	
Clothing	$20	
Household/Gadgets	$100	
Gifts/Donations	$270	
Vacation	$168	This is our lowest vacation spending ever. We pretty much skipped vacation because, you know, the rest of our lives would soon be one giant vacation forever.
Total	$2,583	

End-of-the-Year Balance Sheet

Category	Amount	Comments
Combined after-tax income	$164,000	Bryce gets his third and final promotion. My work has gotten so bad that my boss has a blood clot, my coworker collapses and almost dies at his desk, most of my team are on antidepressants and antianxiety meds, and my best friend gets laid off. I start to realize no one can rely on their job anymore.
Yearly spending	$31,000	
Yearly savings	$133,000	
Savings rate	81%	
Investment gains/losses	8.1%	
Net worth	$1,018,414	

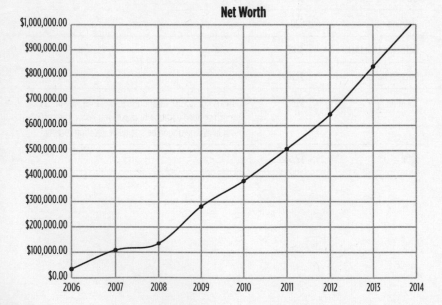

Net Worth

2015

We work for another six months to save up a Cash Cushion and go off to travel the world!

Fast-forward to 2018 (three years after retirement):

We are still traveling the word, spending $40,000 per year, but our net worth has grown to $1.3 million! Even though we're not working, we're making money. At this point, some editor at Penguin Random House named Nina Shield contacts us and asks us whether we'd be interested in writing a book, and the rest is, as they say, history.

APPENDIX C (CHAPTER 15)

In chapter 15, we introduced the idea of using higher-yielding assets to create what we called the Yield Shield. In this appendix, we'd like to provide a few more details about this strategy that didn't quite fit into the narrative flow of the book. Again, this section is completely optional and intended for the math nerds and data wonks out there. So enjoy, ya weirdos!

TOTAL RETURN VS. YIELD

To recap, we are not advocating for a Yield Shield portfolio long term, only for the first five years of retirement to mitigate against sequence-of-return risk. After that, the portfolio should pivot back toward a more traditional indexed portfolio.

Why? Because over the long term a yield-centered portfolio *will* underperform the index.

Whatever vehicle you use to invest to get a higher yield, the underlying companies issuing these securities will be similar: mature, blue-chip corporations with way too much cash that they don't know what to do with besides handing it back to their shareholders. These companies are the Bank of Americas and the Coca-Colas of the index.

And that's great, but investing this way exclusively will ignore the young, faster-growing companies of the index. After all, while a mature company like Ford is unlikely to grow 300 percent in a year, a smaller growth-oriented company like Tesla might, and that's where the outperformance of a total-market index fund like VTI gets its juice. Tesla, after all, doesn't pay dividends.

Dividends Can Be Cut

Also important to know is that while it's true that the yield you get from a portfolio is paid out independent of whether its value goes up or down, it's not guaranteed. It's possible for dividends to be cut, and while companies loathe to do this because it has the double-whammy effect of causing their stock price to plummet, it can happen in the event of extreme financial distress.

SO HOW DID THE YIELD SHIELD DO IN 2008?

So while in theory the Yield Shield protects you, how does it *actually* perform in a recession? Since our retirement in 2015, we've had a few stock market downturns but not a full-blown recession. And definitely nothing like the 2008–2009 Great Financial Crisis. So how do we know that this Yield Shield stuff actually works?

Great question.

Recall that the power of the Yield Shield portfolio comes from its interaction with the Cash Cushion, because it allows you to do something very different and important in a downturn: reduce your portfolio withdrawal rate without reducing your spending.

For an example, let's look at 2008.

Here's how a 60/40 portfolio did, assuming you retired right at the beginning of 2008 with a $1 million portfolio, withdrew $40,000, and continued doing so throughout the storm. You would have been able to fund some of that $40,000 using dividends and interest, but you would also have been forced to sell some assets at a loss.

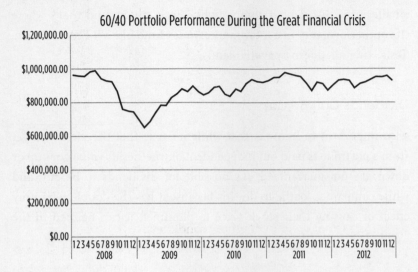

Now let's look at the Yield Shield strategy. For the purposes of this analysis, we are using the American Yield Shield portfolio given in chapter 15.

If we bring up a chart of the income we would have gotten during that time, we can see that it actually stayed relatively steady despite the turmoil. It started at $35,000 the first year, then went down slightly to $33,000 before recovering back up to the $35,000 level a year later.

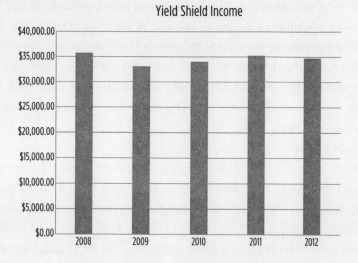

Yield Shield Income

In this scenario, our retiree would *not* have withdrawn $40,000 each year from their portfolio. Instead, they would have harvested the yield and used their cash cushion to make up the difference. How did these two portfolios do under those conditions?

When comparing these two portfolios, the Yield Shield + Cash Cushion strategy actually *beats* a traditional 60/40 portfolio. Yes, it was

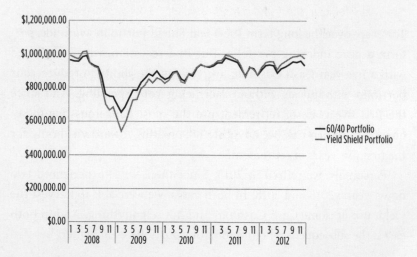

— 60/40 Portfolio
— Yield Shield Portfolio

more volatile, but because we were living off just the yield and the Cash Cushion, we didn't care, and by the end of 2012, our Yield Shield had returned to close to its original $1 million value and was ready to take advantage of the rip-roaring bull market that would have been ahead. Our retiree's five-year Cash Cushion would have been depleted, but that's why you refill it with capital gains when markets rampage, as they did after 2012.

Why is this?

Remember, the Yield Shield strategy isn't some magical investment that doesn't go down in recessions. It simply allows you to do something that every retirement planner agrees works: reduce your portfolio withdrawals in downturns so that you don't sell assets. And it allows you to do it while keeping a relatively small amount of cash sitting on the sidelines. We didn't need to keep hundreds of thousands of dollars out of the market, because that would have been a huge drag on our long-term performance and delayed our retirement.

THE YIELD SHIELD IS NOT A FOREVER PORTFOLIO

To recap, over the long term the Yield Shield portfolio *will* underperform a pure indexing portfolio. But in a recession, when combined with a five-year Cash Cushion, it gives you the ability to reduce your portfolio withdrawals without sacrificing your spending. And since the first five years of retirement are the most dangerous due to sequence-of-return risk, we advocate for pivoting toward yield only for the first five years of retirement.

Personally, we retired in 2015. Since then, we've experienced two down years: 2015 and 2018. In both cases, we were able to harvest the yield, use up some Cash Cushion, and not sell anything. And in both cases, the subsequent rebound took our portfolio even higher.

APPENDIX D (CHAPTER 21)

In chapter 21, I showed you how to project how long it will take for a person or family to become financially independent. To recap . . .

Step 1: Figure out how much this person or family is spending per year.

Step 2: Calculate their FI target by multiplying that number by twenty-five.

Step 3: Figure out their starting balance and their annual savings (how much money they're able to save in a year).

Step 4: Create a simple spreadsheet that tracks the growth of their portfolio.

Step 5: Figure out when their portfolio crosses their FI target.

It's a relatively simple exercise that has become second nature to me, but that's because I do this so often for my blog. If you're still wondering how to do it yourself, allow me to show you how, using the magic of Excel.

Yes, you read that right. It's time to talk about the mind-bending excitement of Excel and Excel formulas. (Now you know why I decided to include this as an appendix rather than in the main chapters.)

First, open up Excel and create the following column headings.

	A	B	C	D	E
1	Year	Balance	Savings	ROI	Total
2					
3					
4					

Next, make a counter on the leftmost column for each year. I type 1 into the first row, then use the "Fill Series" feature to fill in the rest. Consult Excel's Help feature if you're not sure how to do this.

	A	B	C	D	E
1	Year	Balance	Savings	ROI	Total
2	1				
3	2				
4	3				

Next, populate the first row. The first "Balance" value should be the total of your investable assets. This includes cash, 401(k)s, and IRA balances, but not your house equity if you own a home. This is because generally, your primary home's equity can't be used to help you retire, it just provides a place for you to live. This is why retirement planners often refer to home equity as "dead equity."

The next cell, "Savings," is how much you save each year. Again, this includes money that you put into your investment accounts, savings accounts, and retirement accounts, but not your mortgage payments.

The "ROI" (or Return on Investment) column is how much your retirement accounts are growing each year. Make a formula that points back to the "Balance" column and multiply it by your expected ROI. Retirement planners generally use 7 to 8 percent in their projections, but I use 6 percent to be conservative.

Now, create a formula in the "Total" column that adds up all the cells in your row. Your first row should look something like this.

	A	B	C	D	E
1	Year	Balance	Savings	ROI	Total
2	1	Starting Balance	Annual Savings	=B2*0.06	=B2+C2+D2
3	2				
4	3				

And finally, for each column use Excel's "Fill Down" feature to copy your formulas down your spreadsheet, like so.

	A	B	C	D	E
1	Year	Balance	Savings	ROI	Total
2	1	Starting Balance	Annual Savings	=B2*0.06	=B2+C2+D2
3	2	=E2	Annual Savings	=B3*0.06	=B3+C3+D3
4	3	=E3	Annual Savings	=B4*0.06	=B4+C4+D4

SIMPLE EXAMPLE

Say we have a couple who earns $80,000 after tax. This couple spends $40,000 a year, so that means their FI target is $40,000 × 25 = $1,000,000. This couple is just starting out in their journey, so they have zero assets. How long will it take for them to reach financial independence?

Year	Balance	Savings	Return (6%)	Total
1	$0.00	$40,000.00	$0.00	$40,000.00
2	$40,000.00	$40,000.00	$2,400.00	$82,400.00
3	$82,400.00	$40,000.00	$4,944.00	$127,344.00
4	$127,344.00	$40,000.00	$7,640.64	$174,984.64
5	$174,984.64	$40,000.00	$10,499.08	$225,483.72
6	$225,483.72	$40,000.00	$13,529.02	$279,012.74
7	$279,012.74	$40,000.00	$16,740.76	$335,753.50

Year	Balance	Savings	Return (6%)	Total
8	$335,753.50	$40,000.00	$20,145.21	$395,898.71
9	$395,898.71	$40,000.00	$23,753.92	$459,652.63
10	$459,652.63	$40,000.00	$27,579.16	$527,231.79
11	$527,231.79	$40,000.00	$31,633.91	$598,865.70
12	$598,865.70	$40,000.00	$35,931.94	$674,797.64
13	$674,797.64	$40,000.00	$40,487.86	$755,285.50
14	$755,285.50	$40,000.00	$45,317.13	$840,602.63
15	$840,602.63	$40,000.00	$50,436.16	$931,038.79
16	$931,038.79	$40,000.00	$55,862.33	$1,026,901.12

After throwing all that info into our spreadsheet, we can see that this couple can retire in seventeen years (or more accurately, at the end of the sixteenth year), since that's when their "Balance" column crosses their FI target of $1,000,000.

WHAT ABOUT INFLATION?

One question we often get is "What about inflation?" That table doesn't appear to account for it at all. The key is that the conservative 6 percent ROI I use for stock market returns is after-inflation, or real, growth, as we alluded to in chapter 21, whereas the 7 to 8 percent that retirement planners often use is preinflation, or nominal, growth. That's the actual growth of the stock market's value, plus dividends, and it is the most intuitive way of looking at stock market performance. The trouble with using nominal growth is that while it makes the stock market's performance easier to understand, it makes everything else more complicated because you now have to explicitly account for inflation. Specifically, inflation shows up in my analysis in three places:

- ▸ I have to account for the couple's salary's going up with inflation. In other words, they'd be getting yearly cost-of-living raises, and as a result, the amount of money they'd be able to sock away each year would go up with inflation as well.

- ▸ Their portfolios would be growing at the nominal rate rather than the real rate.

- ▸ Your FI target also has to adjust for inflation. After all, even though you're living on $40,000 now, you'll need *more* than that over time since the cost of living is increasing.

So what does that mean for our table? It means we have to add the effects of inflation to the "Savings" and "ROI" columns, as well as add a new column that shows how our FI target changes over time.

Year	Balance	Savings	ROI	Total	FI Target
1	$0.00	$40,000.00	$0.00	$40,000.00	$1,000,000.00
2	$40,000.00	$40,800.00	$3,200.00	$84,000.00	$1,020,000.00
3	$84,000.00	$41,616.00	$6,720.00	$132,336.00	$1,040,400.00
4	$132,336.00	$42,448.32	$10,586.88	$185,371.20	$1,061,208.00
5	$185,371.20	$43,297.29	$14,829.70	$243,498.19	$1,082,432.16
6	$243,498.19	$44,163.24	$19,479.86	$307,141.29	$1,104,080.80
7	$307,141.29	$45,046.50	$24,571.30	$376,759.09	$1,126,162.42
8	$376,759.09	$45,947.43	$30,140.73	$452,847.25	$1,148,685.67
9	$452,847.25	$46,866.38	$36,227.78	$535,941.41	$1,171,659.38

Year	Balance	Savings	ROI	Total	FI Target
10	$535,941.41	$47,803.71	$42,875.31	$626,620.43	$1,195,092.57
11	$626,620.43	$48,759.78	$50,129.63	$725,509.84	$1,218,994.42
12	$725,509.84	$49,734.98	$58,040.79	$833,285.61	$1,243,374.31
13	$833,285.61	$50,729.68	$66,662.85	$950,678.14	$1,268,241.79
14	$950,678.14	$51,744.27	$76,054.25	$1,078,476.66	$1,293,606.63
15	$1,078,476.66	$52,779.16	$86,278.13	$1,217,533.95	$1,319,478.76
16	$1,217,533.95	$53,834.74	$97,402.72	$1,368,771.41	$1,345,868.34

The point at which the couple reaches financial independence is no longer when their net worth crosses $1,000,000 but rather when it crosses the constantly moving FI target, which in this case is $1,345,868.34.

See how much more complicated this analysis becomes? And it still comes out to the same answer: seventeen years. That's why I use a real return rate and do all the math at today's dollars, rather than trying to show the effect of inflation and do all the math using future dollars. Doing it that way just confuses the hell out of everyone, while ultimately arriving at the same answer.

ACKNOWLEDGMENTS

This book talks about *chi ku* and "saving yourself," but we all know nothing in life can be accomplished without support.

We'd like to thank the many people who helped us birth this book baby (okay, that sounded better in my head) and get it out into the world:

To our editor extraordinaire, Nina Shield, thank you for coaxing this book into existence. Without you, this book wouldn't exist. And I mean that. You literally convinced us against our better judgment to write this thing. So, for better or for worse, this book is your fault.

To our superheroine literary agent, Andrea Somberg, thank you for believing in us and trusting our ability to write a book proposal despite our having never written one before. Your bubbly attitude is contagious and your belief in us is confounding.

To our fellow author and organizational guru Fay Wolf, we will never forget the day we found out a Hollywood actress liked our blog enough to tell her editor. Thank you for believing in us.

To copyeditor Aja Pollock, publicist Allyssa Kasoff, marketer Roshe Anderson, and the rest of the TarcherPerigee team at Penguin Random

House, thank you for all your help in getting this book baby out into the world! We couldn't have done it without you.

And special thanks to Kristy's dad for contributing the stories and life lessons that gave this book its heart.

JL Collins, the godfather of FI, of course you know why you're in here. We weren't seriously thinking of writing this book until you told us, "Write the book. Trust me." And now, here we are. Guess we're masochists—just like you. Thank you for your friendship, support, mentorship, and the best damn John Goodman impression ever! FU money all the way!

Vicki Robin, who convinced us that our original shtick of yelling at old people and killing sacred cows wasn't going to cut it, and that my stupid childhood story was, in fact, worth telling, thank you for inspiring us to make this story better.

Pete "Mr. Money Mustache" Adeney, Brandon Bronkhorst, Bill Banholzer, Colby Charles, Rob and Robin Charlton, Alan Donegan, Katie Donegan, Melissa Fournier, Jeremy Jacobson, Lainie Liberti, Justin McCurry, Jennifer Miller, Grant Sabatier, and Joe Udo, thank you all for sharing your stories and advice, proofreading chapters, or helping us with book promotion and marketing. Love you guys!

And last but not least, we want to thank Belgian beer and Portuguese wine, for helping us get through the many grueling hours holed up in our writing cave, wrestling this manuscript into submission. And in the event that this book is unreadable, we reserve the right to change the word "thank" to "blame."

NOTES

Chapter 1: Blood Money

1. "National Average Wage Index," US Social Security Administration, https://www.ssa.gov/oact/cola/AWI.html.
2. "China Average Yearly Wages," *Trading Economics*, https://tradingeconomics.com/china/wages.
3. Yang Wanli, "Rural-Urban Income Gap Narrows," *China Daily*, updated April 22, 2015, http://www.chinadaily.com.cn/china/2015-04/22/content_20509439.htm.
4. David Baker and Natacha Keramidas, "The Psychology of Hunger," *Monitor on Psychology* 44, no. 9 (October 2013), https://www.apa.org/monitor/2013/10/hunger.aspx.
5. R. Radel and C. Clement-Guillotin, "Evidence of Motivational Influences in Early Visual Perception: Hunger Modulates Conscious Access," *Psychological Science* 23, no. 3 (2012): 232–34, DOI 10.1177/0956797611427920.
6. "World Economic Outlook Databases," International Monetary Fund, https://www.imf.org/en/Publications/SPROLLS/world-economic-outlook-databases.

Chapter 2: Peach Syrup, Cardboard Boxes, and a Can of Coke

1. Belle Beth Cooper, "Proof That Constraints Can Actually Make You More Creative," *Fast Company*, March 10, 2014, https://www.fastcompany.com/3027379/the-psychology-of-limitations-how-and-why-constraints-can-make-you-more-creative.

2. Suzanne Goldenberg, "Half of All US Food Produce Is Thrown Away, New Research Suggests," *Guardian*, July 13, 2016, https://www.theguardian.com/environment/2016/jul/13/us-food-waste-ugly-fruit-vegetables-perfect.

3. Kelly Bryant, "You Won't Believe How Much Clothing the US Throws Away in a Year," TakePart, http://www.takepart.com/video/2015/05/29/clothes-trash-landfill.

4. Robert Frank, "The Perfect Salary for Happiness: $75,000," *Wall Street Journal*, September 7, 2010, https://blogs.wsj.com/wealth/2010/09/07/the-perfect-salary-for-happiness-75000-a-year/.

5. Charles Kenny, "We're All the 1 Percent," Foreign Policy, February 27, 2012, https://foreignpolicy.com/2012/02/27/were-all-the-1-percent/.

Chapter 3: Be Educated or Die

1. Yuwen Wu, "China's Class of 1977: I Took an Exam That Changed China," BBC News, December 14, 2017, http://www.bbc.com/news/world-asia-china-42135342.

2. Karim, "Breaking Pencils," Pencils for Africa, February 4, 2014, http://pencilsforafrica.com/breaking-pencils/.

Chapter 4: Don't Follow Your Passion (Yet)

1. Benjamin Todd, "To Find Work You Love, Don't (Always) Follow Your Passion," 80,000 Hours, last updated May 2016, https://80000hours.org/articles/dont-follow-your-passion/.

2. The Writers' Union of Canada, *Devaluing Creators, Endangering Creativity*, https://www.writersunion.ca/sites/all/files/DevaluingCreatorsEndangeringCreativity_0.pdf.

3. *The Daily*, "University Tuition Fees, 2000/2001," https://www150.statcan.gc.ca/n1/daily-quotidien/000828/dq000828b-eng.htm.

4. *The Globe and Mail*, "How Much? A Survey of Salaries in 2002," https://www.theglobeandmail.com/report-on-business/rob-magazine/how-much-a-survey-of-salaries-in-2002/article4096295/.

5. J. Quoidbach, D. T. Gilbert, and T. D. Wilson, "The End of History Illusion," *Science* 339, no. 6115 (January 4, 2013), 96–98.

6. Bureau of Labor Statistics, "Craft and Fine Artists," *Occupational Outlook Handbook*, https://www.bls.gov/ooh/arts-and-design/craft-and-fine-artists.htm.

7. Bureau of Labor Statistics, "Dancers and Choreographers," *Occupational Outlook Handbook*, https://www.bls.gov/ooh/Entertainment-and-Sports/Dancers-and-choreographers.htm.

8. Bureau of Labor Statistics, "Actors," *Occupational Outlook Handbook*, https://www.bls.gov/ooh/entertainment-and-sports/actors.htm.

9. "Is Medical School Worth It Financially?," Best Medical Degrees, https://www.bestmedicaldegrees.com/is-medical-school-worth-it-financially/.

10. Bureau of Labor Statistics, "Physicians and Surgeons," *Occupational Outlook Handbook*, https://www.bls.gov/ooh/healthcare/physicians-and -surgeons.htm.

11. "Schedule of Law School Fees," American Bar Association, https://www .americanbar.org/groups/legal_education/accreditation/schedule-of-law -school-fees/.

12. Bureau of Labor Statistics, "Lawyers," *Occupational Outlook Handbook*, https://www.bls.gov/ooh/legal/lawyers.htm.

13. The College Board, "Average Published Undergraduate Charges by Sector and by Carnegie Classification, 2018–19," Trends in Higher Education, https://trends.collegeboard.org/college-pricing/figures-tables/average -published-undergraduate-charges-sector-2018-19.

14. Bureau of Labor Statistics, "Plumbers, Pipefitters, and Steamfitters," *Occupational Outlook Handbook*, https://www.bls.gov/ooh/construction -and-extraction/plumbers-pipefitters-and-steamfitters.htm.

15. Ann Carrns, "Sweet Smell of Money for Plumbers," *New York Times*, March 24, 2014, https://www.nytimes.com/2014/03/25/your-money/sweet-smell-of-money -for-plumbers.html.

Chapter 5: IOU = I Own You

1. "How Household Savings Stack Up in Asia, the West, and Latin America," *Bloomberg Businessweek*, June 10, 2010, https://www.bloomberg.com/news /articles/2010-06-10/how-household-savings-stack-up-in-asia-the-west-and -latin-america.

2. "China's First Credit Card," Bank of China, http://www.boc.cn/en/aboutboc/ab5 /200811/t20081117_1602019.html.

3. "Credit card," *Encyclopaedia Britannica*, https://www.britannica.com/topic /credit-card.

4. Tae Kim, "Total US Household Debt Soars to Record Above $13 Trillion," CNBC, February 13, 2018, https://www.cnbc.com/2018/02/13/total-us-household-debt -soars-to-record-above-13-trillion.html.

5. Maham Abedi, "Canadian Consumer Debt Just Keeps Growing—but Here's Why It's Not a Problem Yet," Global News, March 12, 2018, https://globalnews .ca/news/4077067/canadian-consumer-debt-equifax-report/.

6. Office of the Assistant Secretary for Planning and Evaluation, "Poverty Guidelines," US Department of Health and Human Services, https://aspe.hhs .gov/poverty-guidelines.

Chapter 6: No One's Coming to Save You

1. *UNH Today*, "As College Graduates Hit the Workforce, So Do More Entitlement -Minded Workers," University of New Hampshire, May 17, 2010, https://www

.unh.edu/unhtoday/news/release/2010/05/17/college-graduates-hit-workforce
-so-do-more-entitlement-minded-workers.

Chapter 8: The Dope on Dopamine

1. P. Brickman, D. Coates, and R. Janoff-Bulman, "Lottery Winners and Accident
   Victims: Is Happiness Relative?" *Journal of Personality and Social Psychology* 36
   (August 1978): 917–27, https://www.ncbi.nlm.gov/pubmed/690806.
2. B. Abler et al., "Prediction Error as a Linear Function of Reward Probability Is
   Coded in Human Nucleus Accumbens," *NeuroImage* 31, no. 2 (June 2006):
   790–95.

Chapter 14: The Magical Number That Saved Me

1. Philip L. Cooley, Carl M. Hubbard, and Daniel T. Walz, "Retirement Savings:
   Choosing a Withdrawal Rate That Is Sustainable," *AAII Journal* 10, no. 2
   (February 1998).
2. "Personal Saving Rate," FRED Economic Data, https://fred.stlouisfed.org/series
   /PSAVERT.

Chapter 18: Inflation, Insurance, and Health Care: Scary Things That Aren't That Scary

1. Irene Papanicolas, Liana R. Woskie, and Asish K. Jha, "Health Care Spending in
   the United States and Other High-Income Countries," *Journal of the American
   Medical Association* 319, no. 10 (March 2018): 1024–39, doi:10.1001/jama
   .2018.1150.
2. Kaiser Family Foundation analysis of 2016 insurer rate filings to state regulators
   (table at end of page): http://www.ncsl.org/research/health/health-insurance
   -premiums.aspx.

Chapter 19. What About Kids?

1. Mark Lino, Kevin Kuczynski, Nestor Rodriguez, and TusaRebecca Schap,
   "Expenditures on Children by Families, 2015," Center for Nutrition Policy and
   Promotion, Miscellaneous Report No. 1528-2015, January 2017, Revised March
   2017. https://www.cnpp.usda.gov/sites/default/files/crc2015_March2017.pdf.

Chapter 21: You Don't Need a Million to Break Free

1. Gordon Green and John Coder, "Household Income Trends: June 2018,"
   Sentier Research, July 2018, http://sentierresearch.com/reports/Sentier
   _Household_Income_Trends_Report_June_2018_07_24_18.pdf.
2. "How Much Do Americans Pay in Federal Taxes?," Peter G. Peterson Foundation,
   April 15, 2014, https://www.pgpf.org/budget-basics/how-much-do-americans
   -pay-in-federal-taxes.

INDEX

Page numbers in **bold** indicate charts or tables; those in *italics* indicate figures or photos.